In the Inner Sanctum

Books by Thomas Hauser

General Non-Fiction

Missing
The Trial of Patrolman Thomas Shea
For Our Children
(with Frank Macchiarola)
The Family Legal Companion
Final Warning: The Legacy of Chernobyl
(with Dr. Robert Gale)
Arnold Palmer: A Personal Journey
Confronting America's Moral Crisis
(with Frank Macchiarola)
Healing: A Journal of Tolerance and
Understanding
With This Ring (with Frank Macchiarola)
Thomas Hauser on Sports
Reflections

Boxing Non-Fiction

The Black Lights: Inside the World of
Professional Boxing
Muhammad Ali: His Life and Times
Muhammad Ali: Memories
Muhammad Ali: In Perspective
Muhammad Ali & Company
A Beautiful Sickness
A Year at the Fights
Brutal Artistry
The View from Ringside
Chaos, Corruption, Courage, and Glory
I Don't Believe It, but It's True
Knockout (with Vikki LaMotta)
The Greatest Sport of All
The Boxing Scene
An Unforgiving Sport

Boxing Is . . .
Box: The Face of Boxing
The Legend of Muhammad Ali
(with Bart Barry)
Winks and Daggers
And the New . . .
Straight Writes and Jabs
Thomas Hauser on Boxing
A Hurting Sport
A Hard World
Muhammad Ali: A Tribute to the Greatest
There Will Always Be Boxing
Protect Yourself at All Times
A Dangerous Journey
Staredown
Broken Dreams

Fiction

Ashworth & Palmer
Agatha's Friends
The Beethoven Conspiracy
Hanneman's War
The Fantasy
Dear Hannah
The Hawthorne Group
Mark Twain Remembers
Finding the Princess
Waiting for Carver Boyd
The Final Recollections of Charles
Dickens
The Baker's Tale

For Children

Martin Bear & Friends

In the Inner Sanctum

Behind the Scenes at Big Fights

Thomas Hauser

The University of Arkansas Press
Fayetteville
2022

ISBN: 978-1-68226-214-6
eISBN: 978-1-61075-783-6

26 25 24 23 22   5 4 3 2 1

Manufactured in the United States of America

⊗ The paper used in this publication meets the minimum requirements of
the American National Standard for Permanence of Paper for Printed Library
Materials Z39.48–1984.

Library of Congress Cataloging-in-Publication Data

Names: Hauser, Thomas, author.
Title: In the inner sanctum: behind the scenes at big fights / Thomas Hauser.
Description: Fayetteville: The University of Arkansas Press, 2022. | Summary: "In
    the Inner Sanctum, Thomas Hauser's latest essay collection, explores the fight
    night in boxing. Hauser chronicles the most dramatic hours in boxers' lives-the
    very moment when a fighter's physical well-being and financial future are on the
    line, when the fighter is most at risk and most alive"— Provided by publisher.
Identifiers: LCCN 2022006843 (print) | LCCN 2022006844 (ebook) |
    ISBN 9781682262146 (paperback) | ISBN 9781610757836 (ebook)
Subjects: LCSH: Boxing—United States—History—21st century. | Boxers
    (Sports)—Psychology.
Classification: LCC GV1125 .H2933 2022 (print) | LCC GV1125 (ebook) |
    DDC 796.830973—dc23/eng/20220321
LC record available at https://lccn.loc.gov/2022006843
LC ebook record available at https://lccn.loc.gov/2022006844

For Billy Costello, Mike Jones, Victor Valle, and Saoul Mamby

The first time I was in a fighter's dressing room before and after a fight was with Billy Costello in 1984 while I was researching The Black Lights—an experience dealt with at length in the pages of that book. To excerpt it here wouldn't do justice to the people involved.

Mike Jones, Billy Costello, Victor Valle, and Saoul Mamby gave generously to me of their time and knowledge. They were the foundation stone for everything that followed for me as a boxing writer. I'll always be grateful to them.

Contents

Introduction

I often ask myself what it would mean for boxing history if someone had been in Joe Louis's dressing room before and after he fought Max Schmeling at Yankee Stadium on June 22, 1938, writing down everything of consequence that happened and was said that night. Or with Sugar Ray Robinson for one of his big fights. Or in Jack Johnson's dressing room before and after his conquest of James Jeffries.

I've been privileged in that, over the years, scores of fighters—some of them elite, others club fighters—have allowed me that access.

The first time I was in a fighter's dressing room before and after a fight was with Billy Costello in 1984. Thirteen years passed before I did it again, this time with Shannon Briggs when he fought George Foreman. Next, it was with Michael Grant when he challenged Lennox Lewis for the heavyweight championship. And after that, with Roy Jones Jr. when he wrested the WBA heavyweight crown from John Ruiz.

Then something wonderful happened. Fighters and their teams started coming to me, asking if I'd like to write about the inner workings of their own journey on fight night. Over the years, I've done it more times than I could have imagined. It's a privilege that I never take for granted.

I've been with Manny Pacquiao in his dressing room before and after four of his biggest fights. With Canelo Álvarez on five occasions and with Roy Jones on six. Evander Holyfield, Bernard Hopkins, Miguel Cotto, Gennady Golovkin, Ricky Hatton, Kelly Pavlik, Sergio Martínez, Tim Bradley, James Toney, and Jermain Taylor are among the many elite fighters who have invited me to share the most dramatic moments of their lives. I've also recounted the fight-night experiences of club fighters and journeymen who are equally important to the fabric of the sport.

The articles I've written about boxing have been collected in twenty-four volumes, many of them published by the University of Arkansas Press. The essays in this book have been adapted from those pieces.

In the Inner Sanctum consists of thirty-five articles, each one built around my experience in a fighter's dressing room on fight night. They're a representative sampling of my efforts to chronicle the moments when a fighter's physical well-being and financial future are on the line, when the fighter is most alive and most at risk.

In the Inner Sanctum

Bad judging is an accepted part of boxing. It shouldn't be.

Shannon Briggs, the Judges, and George Foreman's Last Fight

George Foreman vs. Shannon Briggs— November 22, 1997

On November 22, 1997, forty-eight-year-old George Foreman fought twenty-five-year-old Shannon Briggs at the Trump Taj Mahal Hotel and Casino in Atlantic City for what was styled as the lineal heavyweight championship of the world.

Foreman had claimed the World Boxing Association and International Boxing Federation heavyweight titles at age forty-five with a stunning tenth-round knockout of Michael Moorer on November 5, 1994. Four months later, he was stripped of the WBA belt for refusing to make a mandatory defense against Tony Tucker. Then, after successfully defending his IBF crown against Axel Schultz, he was stripped of that belt as well for not fighting a mandated rematch against Schulz.

That left Foreman without a major sanctioning-body title. But he was still George Foreman. And by virtue of his victory over Moorer, he was still the lineal heavyweight king. Victories over Crawford Grimsley and Lou Savarese (both of whom were undefeated at the time) followed. That set the stage for Foreman vs. Shannon Briggs.

Foreman's credentials were self-explanatory. Explaining Briggs was a bit more complicated.

Despite occasional erratic behavior, Shannon was personable, articulate, and smart. Part of his adolescence was spent in relative comfort. But there was a time when he was forced to deal with a mother who fell victim to substance abuse and a stint of homelessness on the streets of New York.

Once, Briggs had been touted as a rising star. He was a United States Amateur National Champion and a top prospect for the 1992 United States Olympic boxing team until a hand injury took him out of the Olympic trials. His manager, Marc Roberts, had invested over a million dollars in his career as Shannon fought his way to a 29–1 professional record with 24 knockouts.

But the fact that Foreman was willing to fight Briggs underscored the doubts that existed regarding Shannon's merits as a fighter. Most of the fighters Briggs had beaten were mediocre. And the one time he'd stepped up the level of competition (on an HBO telecast featuring "young heavyweight stars"), Shannon was knocked out in the third round by Darroll Wilson.

Briggs, HBO commentator Jim Lampley told a national audience, "folded like an accordion."

Shannon said the loss to Wilson was due to an asthma attack that he suffered in the ring. Teddy Atlas (who trained Briggs for the fight) said that Shannon quit.

"I think Shannon has talent," Atlas said. "And I worked very hard to give him a foundation, so he'd have the boxing mechanics and mental strength necessary to face an opponent in the ring. But Shannon was always more interested in finding the easy way to do things. Physically, he worked hard, but mentally it was all a big con with him. He was great at shmoozing investors with Marc Roberts. You can con investors. But sooner or later in boxing, you meet an opponent who you can't con in the ring, like Darroll Wilson. I never said Shannon didn't have asthma. What I said was, Shannon didn't have an asthma attack that night. But a weak mind and panic can bring on a lot of things. I tried to help Shannon become a real fighter. Not a phony, a real fighter. And the sad thing is, Shannon could have done all the stuff he wanted to do outside the ring and still become a fighter."

After Atlas made those comments, Briggs responded, saying, "Teddy played an important role in my development as a boxer and as a person. I had a lot of love for Teddy and a lot of respect for Teddy, and some of the things he said hurt me a lot. You know what I'm talking about. That I quit against Darroll Wilson, that I lack character. If you look at the other side of things, I wasn't always happy with Teddy. Teddy talks a lot about character and discipline, but he isn't always as disciplined as he should be. If I did some of the things Teddy has done, if I'd gotten into some of the fights outside the ring that Teddy has gotten into, he would have been on me like a ton of bricks and I would have deserved it. There were lots of times when I thought Teddy was wrong about something. There were lots of times when I felt Teddy was much too into controlling other people and not enough into controlling himself. But whatever problems I had with Teddy, I didn't go public with them. And he did. He said a lot of very negative things about me to the media, and I felt betrayed. It hurt a lot. And it hurt more because he walked out on me after a loss when I was down. Teddy is still part of my thinking. I got some very good things from him, and you don't just break up with someone and forget about them completely. But I have to admit, I'm still bitter about some of the things Teddy said about me."

The view of the ocean from the boardwalk in Atlantic City is spectacular. One can gaze out at the water and see Herman Melville's "great shroud of the sea" as it rolled on thousands of years ago. But turn away from the ocean and a vastly different scene beckons. Large gaps of urban decay are visible between the hotel-casinos that mark the skyline. Panhandlers solicit the tourists walking along the boardwalk. The Miss America Pageant (once Atlantic City's showcase event) is gone. Seedy shops and 99-cent discount stores proliferate.

The Trump Taj Mahal, where Foreman–Briggs was contested, stood on the dividing line between those two worlds.

Foreman had handpicked Briggs because George felt he could break Shannon's will. If a fighter quits in the ring, as it was alleged Briggs had done against Wilson, one of two things happens. Either quitting becomes part of his personality, like a circuit breaker that trips whenever he's in trouble, or he hates having quit so much that he vows never to quit again.

That led to two questions: (1) Were Briggs's physical skills so superior to those of the now-forty-eight-year-old Foreman that Shannon's will wouldn't be tested? (2) If Foreman tested Briggs's will, would Shannon quit?

In sum, while the promotion was largely about Foreman, the crucial questions regarding the outcome of the fight revolved around Briggs.

"I'm not looking for a knockout," Shannon said, sitting in his hotel room shortly before leaving for the arena on fight night. "If it happens, fine, but my mind isn't set on it. I envision using my jab, using my legs, fighting within my boundaries. If it turns into a test of brute strength,

I'm in trouble. But that's not what the fight will be about. People say that George handpicked me as his opponent. But what they lose sight of is, I picked George too."

Then Briggs turned pensive.

"When George goes into the ring, he believes God is behind him and that gives him strength. I have a different view of religion. I don't think God takes sides in sports contests. This is the biggest fight of my life, and I feel like it's all on me."

By virtue of his marketing power, Foreman had dictated the details of the promotion. That continued well into fight night. George wanted privacy. And he ran a tight ship. When Donald Trump went to Foreman's dressing room to wish George well, he was barred from entering by the fighter's personal security detail.

Briggs's dressing room was a less exclusive venue. At 9:00 p.m., sixteen people were scattered about. An hour later, that number had dwindled to ten. By the time Shannon made his way to the ring, his following was down to three cornermen. Then the bell rang and he was alone with Foreman.

Briggs had watched Foreman on television but had never seen him fight in person. After the press conference announcing their fight, he'd expressed surprise that George wasn't as big as he'd thought he was. Now he was experiencing Foreman was up close and personal—a massive presence who'd had thirty-two professional fights before Shannon was born.

Against Briggs, Foreman moved inexorably forward for twelve rounds. Shannon retreated as George advanced whether Foreman was punching or not. That allowed George to rest when he wanted to.

Briggs's jab was mostly a stay-away-from-me jab. He rarely threw his right hand with conviction. In round three, he was on the receiving end of some punishment, and it looked for a moment like he might go down. In round eight, Foreman landed a series of sledgehammer blows. But again, Shannon stayed on his feet.

It appeared to virtually every onlooker that Briggs didn't come close to doing what he had to do to win the fight. Then came the decision.

Steve Weisfeld's scorecard was announced first: 114–114.

There was amazement at ringside. What fight had Weisfeld been watching?

Then ring announcer Michael Buffer read the scores of judges

Lawrence Layton and Calvin Claxton—117–113 and 116–112 respectively. Sanity, it appeared, had been restored. Until Buffer intoned the words, "For the NEW lineal champion of the world . . ."

Foreman had won the fight but Briggs got the decision.

"I was lucky," Shannon told this writer in his dressing room after the bout. "The judges were nice to me."

The decision was inexplicable by any honest measure. Foreman had dominated the fight. He outboxed Briggs. He outpunched Briggs. He landed 284 punches to Briggs's 223. And his were the harder blows.

"We polled over a hundred media people, boxers, trainers, and managers who watched the fight," Foreman's co-promoter, Jeff Wald, said afterward. "Not one of them scored the fight for Briggs. This wasn't even a controversial fight. A controversial fight is when you argue and disagree. Outside of two judges, there is no disagreement."

Wald, of course, had an axe to grind. He was Foreman's co-promoter, and his reference to a hundred-person survey might have been hyperbole. But as Tim Layden wrote in *Sports Illustrated*, "The stink lingered after the decision. So egregious was the verdict in Atlantic City that it left even the most jaded fight fans shaking their heads and gave rise to allegations of corrupt judging involving Briggs's manager, Marc Roberts; Roberts's promotional company, Worldwide Entertainment & Sports; and New Jersey boxing commissioner Larry Hazzard."

Those looking for clues with regard to the scoring also took note of the fact that, subsequent to raising millions of dollars through a 1996 offering of Worldwide Entertainment & Sports stock, Roberts had been involved with two major fights in New Jersey. Foreman–Briggs was the second. The first was a December 14, 1996, bout between Tim Witherspoon and Ray Mercer (another WWES fighter). That bout resulted in an absurdly lopsided decision for Mercer, and the most lopsided scorecard was turned in by Calvin Claxton.

Foreman was gracious in defeat. "He's a good kid," George said of Shannon in the ring after the fight. "He just lost his mother. He stayed in there with me. I wish him well." Roy Foreman (George's brother) was equally kind, adding, "Shannon Briggs is a nice young man. The decision wasn't his fault. Shannon didn't score the fight."

Foreman never fought again. He retired from boxing the following year with a career record of 76 wins against 5 losses with 68 knockouts.

Briggs fought for nineteen more years and, at age forty-eight, is threatening to fight again. His record as of this writing stands at 60–6–1 with 53 KOs.

Meanwhile, in his first fight after decisioning Foreman, Briggs relinquished the lineal crown when he was knocked out in the fifth round by Lennox Lewis. Eight years later, Shannon won the WBO heavyweight title with an eleventh-round stoppage of Siarhei Liakhovich. But he lost it by decision in his next outing against Sultan Ibragimov.

"I feel like I've been successful in boxing," Briggs said after his loss to Ibragimov. "I didn't achieve the status of a Mike Tyson or a Lennox Lewis, but I'm happy with what I achieved. Coming from where I came from, homeless in Brooklyn, sleeping in shelters, everything I did was an accomplishment. How many kids come from where I did and break the cycle? People who've been comfortable all their life and were given everything when they were young think it's easy to break away from a bad situation. They say stupid things like, 'Just go out and work hard.' But most people who come from where I came from wind up doing what their parents did and living like their parents lived. I don't care what anyone else says. I made good. I'm proud of what I've accomplished. And I was the lineal heavyweight champion of the world whether people like it or not."

The Night Lennox Lewis Vanquished the Heir Apparent

Lennox Lewis vs. Michael Grant— April 29, 2000

The mid-twentieth century gave birth to a new breed of athlete—men who were big, well coordinated, and faster than men their size had been before. By the start of the new millennium, athletes had further honed their natural gifts and were even bigger than their predecessors.

Two heavyweights personified this trend—Lennox Lewis and Michael Grant. When they met in the ring at Madison Square Garden on April 29, 2000, Lewis was the reigning heavyweight champion. But Grant was seen in some circles as the heir apparent to the throne.

After winning a gold medal at the 1988 Olympics, Lewis advanced through the heavyweight ranks and annexed the WBC heavyweight crown by decision over Tony Tucker. Next, he defeated Frank Bruno and Phil Jackson. Then, shockingly, he was knocked out by Oliver McCall.

The road back for Lennox began with knockout victories over Lionel Butler, Justin Fortune, and Tommy Morrison. Then came a narrow majority decision over Ray Mercer at Madison Square Garden. In 1997, Lewis avenged his loss to McCall and reclaimed a portion of the heavyweight throne. Victories over Henry Akinwande, Andrew Golota, Shannon Briggs, and Zeljko Mavrovic followed. That set the stage for a return to Madison Square Garden and a March 13, 1999, title unification bout against Evander Holyfield. The widespread belief was that Lennox deserved the nod that night. But the judges ruled the contest a draw. Eight months later, Lewis won a unanimous decision over Holyfield in Las Vegas. In his next fight—on April 29, 2000—he fought at Madison Square Garden for the third and final time.

The opponent was Michael Grant: twenty-seven years old, undefeated in thirty-one bouts, six feet, seven inches tall, 250 pounds. There were questions regarding Grant's skills. He'd turned pro six years earlier with only twelve amateur bouts to his credit. In many respects, he was still a "project." But boxing insiders marveled at his strength, coordination, and stamina. Some observers called him the best pure athlete ever to come into boxing.

HBO (which set the agenda for boxing in those days) was high on Grant. The cable giant had televised his five most recent outings during the preceding two years; fights in which Grant knocked out David Izon, Obed Sullivan, Ahmad Abdin, and Andrew Golota, and decisioned Lou Savarese.

On February 8, Grant and Lewis attended a press conference at Madison Square Garden to announce their April 29 battle. There were the usual speeches before the fighters had their say. Don Turner (Grant's trainer), advisor Craig Hamilton, and attorney Jim Thomas spoke for Team Grant. Promoter Panos Eliades, manager Frank Maloney, and trainer Emanuel Steward advocated for Lewis. In the middle of the speeches, Turner pumped his fists spontaneously into the air. Joy and anticipation were etched on his face.

There was an interesting energy in the room. Most of the boxing media had come to the press conference believing that Lewis would beat Grant. But there was a growing sense that maybe Grant's time had come; that Holyfield–Lewis had been about boxing's past, and Lewis–Grant would be about boxing's future.

Michael Katz, then the dean of American boxing writers, had been skeptical about Grant for most of the fighter's pro career. Now Katz opined, "One way or the other, one of them won't be standing at the end. I think Grant will win."

HBO Sports vice president Lou DiBella (the network's point person on boxing) was also at the press conference. On his way out of the Garden, with excitement in his voice, DiBella said simply, "I think we're in for a changing of the guard."

When the day of reckoning came, Grant awoke in his room at the Grand Hyatt Hotel in Manhattan at 6:00 a.m. He lay in bed, listening to gospel music for two hours. Then he ordered breakfast from room service. Fruit salad, scrambled egg whites, and ham. At ten o'clock, Don Turner came to the room and the two men talked for twenty minutes. That was followed by a light snack.

At 12:30, Grant went down to the hotel lobby and sat in a large cushioned chair for an hour surrounded by friends.

"There have been other fights where I was more relaxed than this one," he acknowledged. "But this is okay. I'm cool with it. I know this is for the heavyweight championship of the world. But I'm focusing on the fight, not the belt."

For the first time in his pro career, Grant would be the underdog in one of his fights. Lewis had been installed as a 5-to-2 betting favorite. The prevailing view was that Lennox's boxing skills gave him an edge. Also, Grant might be stronger, but Lewis was believed to be the harder puncher.

Grant's advantage, such as it was, lay in his stamina. In the past, he'd worn opponents down. And some of Lewis's past performances had raised doubts regarding his own stamina. The early rounds were expected to belong to the champion and the late rounds to the challenger. The outcome would hinge on what happened early and, if that wasn't dispositive, on how early it got late.

The objective in the Lewis camp was that there not be any late rounds. Emanuel Steward's plan was for Lennox to jump on Grant. But Craig Hamilton had a different view. Standing in the hotel lobby, Hamilton observed, "When you're in the center of the ring looking at Michael and the referee is giving final instructions, Michael can look very imposing. Lennox could be forgiven for asking himself at that moment, 'Do I really want to jump on this guy? Maybe I should just use my superior boxing skills.'"

"It won't be easy," Don Turner added. "Lennox has plenty of guts. He's not that good when he's backing up; most fighters aren't. But he's very good coming forward. Michael has to fight a hungry fight. If Michael lays back, Lennox controls the fight and outboxes him. Michael has to back Lennox up and make it an action fight to win. He has to impose his will. Get off first. Initiate everything. Dictate the rhythm of the fight. If Michael does what he's capable of doing, he doesn't have to worry about what Lennox is doing. We know about Lennox. This fight is about Michael."

At two o'clock, Grant went for a walk. An hour later, Turner, Hamilton, Thomas, and associate trainer Bobby Miles walked over to Madison Square Garden to arrange for last-minute ticket requests and check out the ring. Meanwhile, Michael returned to the hotel, had a

three o'clock snack, took a nap, and spent the rest of the afternoon in his
suite with his wife and a few friends. At seven o'clock, he ate his final
pre-fight meal. Like every fighter who ever fought for the heavyweight
championship of the world, he had dreams.

"I like Lennox," Michael had said earlier. "I think he's a gentleman.
He's not an open person; he's very private. But if we were neighbors,
there'd be a connection. We'd be in each other's homes from time to
time."

Now Grant was focusing on the task ahead. "I know what I have
to do when we fight," he said. "This is a wonderful opportunity for me.
When I'm champion, I won't change. My character won't change. But
when I win the title, my life will."

At 8:45 p.m., wearing a dark-blue jogging suit and gray peak cap,
Grant arrived at Madison Square Garden with Turner, Thomas, and Miles.
His assigned dressing room was twenty-four feet long and twenty feet
wide with a scuffed gray linoleum floor and white cinderblock walls.
Nine lilac-colored folding chairs were scattered about. A TV monitor
was affixed to the wall by the door.

Grant crossed the room to a blue rubdown table and seated himself in
an upright position with his legs dangling over the side. Then he lowered
his head in contemplation.

"The most nervous I ever was before a fight was before my first
amateur fight," Michael had once said. "I remember being in the locker
room, banging the back of my head against my locker, saying, 'I can't
believe I'm doing this.'"

He looked nervous now. Very nervous.

An inspector from the New York State Athletic Commission came
into the room and handed a pair of latex gloves to each of Grant's cornermen. A Commission physician who had entered with the inspector took
Michael's blood pressure.

At 8:58, Grant lay down on the rubdown table with a half-dozen
towels beneath his head and closed his eyes. Two minutes later, another
Commission inspector came in and asked for a urine sample. Michael got
up, went into the adjacent lavatory, provided a sample, and returned to the
rubdown table where, once again, he lay down and closed his eyes. The
table was a foot too short. His feet and then some dangled over the end.

The monitor on the wall heralded the start of the evening's pay-per-view telecast. Several members of Team Grant watched as Wladimir Klitschko knocked out David Bostice in two rounds. Next, Arturo Gatti KO'd Eric Jakubowski, also in two. Michael slept—or pretended to sleep—through it all.

At 9:43, the monitor showed Lennox Lewis arriving at Madison Square Garden. Three minutes later, someone from HBO came into the room and asked if it would be possible to wake Michael for an interview. The answer was "no."

At ten o'clock, an hour after Grant lay down and closed his eyes, Turner roused him gently.

At 10:05, New York Jets receiver Keyshawn Johnson entered the room and approached Grant. "You came this far," the NFL star exhorted. "You're gonna get it done, definitely."

Paul Ingle vs. Junior Jones, the next-to-last fight of the evening, came onto the TV monitor.

Turner began taping Michael's hands. Fifteen minutes later, he was done and a Commission inspector initialed the wraps.

At 10:30, Grant and Turner left the dressing room and walked to a nearby freight-loading area where Michael jumped rope for three minutes. Four times, the normally agile fighter missed a beat and the rope slid off his shoe against the floor. That was cause for Turner to be concerned about his fighter's state of mind.

The trainer led Grant back to the dressing room and took him through a series of stretching exercises. The positive energy so abundant at the February 8 kickoff press conference was gone. The room was silent. There was no aura of confidence and no crackle of electricity to signify that this was a fight for the heavyweight championship of the world.

Grant began loosening up. For the first time since he'd entered the room earlier in the evening, his face transformed into the face of a fighter. His eyes grew more focused, angry and intense.

Then the look receded.

Paul Ingle KO'd Junior Jones in the eleventh round.

Grant put on his protective cup and trunks and gloved up. Cutman Joe Souza applied Vaseline to his face.

At eleven o'clock, referee Arthur Mercante Jr., who would preside over the title fight, came into the room to give the fighter his final pre-fight instructions. Two minutes later, Mercante was gone.

Someone turned on a portable CD player. Gospel music sounded.

Bobby Miles put on a pair of handpads. For the next six minutes, Grant hit the pads as Miles gave instructions.

"Jab, hook to the body. . . . Jab, hook to the body, follow with a right."

When they were done, Michael began pacing in a circle. Now it was just a matter of time.

But something was missing. The room seemed strangely unalive.

Miles put the handpads on again and Grant pounded them for another two minutes. It was 11:15 p.m.

"Three minutes," a voice from doorway sounded.

Everyone in the room joined hands in a circle, readying for prayer.

"Be sincere, please," Michael implored them.

They prayed together. Then Grant turned for a silent moment of his own.

"I always shed a tear before a fight," Michael had once said. Now he appeared to be shedding many of them.

The room still didn't feel right.

There would be no violent transfer of power that night. Lewis knocked Grant down three times in the first round and ended matters in the second stanza.

Grant never fought for the heavyweight title again. In his next outing, he suffered a broken ankle, occasioning a first-round stoppage at the hands of Jameel McCline. After that, he did what he could to rebuild his career. He worked hard in the gym. He took seven fights for small money, winning all of them. Every step was aimed at getting back on HBO. When he did, it was against Dominick Guinn in a crossroads bout for both men. Guinn won. Grant then reeled off eight more victories in succession before losing a twelve-round decision to Tomasz Adamek. He finished his career with a 48–7 (36 KOs) ring record.

"The problem," Bobby Miles said as Grant's career wound down, "is that Michael doesn't really like boxing. It's just not something he likes to do. And he still thinks like an athlete, not a fighter. In most sports, there's a code of sportsmanship and gentlemanly conduct. If you're a fighter, you have to approach each fight like a gladiator in the Roman Coliseum.

You have to be mean. You're fighting for survival. Tyson, Duran, guys like that; they understand. All great fighters do. Ray Leonard might have smiled and said nice things, but in the ring he was a mean son-of-a-bitch. Michael just isn't mean enough."

And Craig Hamilton added, "It's not a question of courage. Every time in his career that Michael has been knocked down, he's gotten back up. But he lacks confidence, and confidence is crucial to a fighter. What can I say? Michael wasn't cut out to be a fighter. The fact that he got as far as he did in boxing is testament to what a great athlete he is. He could have accomplished so much more if he'd had the temperament of a fighter. But he doesn't, and that's that."

Meanwhile, Lewis's knockout of Grant solidified Lennox's standing as the preeminent heavyweight in the world. By the time his ring career ended with a victory over Vitali Klitschko three years later, people in the know understood that he would have been competitive against the best of any era.

There was a time when Roy Jones was the best fighter in the world and acclaimed as one of the greatest fighters ever.

Roy Jones: "Y'all Musta Forgot"
Roy Jones vs. John Ruiz—
March 1, 2003

Roy Jones fought too long. He was knocked out on the downside of his career by Enzo Maccarinelli, Denis Lebedev, and Danny Green and struggled against club fighters who wouldn't have made the cut as sparring partners when he was young. That's sad for a lot of reasons, one of which is that some people have forgotten how good Jones was in his prime.

There was a time when you could have asked ten fighters, "Who's the best fighter in the world?" And without hesitation, every one of them would have answered, "Roy Jones."

Sugar Ray Robinson, for whom the phrase "pound for pound" was invented, was a classic fighter. Robinson fought conventionally. He just did it better than anyone else. Jones was different. He moved beyond the framework of convention. Like Muhammad Ali, he deconstructed the art and science of boxing and reassembled the pieces to his liking.

The young Roy Jones beat Bernard Hopkins and James Toney. In a highlight-reel moment that encapsulated his brilliance, he knocked out Virgil Hill with a single punch—a right hand *under* the jab. Against Glen Kelly, standing with his back to the ropes and both hands behind his back, Jones flashed a right hand that put Kelly down for the count. Figuratively speaking, he knocked Glen out with his hands behind his back. The sole blemish on Jones's record was a 1997 loss by disqualification to Montell Griffin. Four months later, he KO'd Griffin in the first round.

"Boxing isn't a game," Jones said. "It's a deadly violent sport. But God put fighting in me. It's what I was born to do."

The high point of Jones's career came on March 1, 2003, at the Thomas & Mack Center in Las Vegas. On that night, fourteen years after beginning his journey through the professional ranks as a junior-middleweight, he defeated John Ruiz to claim the WBA heavyweight crown.

Prior to Jones–Ruiz, Jones was in danger of becoming a victim of his own success. Enabled by a sweetheart deal with HBO, he'd stepped away from the toughest available competition to fight lesser opponents. Writing about Roy's 175-pound title defense against Clinton Woods, Steve Bunce of *The Guardian* had declared, "This is not part of a sporting tradition. It's just the latest Jones fight where he has taken the most money for the least risk." Larry Merchant of HBO observed, "Roy Jones seems to think that stiff competition means fighting only stiffs." Thom Loverro of the *Washington Times* added, "Roy Jones is an artist, but he doesn't want to get any paint on himself."

Jones was aware of the criticism. In response, he recorded a rap song titled "Y'all Musta Forgot":

> They got the nerve to say I ain't fight nobody
> I just make 'em look like nobody
> Y'all musta forgot!
> Let's look back at my whole career
> Cuz y'all musta forgot!
> The "best pound for pound" is mine
> Hit Percy Harris with four hooks at one time
> Y'all musta forgot!
> When I beat Bernard Hopkins and won the IBF
> The right was hurt, beat him with the left
> Y'all musta forgot!
> You remember the left hook that James Toney got
> Sucka move that I stole from a gamecock
> Y'all musta forgot!
> Will there be another Roy Jones?
> Probably not
> Topped Virgil Hill with a body shot
> See y'all musta forgot!

But rapping wouldn't silence the critics. So Jones took an audacious step. He had eyed the heavyweight division since the mid-1990s when he considered fighting Evander Holyfield and Mike Tyson. Now, with

47 victories and 1 loss (by disqualification) on his ring ledger, he moved up to heavyweight to challenge John Ruiz for the WBA title.

The fight was promoted by Don King as a modern-day version of David versus Goliath.

"Roy Jones is challenging destiny," King declared at the kickoff press conference. "He's undaunted in spirit. He has indomitable courage. He's not ordinary Roy Jones. He's Superman Roy Jones. Roy is faster than a speeding bullet and more powerful than a locomotive. He can leap tall buildings in a single bound."

Jones concurred, adding, "I've accomplished all that I can at light-heavyweight. People are tired of seeing races between a Porsche and a Volkswagen. They have to take me out of my weight class to even consider someone beating me."

The odds were 9-to-5 in Jones's favor, but boxing insiders were divided on the outcome. Many people who considered Roy number one in the world "pound for pound" thought that Ruiz would inexorably wear him down. That belief rested in large measure on the logic that, in Jones's previous four bouts, he had fought Derrick Harmon, Julio González, Glen Kelly, and Clinton Woods, while Ruiz had been up against Kirk Johnson once and Evander Holyfield three times."

"John Ruiz is easy to beat when you're watching him on television in your living room," Holyfield said.

"I don't think much of John Ruiz as a fighter," Lennox Lewis added. "But there's one thing I'll say for him. You should never underestimate someone who goes thirty-six rounds with Evander Holyfield."

"My main thing will be to work the body," Ruiz noted confidently. "I don't want to go head-hunting and miss all over the place. My strength is my strength. I'm a lot stronger than anyone Jones has fought, and it will be a new experience for him to be in the ring with someone like me. His flurries and pitty-pat punching won't work at heavyweight."

But Jones was confident. "I'll do what I have to do to win," he promised. "If I need to attack, I'll attack. If I need to box, I'll box. A lot of people say that Ruiz's punching power will change my mind, but I'm going to be asking chin questions too. The surprise will come when I hit him hard. Ruiz is measuring me against Evander Holyfield and Kirk Johnson, but I ain't them."

"Roy will see Ruiz's punches coming," Alton Merkerson (Jones's trainer) added. "But Ruiz won't see Roy's punches coming. And when Ruiz watches the tape after the fight, he'll realize that he was hit with things that no one ever threw at him before."

Ruiz weighed in for the bout at 226 pounds. Jones tipped the scales at 193 wearing an estimated three pounds of clothes. That was well above his previous high of 175 pounds. But conditioner Mackie Shilstone, who helped Jones prepare for Ruiz, explained, "Roy came to me at 192 pounds with 8.7 percent body fat. All we did was change the composition; bring his body fat down to 6 percent."

"Look at me," Jones proclaimed. "The little man ain't so damn little."

Dr. Margaret Goodman, who administered the pre-fight physicals, observed, "I've never seen a fighter in better condition than Roy Jones is in now. He's got the head of a middleweight on the neck and body of a heavyweight. His body is absolutely phenomenal."

One night before the fight, Jones deviated from ritual. Almost always, he watched martial-arts action films in his hotel suite to prepare mentally for the battle to come.

"The movies get my mind right," he explained. "They help me visualize. The people in them move in a way that's very precise. They never get tired. Their breathing is controlled. Their focus stays the same. He who loses form first loses."

Jones had brought eighteen martial-arts videos to Las Vegas. But now, on the night before the biggest fight of his professional career, he watched tapes of himself as an amateur instead.

"I want to remind myself that Roy Jones is still Roy Jones," he said. "Tomorrow night, I might be fighting like I did when I was young."

Translation: Jones was planning to set down more on his punches than he had in recent fights.

On fight night, Jones arrived at the Thomas & Mack Center at 6:25 p.m. He was wearing a blue-and-white North Carolina basketball warm-up suit over jersey number 23 (Michael Jordan's old number). Soon after his arrival, his dressing room was jammed.

Alton Merkerson and Roy's other cornermen were there. Two Nevada State Athletic Commission inspectors sat near a group of fighters that included Derrick Gainer, Vince Phillips, Billy Lewis, and Gabe

Brown. Al Cole and David Izon had fought each other in the evening's first preliminary bout. Now they sat side by side with Izon holding an icepack to reduce the swelling around his right eye.

The room seemed as hot as a sauna. Jones opened a folding metal chair and sat down facing away from his locker. Rap music blared. Occasionally, Roy drank from a bottle of mineral water. Now and then, he intoned the lyrics of the music and glanced at preliminary fights on the television monitor in a corner of the room. Mostly, he alternated between quiet contemplation and relaxed conversation.

HBO Boxing production coordinator Tami Cotel entered the room and asked Roy if he'd be willing to weigh in on an HBO scale.

"Tell me why I should do it," Jones countered.

"We always do it before a big fight."

"That's not good enough."

Cotel tried again.

"We want to compare your weight with what other great champions like Jack Dempsey, Joe Louis, and Rocky Marciano weighed when they won the heavyweight title."

That appealed to Jones, who agreed to get on the scale.

One hundred ninety-nine pounds. Subtract three pounds for clothes, and he weighed 196. That was more than Dempsey or Marciano ever weighed in the ring and a pound less than Joe Louis weighed when he captured the heavyweight crown.

"It's out now," Merkerson chortled. "I knew the scale at the official weigh-in was light."

At 7:38 p.m., with a member of the Ruiz camp present, Merkerson began wrapping Jones's hands. As that task progressed, Jay Nady, who had been assigned to referee the fight, entered with Nevada State Athletic Commission executive director Marc Ratner to offer the normal pre-fight instructions.

"Any questions?" Nady asked at the close of his remarks.

"We want to fight clean," Merkerson responded. "I know you'll do your best, sir."

"I'll stay on top of it," Nady assured him.

When the taping was done, an inspector initialed the wraps. Then Jones put on a protective cup, brown trunks, and tasseled brown-and-white ring shoes. At 7:50 p.m., he turned off the music and summoned everyone to room center. Hands joined together in prayer, asking first that no one be hurt in the fight and only then for victory.

After the prayer, Jones turned the music on again and stood in front of his chair. Slowly, he shifted his weight from one foot to the other. Then he sat down and silently mouthed the lyrics to the music.

Jones, not Merkerson or anyone else, was dictating the pace of everything. Throughout his time in the dressing room, he rarely left his chair. He never warmed up in the conventional sense; never stretched, shadow-boxed, or hit any pads.

"It's known as 'the slows,'" Merkerson explained. "The theory is that muscles work better if the body is hot but, at the same time, energy should be conserved."

At eight o'clock, Ratner returned with the gloves that Jones would wear during the fight. Fifteen minutes later, Roy gloved up with a Ruiz cornerman present.

Then Merkerson moved to the center of the room. "What time is it?" he shouted.

"Jones time," the chorus responded.

"What time is it?"

"Jones time!"

"What time is it?"

"Jones time!"

Then the Q and A changed.

"Whose house?"

"Jones house!"

"Whose house?"

"Jones house!"

"Whose house?"

"Jones house!"

"And the new!"

"Heavyweight champion of the world."

"And the new!"

"Heavyweight champion of the world."

"And the new!"

"Heavyweight champion of the world."

Merkerson turned to Jones.

"Let's go to work," he told the fighter.

What followed wasn't a great fight, but it was a great performance. Roy Jones asked a lot of questions, and John Ruiz didn't have the answers.

For most of round one, the combatants fought on even terms. Then, toward the end of the round, Ruiz landed a clubbing right hand and Jones fired back harder. As early as round two, Ruiz was no longer bulling forward as planned and was fighting more cautiously.

Jones didn't run. Instead, he stood in the center of the ring, often directly in front of Ruiz, feinting, looking to counter, getting off first when he wanted to, setting down on his punches more than in recent fights and controlling the flow of the action. In recent years, Roy had averaged only eight jabs per round. Against Ruiz, it was nineteen.

As the rounds went by, Jones–Ruiz took on the look of a Roy Jones light-heavyweight title defense. He broke Ruiz's nose in round four. Then, with eighteen seconds left in the round, he landed a lightning-bolt right to the temple that staggered Ruiz.

At that point, Ruiz looked like a beaten fighter. And for the rest of the night, he looked like a fighter who knew he was beaten. There were times when Jones fought more like a heavyweight than Ruiz did.

"I don't hit that hard," Jones said mockingly after the bout. "Everyone knows that. So when you fight me, go ahead. Charge! Attack! It was a punch from the referee that broke John's nose."

The scoring of the judges was anticlimactic: 118–110, 117–111, 116–112. The only reason it was that close was that Jones took the final three rounds off. People had expected an ugly fight, but Roy's performance was beautiful. It left no doubt that he was pound-for-pound the best fighter in the world.

That was reaffirmed when no less an authority than Emanuel Steward declared that Lennox Lewis was still the #1 heavyweight in boxing but Jones was far superior to many heavyweight champions of the past. Then Steward went further, saying that, if Jones could be transported back in a time machine, he would beat the smaller heavyweight greats like Jack Dempsey and Rocky Marciano.

Evander Holyfield was boxing's consummate warrior and as pure a fighter as there ever was in the sport.

The Night You Knew It Was Over for Evander

Evander Holyfield vs. James Toney— October 4, 2003

All good things must come to an end. For Evander Holyfield, the end of his days as an elite fighter came on October 4, 2003, when he fought James Toney in Las Vegas.

The public perception of Holyfield crystalized on July 12, 1986, when he outwilled Dwight Muhammad Qawi over fifteen brutal rounds to claim the WBA cruiserweight crown. After that fight—bruised, battered, and badly dehydrated—Evander was taken to the hospital for overnight observation.

"I lay in that bed," Holyfield later remembered. "And even though I won, I said out loud, 'Oh, Lord; I don't know if I want to do this anymore.' But to be a true success, you have to endure hardship. Being a warrior isn't just being destructive. A warrior is a man who takes it to the end and doesn't quit."

Four years later, Holyfield knocked out James "Buster" Douglas to become undisputed heavyweight champion of the world. More historic triumphs followed, highlighted by a 1993 victory over Riddick Bowe and two conquests of Mike Tyson.

"I'm really not interested in being the baddest man on the planet," Evander said after knocking out Tyson in the eleventh round of their first encounter. "My only interest is being the best man in the ring."

During the course of his career, Holyfield defeated Tyson, Bowe, Douglas, George Foreman, Larry Holmes, Michael Moorer, Pinklon Thomas, Michael Dokes, John Ruiz, Hasim Rahman, and Frans Botha. That's eleven men who held a major heavyweight championship belt at one time or another.

"I fight people who fight back," Evander said. "My whole career, I've fought people when they were at their best. You can't prove anything to me by doing it to someone else. You got to do it to me. And I don't look to beat somebody because he makes mistakes. I want to be better."

But as he readied to fight James Toney, Holyfield's career was on the decline. In the previous five years, he'd won twice in seven bouts. He was fifteen days shy of his forty-first birthday and hadn't scored a knockout since 1997.

"This will be Holyfield's last fight," Toney pledged. "I'm retiring him. He's past his prime. He's had his time. He can grab his Bible, bring his choir, do whatever; it don't matter. He's in trouble. It's going to be a bloody night. I'm gonna give this old southern boy an ass-whupping."

But talking doesn't win fights. And the Holyfield camp was confident. Although Toney was six years younger than Evander, Team Holyfield believed that their man was the better fighter, could punch harder and, given his reach advantage, would be able to control Toney with his jab. Moreover, Holyfield had been hit lots of times by people who punched harder than Toney. James had never been hit by anyone who punched as hard as Evander.

In the days leading up to the fight, Holyfield said of Toney's trash-talking, "Everyone has the freedom to say what they want. Some can back it up and some can't. The question is, can he take what I give him? Toney says he's going to stand in front of me and fight me. I look forward to that. That's great. That means I won't miss. If he doesn't move, I'm gonna wind up moving him. He may stand there, but it won't be for long.

"People say they don't want to see me hurt," Evander added, acknowledging the talk about his decline. "I don't want to see me hurt either. But they've tried to bury me two or three times before and found out that I wasn't dead. For the last ten years, people been popping the same question at me: 'When you gonna quit?' They started asking after I fought Riddick Bowe the first time. So I went out and beat Bowe in the rematch, and they still said I should retire. They've been singing the same song ever since. And when they're not singing, they've been threatening that I'm gonna get carried out on my back. But I'm still standing. I'm still here. Ain't nothing changed. I've set a goal to retire as undisputed heavyweight champion of the world."

Still, looking realistically at the situation, Holyfield was going into the fight against Toney as a gatekeeper for the heavyweight division.

If he won, he would reemerge as a contender. If he lost, James would become the contender and Evander would be relegated to "opponent" status.

At 10:30 a.m. on the day of the fight, Evander sat in his palatial three-bedroom suite at the Mandalay Bay Resort and Casino. Attorney Jim Thomas, conditioning coach Tim Hallmark, and several friends from Atlanta were with him. Wearing blue workout shorts and a gray T-shirt, he eyed a plate of steak and eggs and a stack of pancakes that conjured up the image of a tall office building.

There was no sign of nerves. Everyone was relaxed and confident. One reason for the confidence was that, subsequent to Evander's second fight against Lennox Lewis, he'd been plagued by an ailing left shoulder that left him unable to throw effective left-hand leads or hook off his jab. But after being outpointed by Chris Byrd in December 2002, he'd undergone surgery to repair a torn rotator cuff. Now the shoulder was fully healed.

Holyfield and Toney had both looked good at their final pre-fight physicals. Evander weighed in at 219 pounds and seemed to be in the best shape possible for a fighter on the verge of turning forty-one. Toney had come in a bit heavy at 217.

"It don't matter what Toney weighs," Holyfield said when the subject arose during breakfast. "If I start paying attention to what he weighs, it means I'm not paying enough attention to what I'm gonna do."

Evander stood up from the table and demonstrated how, when Toney turned his head and shoulders on the inside to avoid punches, he exposed his ribs.

"You break something if you hit a man there," he noted.

At noon, Holyfield went outside for a short walk. A half hour later, he returned and sat down on the sofa to watch the playoff game between the New York Yankees and Minnesota Twins. Then the conversation turned to an overview of his career.

"I've been boxing for thirty-two years," Evander reminisced. "I've had my ups and I've had my downs, but it's been good. The fight that meant the most to me was the first fight against Tyson. I knew I could beat him, but the public didn't. The fight I learned the most from was my first fight against Qawi. Before that fight, I wasn't sure if I belonged in the ring with him."

Then came a familiar refrain: "When I become undisputed heavy-weight champion of the world again is when I close the book on being a fighter. I might not get it when I want it, but I'll get it. The only way I won't reach my goal of becoming heavyweight champion of the world again is if I quit. And I won't quit."

Holyfield stayed in his hotel suite for the rest of the afternoon. Then, after the Atlanta Braves (his hometown team) secured game four of their playoff series against the Chicago Cubs, he traveled down a service elevator and through back passageways with trainer Don Turner and several other team members to the Mandalay Bay Events Center. At 5:25 p.m., he arrived in a room with plush ivory carpeting, a sofa, club chairs, and a large-screen television. It looked like the dressing room for a concert performer.

Evander sat on the sofa, directly opposite the television. The first pay-per-view fight of the evening—Cruz Carbajal versus Gerardo Espinoza—was underway. Holyfield watched impassively. The atmosphere in the room was like a handful of friends sitting at home in someone's living room watching a fight. Except soon, one of the friends would get up off the sofa to fight in the main event.

Long stretches of time passed without anyone saying a word. Evander watched silently. Everyone else followed his lead. Espinoza got beaten up. The fight ended with a left hook to the body that left him writhing in pain on the canvas.

Holyfield stood up from the sofa, walked over to a six-foot mirror, and threw a handful of punches in exaggerated slow-motion.

At 5:50 p.m., Nevada State Athletic Commission executive director Marc Ratner entered the room with Jay Nady, who would be refereeing the main event. Nady gave Evander his preliminary instructions and closed with, "Good luck. It's an honor to be in the ring with you."

After Nady and Ratner left, Evander went into the adjacent bathroom to provide a urine sample for a commission inspector. Then he returned, turned off the sound on the television, and inserted a tape of gospel music into a cassette player.

"All praise to the King. . . . Praise to Jesus. . . . Nothing compares to His love."

Holyfield put on high-top fight shoes and began lacing them up, singing along with the music.

"My Jesus, my Savior. . . . Glory to His name."

A look of rapture came over Evander's face and his body began to sway. The mundane work of lacing shoes took on the aura of a devotional act.

On the television screen, Joel Casamayor versus Diego Corrales began.

"Lift up your hearts to Jesus. . . . Glory unto His name."

At 6:05 p.m., Don Turner began taping Evander's hands.

No one spoke. Holyfield's eyes were closed. His head swayed to the music as he sang.

"We lift up our hands and bless Your Holy Name. . . . Blessed be the name of The Lord."

Turner worked efficiently. When the taping was done, Tim Hallmark stood opposite Evander and led him through a series of stretching exercises.

Casamayor–Corrales unfolded silently on the screen.

"Blessed be the name of the Lord. . . . Because He is worthy to be praised and adored . . . Hallelujah."

The stretching exercises ended. Holyfield pulled his protective cup up over his gym shorts. Blood was gushing from gashes on Diego Corrales's cheek and inside his mouth. After the sixth round, ring doctor Margaret Goodman stopped the fight.

"Good stoppage," Don Turner said.

It was almost time.

Everyone in the room joined hands in prayer.

"We lift up our hands and bless Your Holy Name. Blessed be the name of the Lord for He is worthy to be praised."

Then came the carnage.

Holyfield–Toney was a sad fight for people who cared about Evander.

"If a fight can be made," Evander once said, "I can win it." But as Larry Holmes has observed, "Sometimes the mind makes a date that the body can't keep." Holyfield–Toney was a reality check for Evander and the check bounced.

Holyfield came out hard in round one and looked pretty good at the start. But Toney was difficult to hit flush. Finally, in round three, Evander whacked James with his best right hand. And nothing happened. Then, in round four, Toney hit Holyfield back solidly and Evander wobbled.

Thereafter, Toney beat Holyfield up. By round seven, he was hitting

Evander at will with right hands. In the past, Holyfield had been on the opposite side of the same equation. Once, he had been the young fighter facing aging lions like George Foreman and Larry Holmes. And of course, there were times when Evander had taken beatings and come back to prevail.

But not this time.

By round eight, Holyfield's face was swollen and blood was streaming from his mouth. In round nine, a barrage of blows punctuated by a brutal body shot put him on the canvas. Most likely, Nady would have allowed the fight to continue. After all, Evander was boxing's consummate warrior. But as Holyfield rose, Don Turner stepped into the ring and halted the punishment. For only the second time in his ring career, Evander had been knocked out.

Whatever else Turner might have done in boxing, that was his finest moment.

All three judges had Toney comfortably ahead at the time of the stoppage.

In his dressing room after the fight, Evander glanced at his image in the mirror, opened a bottle of water, and took several gulps. Then he slumped in a chair.

"I got beat up," he said to no one in particular. "The body shots got me. Toney got off before me. He outhustled me. He beat me to position. I found myself thinking, not reacting. I was a step behind all night."

Holyfield bowed his head, not in prayer but in disappointment. For the moment, the emotional pain seemed worse than the physical.

"I don't have no excuses," he said. "My shoulder didn't bother me. I fought like I had a hurt shoulder, but the left arm was fine. The shoulder wasn't hurt at all. But I'm not ready to retire. I'll go home, rest a while, and look for a signal from the Lord."

There was a post-fight press conference marked by a standing ovation from the media in Evander's honor. Then he journeyed through a maze of back corridors and up to his suite on a service elevator.

"I feel good," he told the friends who gathered around him in the living room. "I got beat; that's all. I got my head up, so don't you all be sad."

That would have been a good time for Holyfield to end his career as an active fighter. But he didn't. He fought ten more times over the next eight years, beating Jeremy Bates, Fres Oquendo, Vinny Maddalone, Lou Savarese, Frans Botha, and Brian Nielsen, while losing to Larry Donald, Sultan Ibragimov, and Nikolai Valuev. He also fought Sherman Williams and was trailing on points when the bout was stopped and ruled "no contest" after Evander was cut by an accidental head butt.

But those fights were fought without Don Turner in his corner. The two men had worked together for sixteen fights against the likes of Mike Tyson, Riddick Bowe, and Lennox Lewis. Since 1994, Turner had readied Evander for battle and watched his back once the fighting began. Now his services were terminated.

"Toney was slick and hard to hit," Holyfield explained after Turner was fired. "So I was playing possum to lure him in. But Don didn't understand that and didn't have faith in me as a fighter so he stopped the fight. I can't have a trainer who doesn't believe in me."

Turner, not surprisingly, had a different take on things.

"Evander only hears what he wants to hear," the trainer responded. "And if you don't tell him what he wants to hear, you're gone. I'm a big fan of reality. And the reality is that Evander isn't what he used to be. I told him so and got fired. But I'd rather lose my job than go to a funeral."

After his 1947 outing against Jersey Joe Walcott, Joe Louis lamented, "I saw openings I couldn't use. A man gets old; he don't take advantage of those things as fast as he used to." Louis was thirty-three years old at the time. When Roy Jones stepped into the ring for his second fight against Antonio Tarver, he was thirty-five.

From Invincible to Vulnerable
Roy Jones vs. Antonio Tarver—
May 15, 2004

On May 15, 2004, Roy Jones and Antonio Tarver met in the ring at the Mandalay Bay Events Center in Las Vegas in a rematch of their November 8, 2003, encounter.

Jones had burst upon the scene as a nineteen-year-old prodigy at the 1988 Seoul Olympics and been widely recognized as the best fighter in the world for a decade. Boxing's pound-for-pound rankings were divided into two categories—Jones and everyone else.

Jones at his peak gave the impression of being able to ride bareback on a tornado without wrinkling his gleaming satin trunks. He fought championship-caliber opposition and, at times, made boxing look like a game instead of the brutal competition that it is. He was one of the most gifted fighters of our time.

Boxing legacies are written in the ring. Jones won his first world title by beating Bernard Hopkins and his second by outclassing James Toney. He won championships against opponents whose weight ranged from 160 to 226 pounds and, during the course of his career, defeated seventeen men who held world titles. The sole blemish on his résumé at the time he fought Tarver was a loss by disqualification against Montell Griffin in 1997. Four months later, he knocked Griffin out in the first round.

Jones had his critics. Great fights are marked by a dramatic ebb and flow. And the entertainment value inherent in boxing comes in significant part from risk. Jones had developed a style that, given his extraordinary talents, was as close to risk free as possible.

Lou DiBella (who helped build Jones as an attraction while vice president for programming at HBO Sports), declared, "Roy Jones is the most careful great fighter I've ever seen." And as 2003 came to a close, HBO Boxing analyst Larry Merchant observed, "I don't get a feeling of magic from Roy Jones anymore. Early in his career, I felt there was a certain magic; that he was a like a brilliant jazz musician running off riffs of punches that nobody had ever seen before. But as Roy moved up in weight, you didn't see that as often. His fights took on a pattern of opponents trying to pressure him, and Roy using his intelligence and very fast hands to discourage them. And what upsets a lot of boxing people is, he won't even try to close the show. That is, we're into the tenth round of a championship fight; Roy is ahead nine rounds to one; and he's content to play it out and walk away with a decision. In Roy's mind, it's, 'Why should I give the other guy a chance? If I try to knock him out, he might hit me with a big punch.' But it isn't very entertaining. Roy sucks the drama out of his fights by dominating his opponents in the first six rounds and coasting in the last six. From an entertainment point of view, instead of building to a climax, Roy builds to an anti-climax. Is it because he's so good? Yes. Is it because he's so smart? Yes. But it turns a lot of people off."

Jones's detractors wouldn't concede his greatness until he proved to their satisfaction that he had a fighting heart. In Roy's defense, Evander Holyfield, boxing's consummate warrior, opined, "You don't get down on a person because he's so talented that he hasn't been put in a position where he has to go through fire to win."

Then Holyfield was asked if, in his view, Jones would walk through fire if he had to.

"I don't know," Evander responded. "It don't matter how good a fighter is or what he has done before. Until he's faced with that moment for the first time, you don't know what he'll do because he doesn't know himself. He might think he knows, but he don't."

Thus the ultimate question: "On a night when Jones was brutally tested, when he was hurt, when his body ached, when he felt like he had nothing left; on that night, would Roy Jones just try to survive or would he walk through fire to win?"

Enter Antonio Tarver.

Jones and Tarver first met in the ring as thirteen-year-olds at the

Sunshine State Games in Gainesville, Florida. It has been said that, when boxers talk about long-ago amateur fights between them, there are three versions of what happened—one from each fighter and the truth.

"I beat his ass," Jones said of their 1982 encounter. "I chased him around the ring, beating on his ass, and won all three rounds."

"We had a very very competitive fight," Tarver countered. "And Roy won a split decision."

In November 2003, they met again. Tarver, by that time, was a former world amateur champion, Olympic bronze medalist, and 175-pound beltholder. The sole blot on his pro ledger was a loss by decision to Eric Harding, avenged by knockout two years later.

The general view was that Tarver was the second-best light-heavyweight in the world. But he was about to face a man who some thought was the best light-heavyweight ever. Jones had won twenty-three world championship fights. Tarver had fought twenty-two bouts in his entire pro career. Jones was a 7-to-1 betting favorite.

But as Jones–Tarver I approached, Roy found himself in a situation that he couldn't fully control. Six months earlier, he'd gone up in weight to fight John Ruiz for the WBA heavyweight crown. That night, he'd tipped the scales at 196 pounds. Now, for the first time in history, a heavyweight beltholder was going down in weight to fight for the light-heavyweight title. That meant, thirty hours before Jones–Tarver I, Roy had to weigh in at 175 pounds.

Not even Roy Jones could defy the laws of nature.

Jones called making weight for Jones–Tarver I the hardest thing he'd done in his life. By his own admission, he'd underestimated how difficult it would be to get back down to 175 pounds. "It's one of the worst times I ever had," he acknowledged. "You sacrifice so much, you want to kill somebody. I had to run more, diet more. You're hungry and thirsty half the time."

And there was another problem. In mid-October, Jones had gone to a dentist to have a cavity filled and another tooth capped. The filling and cap had bothered him ever since. He hadn't returned for corrective dentistry out of fear of making the situation worse. But for three weeks leading up to Jones–Tarver I, the pain interfered with his sleep.

In sum, fighting Tarver in 2003, Jones had been physically debilitated. "In the seventh round," he later acknowledged, "I told myself, 'This ain't working.' And in the eighth round, I was so tired, I told myself, 'This dude could stop me. If he ever could stop me, it would be now.'"

Then, in round nine, Jones dug deep and unveiled a new weapon in his arsenal—his heart. And in rounds nine through twelve, he showed the world that Roy Jones wasn't just a front-runner who outclassed opponents. Roy Jones was a fighter who summoned up strength when there appeared to be none, sucked up his guts, and did what had to be done on a bad night to win against a strong, skilled opponent.

Jerry Roth scored Jones–Tarver I a draw. Glen Hamada and Dave Harris gave Roy the nod by 117–111 and 116–112 margins.

That set the stage for Jones–Tarver II.

Roy knew that he was in for a tough fight. He was thirty-five years old now, the same age as Tarver. But the two men had different skill sets. It's axiomatic in boxing that a fighter loses speed and reflexes before he loses power. And without his preternatural speed and reflexes, Roy was no longer a spectacular fighter.

In truth, Jones likely had been slowing down before the first Tarver fight. There were inklings of it when he fought John Ruiz. But Ruiz was so slow that no one noticed. And Roy had put on twenty pounds of muscle for that fight, which likely contributed to slowing him down. Then, in Jones–Tarver I, the assumption in most circles was that Roy had been hampered by difficulty in making weight and complications from his oral surgery. But Alton Merkerson, Roy's trainer, sounded a cautionary note.

"Coach Merk" had known combat throughout his life: growing up on the mean streets of Chicago, as a career military officer in Vietnam, and in boxing. He and Jones had bonded at the 1988 Olympics when Merkerson helped guide Ray Mercer, Andrew Maynard, and Kennedy McKinney to gold medals. After Jones turned pro, Merkerson was his most constant ally. "If I had to go to war," Roy said, "I'd want Coach Merk with me first."

"I worked with Roy in 1988 on the Olympic team," Merkerson noted. "And I'll tell you what I see in Roy at the age of thirty-five. The ring generalmanship, he still has it but it's not as sharp as it used to be. He's just getting older. He can't do the things that he did when he was younger. You just lose it after a time when you get older. It's going to happen, as sure as you live and die."

★★★

The first arrivals in Roy Jones's dressing room on fight night—May 15, 2004—were Merkerson, former Olympic boxing coach Kenny Adams, cutman Richard Lucey, cornerman Mario Francis, and conditioning coach Mackie Shilstone. Jones, wearing a black Air Jordan warm-up suit with red-and-white trim, arrived at 6:30 p.m. with a half-dozen entourage members.

Bruce Seldon and Gerald Nobles were engaged in an inartistic heavyweight undercard fight that could be seen on a silent television monitor at the far end of the room.

"I'm good tonight," Roy announced. "Ready to go."

He seemed relaxed and confident.

"Some classic [NBA playoff] basketball games this week," he was told.

Roy's face lit up. "A lot of them," he said.

By seven o'clock, two dozen people were in the room, many of them constant presences in Roy's life, including fighters Billy Lewis, Derrick Gainer, Lemuel Nelson, and Al Cole.

Seldon–Nobles ended and was followed by Zab Judah versus Raphael Pineda.

Roy changed into his fighting clothes. Gray trunks with red-and-white trim. Gray-and-white shoes with red, white, and gray tassels.

At 7:20, John McClain (Laila Ali's husband and one of Tarver's seconds) entered the room to watch Merkerson tape Roy's hands. Ten minutes later, rap music sounded.

"The champ is here! The champ is here! The champ is here!"

Jones pulled up a chair beneath the television monitor and watched impassively, arms folded across his chest. From time to time, he chatted with Gainer, who was standing beside him.

Judah versus Pineda ended.

Roy rose and walked the length of the room, back and forth several times. Then everyone gathered in a prayer circle, with each person reaching forward so the outstretched arms were like the spokes of a wheel with their hands forming the hub.

Al Cole led the group in prayer.

Roy circled the room and embraced everyone, one person at a time.

Minutes later, Jones and Tarver were in the ring, facing each other.

"I gave you your instructions in the dressing room," referee Jay Nady told the fighters. "Do you have any questions?"

"I got a question," Tarver sneered. "Do you got any excuses tonight, Roy?"

The bell for round one rang, and the fight began with Jones stalking and Tarver keeping his distance. Not much happened, although Roy had an 8-to-2 edge in punches landed. It was his round.

In round two, Tarver began to stand his ground. Then, midway through the stanza, Jones scored with a quick right hand and followed with a hook that was more of a slap than a punch. As he did, he drew his head back a bit and raised his right hand in a defensive posture. He thought that the right side of his face was protected.

It wasn't. And Tarver landed with the precision of a gangland hit.

"We both threw at the same time," Antonio said later. "And I turned it over shorter than he did. It was an overhand left, right on the kisser. I would have knocked anyone out with that shot. It was a perfect punch."

Jones plummeted to the canvas, tried to rise, pitched forward onto his right shoulder, and forced himself to his feet at the count of nine through an act of incredible will. But Jay Nady waved his arms. The fight was over.

In boxing, as in the rest of life, one moment of violence can change everything.

One of Jones's cornermen put a stool beneath him. Dr. Margaret Goodman entered the ring, knelt beside the fighter, and took his hand.

"Are you okay?"

"I'm cool, baby," Roy told her.

"I'm so sorry."

"Hey, it happens."

Dr. Goodman began to probe.

"Do you have a headache?"

"I don't have a headache."

"Are you dizzy?"

"I'm not dizzy."

"Are you nauseous?"

"I'm not nauseous."

From a neurological standpoint, Jones was responsive and alert. His pupils were equal and reactive.

Derrick Gainer stood nearby, visibly shaken and crying. "Is he okay?"

"He's fine," Dr. Goodman assured him. Then she turned her attention back to Roy.

"I want you to sit here," she instructed. "A lot of people will want to talk with you. But I want you to rest for a minute. Let's take your gloves off."

The gloves were a way of buying time. Cornerman Mario Francis removed them. As he did, Jones watched a replay of the knockout on one of the giant screens above.

"How are you doing now?" Goodman queried.

"I'm cool."

It's a humbling experience to be knocked out by another man in front of millions of people. But one-punch knockouts happen in boxing. Ask Lennox Lewis, who was starched by Oliver McCall and Hasim Rahman. Ask Larry Holmes, who, in today's world, most likely wouldn't have been allowed to continue after being knocked woozy by Earnie Shavers and Renaldo Snipes in fights that he ultimately won. Ask Roberto Duran, who suffered a one-punch knockout at the hands of Thomas Hearns.

There were a lot of broken hearts in Roy Jones's dressing room after the fight.

Roy sat on a chair, looking straight ahead with a pile of towels beside him. Conversations were going on around the room, but he was the focus of attention.

"I had him where I wanted him," Roy said. "I was doing what I wanted to do. I was faster than last time. I was stronger than last time. I just got caught. I guess God wanted me to go through this at least one time."

Roy took a breath and let it out slowly.

"One shot. I know exactly what happened. I threw a right hand and tried to come back with the left. He read it and fired his gun first. My right hand was up and I couldn't see the punch coming. No excuses. He caught me with a good shot."

Félix Trinidad, who had suffered his own bitter disappointment at the hands of Bernard Hopkins three years earlier, entered the room.

There's a fraternity among great fighters. Jones rose and the two men embraced.

"I'm sorry," Trinidad said. "You are a great fighter."

Roy sat down again.

"Nothing like this ever happened to me before. It hurts. It feels hard, but there's no physical pain. . . . Hey—that's how life goes sometimes. I'll deal with it. Take it as it comes. . . . Shit."

One of the entourage members sought to boost Roy's spirits.

"The referee was looking to stop the fight. He never gave you a chance."

Alton Merkerson shook his head.

"The guy that's talking to Roy now doesn't know shit about boxing," Coach Merk said. "Believe me—if something happened that was wrong, I'd be the first one to let everyone know about it. But I can't fault the referee. He was looking after Roy's best interests. Roy was hurt. There's a chance he could have weathered the storm, but he was still shook when they stopped it."

Merkerson shook his head again.

"No use crying over spilt milk. Tarver's a good fighter."

"What do you think about the stoppage?" Jones was asked.

"When you're in there, you want to go on," Roy answered. "But I can't say the referee did the wrong thing. Hey—it happened. In your heart, you always know it can happen, even though you hope it never will."

"This doesn't change who you are," a friend said. "You're still every bit as good a person as you are a fighter."

Jones smiled. "Tonight, I'm a better person than I was a fighter."

Then Roy turned toward Derrick Gainer, who had begun crying again.

"Don't be sad," Roy told him. "God is good."

The pre-fight buildup to Bernard Hopkins vs. Jermain Taylor was nasty versus nice. Once the bell rang, that didn't matter.

The Changing of the Guard
Bernard Hopkins vs. Jermain Taylor— July 16, 2005

On July 16, 2005, Jermain Taylor—"The Pride of Little Rock, Arkansas"— won a split-decision victory over Bernard Hopkins at the MGM Grand in Las Vegas to claim the undisputed middleweight championship of the world. It wasn't easy.

Like most fighters, Taylor came from hard origins. His father abandoned the family when Jermain was five, leaving Jermain, his mother, and three younger sisters behind. The children were raised largely by their maternal grandmother, who was murdered by her own son (Jermain's uncle) when Jermain was nineteen.

"He had a bad drug problem," Jermain later recalled. "He wanted money and she wouldn't give it to him, so he cut her throat and then killed himself. I was at the Goodwill Games when it happened. They told me about it when I got home. I heard what they were saying but it wasn't real. Then I went into her bedroom. There was blood all over the sheets, all over the floor, and I realized that what they were saying was true. I'd won a bronze medal at the games and, at the funeral, I put it in her casket."

Taylor won National Golden Gloves championships at 156 pounds in 1998 and 1999 and was a 156-pound bronze medalist at the 2000 Olympic Games.

"In the amateurs, I was ignored most of the time because I come from Arkansas," he noted years later. "I was skipped over a lot when boxers were chosen for teams that went to tournaments because Arkansas is small and doesn't have much boxing. Then I started winning national tournaments and it was like, 'Wow! Look at Jermain.'"

Taylor came into the Hopkins fight as an immensely likeable twenty-six-year-old man. He was down to earth, good looking, personable, and unfailingly polite.

Meanwhile, boxing fans were familiar with the Hopkins saga. At age seventeen, Bernard was sentenced to five to twelve years in prison for multiple street crimes. Fifty-six months later, he was released and his life began anew.

"When I got home from Graterford State Penitentiary," Hopkins later reminisced, "it wasn't like I knew I was going to be middleweight champion of the world someday. It was, I got eight years of parole and I don't ever want to go back there again."

Ultimately, he became boxing's pound-for-pound champion and entered the Taylor fight with twenty successful title defenses for the third-longest unbroken championship reign in boxing history (ten years, eighty-two days).

"I'm in the hurt business," Hopkins said. "I'm not looking to come out of this squeaky clean every time I step into that ring. While the fight's going on, the fight business is not about, 'Are you okay? Are you all right? Did I hit you too hard?' It's legal to hit a guy in the Adam's apple. A shoulder can be hit. Trust me; whatever limb you give me, I'm punching it. I'll do anything to win."

Often, the public hears a fighter say, "I'm in the best shape of my life," and then watches as the fighter comes into the ring physically unprepared for battle. That never happened with Hopkins. Over the years, he maintained his body through a mix of hard work and extraordinary discipline and turned himself into a finely honed precision weapon. His superb defensive skills allowed him to dictate the pace of fights. No boxer's defense is "impenetrable" but Bernard's came close.

There were times when Hopkins was charming. But often that gave way to something ugly. Bernard approached many of his dealings in boxing, in and out of the ring, as though they were street confrontations.

Hopkins and Taylor had been on each other's radar screen for several years. Bernard was the undisputed middleweight champion. Jermain was seen by many as the heir apparent. The negotiations leading up to their fight were acrimonious. Hopkins had once been promoted by Lou DiBella. Then he left DiBella, made ugly allegations of financial wrongdoing by the promoter, and wound up on the losing end of a $610,000 jury verdict in a libel action that DiBella brought against him in federal court. DiBella was now Taylor's promoter.

At the final pre-fight press conference, Hopkins seemed to be looking past Taylor as he talked about moving up in weight to fight Antonio Tarver or Roy Jones next. He also commented on Taylor's persona, saying, "Jermain Taylor and I are both African Americans but that's where the similarity ends." A mocking appraisal followed, highlighted by, "Jermain uses words like 'golly gee.' That's not my style."

"As a child, I had a real bad speech problem," Taylor said when it was his turn to talk. "I stuttered a lot. I still do it some, so it's hard enough for me to talk without trying to talk trash. Bernard Hopkins might outtalk me, but I'm gonna outfight him. I want to be number one. And now that I got that chance, I'm gonna take it. I'm a lot faster than Bernard, faster and stronger. However he brings it, I'm going to take it to him. I know how Bernard fights. If he wants to make it a dirty fight, then it's going to be a dirty fight because I ain't backing down from nobody. My time is now, and Bernard is ready for the taking. There's been a lot of ups and downs in my life, a lot of hurt. I've had to step up to the plate when it wasn't my time. All that has prepared me for this moment. This is what I've wanted since I first started boxing."

Two days later, there was an uglier confrontation. Hopkins had made his hatred for DiBella a subplot to Hopkins–Taylor. At the final pre-fight press conference, he'd proclaimed that beating DiBella's fighter would be "like a second erection."

That ugliness burgeoned out of control at the fighter weigh-in. The temperature outside the MGM Grand Garden Arena was a blistering 110 degrees. Taylor stepped on the scale with Pat Burns (who'd trained Jermain from his first day in the pro ranks) beside him. Perfect weight, 160 pounds. Hopkins followed, also 160.

"Face off the fighters," someone instructed.

But instead of moving to a staredown with Taylor, Hopkins approached DiBella.

Bernard knows how to place his punches, in and out of the ring. In both venues, he has been known to go low. Twelve years earlier, after being disabled in a skiing accident, DiBella's brother had taken his own life. DiBella had shared that information with Hopkins in earlier years when the fighter and promoter had been friends. Now. . . .

"You're going to kill yourself tomorrow night," DiBella says Hopkins told him. "It's the end of your life tomorrow night. You know about people killing themselves. You'll slit your throat or take pills and not wake up on Sunday morning."

Then Hopkins moved toward Taylor, who was tying his shoes, and stood over him.

"You're a puppet," Bernard sneered.

Taylor stood up and the two men were nose to nose with perhaps two inches between them.

"I ain't no one's puppet, you ugly motherfucker."

They stood that way, jawing at one another, until calmer heads separated them.

Afterward, Taylor was pleased with the confrontation. "There was a whole lot of motherfucking going on," he said on the way back to his hotel room. "Bernard got in my face, and my first reaction was to step back and throw an uppercut. I got two sides. I'll beat him in a street fight too. Man, we were so close, our lips were almost kissing. I said to myself, 'This won't look good to my wife.'"

Pat Burns had a similar take on the situation.

"Bernard is trying to get his courage up; that's all," Burns offered "Some guys drink to get that liquid courage. Some guys do it like this."

Then Burns turned to this writer.

"Listen to me," he said. "Look at me, because what I'm about to tell you is very important. Jermain will not be intimidated by Bernard Hopkins. There is no intimidation factor here at all. Zero. None."

★★★

Shortly after 6:00 p.m. on Saturday night, Jermain Taylor arrived at his dressing room at the MGM Grand Garden Arena. The early odds had been 2-to-1 in Hopkins's favor, reflecting both his greatness and doubts regarding Taylor's seasoning as a fighter. The champion was still favored but the odds had dropped to 3-to-2.

Taylor sat quietly beside Burns on a sofa and watched as an undercard fight unfold on the large television screen in front of them. Dennis Moore (a Little Rock police officer and friend of Jermain's) stood guard by the dressing room door. Cutman Ray Rodgers was readying the tools of his trade. Ozell Nelson (who taught Taylor the rudiments of boxing when Jermain was a boy), Dan Lowry (who ran the gym in Little Rock where Ozell first trained Jermain), and Joey Burns (Pat's brother) joined them. So did Pat's twelve-year-old son, Ryan. Well-wishers came and went.

At 6:30, Burns closed the door to all but essential personnel. Five minutes later, referee Jay Nady came in to give Jermain his pre-fight instructions. The Taylor camp was happy with the choice of Nady as the referee. He was a big no-nonsense guy who ran a tight ship and, it was hoped, would keep fouling by Hopkins to a minimum. "This is for every belt that I know of," Nady began. The pro forma instructions followed.

At 6:55, Ozell Nelson went to Hopkins's dressing room to oversee the champion's hands being wrapped. While he was gone, Naazim Richardson (on behalf of Hopkins) watched Pat Burns do the same with Jermain. At 7:20, the taping was done.

"Except for the commission inspector," Burns said, "all cell phones off, please."

Everything in the dressing room was business-like and low key. There was no music.

Jermain put on his University of Arkansas—red trunks.

Lou DiBella came in and sat on a chair in the corner.

Jermain went into an anteroom the size of a small boxing ring with a carpeted floor and cinderblock walls. Under the watchful eye of Burns and training assistant Edgardo Martinez, he shadow-boxed and worked the pads with Martinez.

At 7:45, Naazim Richardson returned and Jermain gloved up.

Taylor, Burns, and Martinez went back into the anteroom. Work resumed with Burns giving advice in a reassuring yet authoritative tone.

"Make sure your feet and hands work together. . . . He won't be able to stop the jab. The moment you sense he's trying to counter the jab with a jab, double up. . . . The last fifteen seconds of each round, you'll have already won it and he'll try to steal it. Don't give up anything cheap. . . . Punch him anywhere you can. . . . Speed kills. If he's doing forty, you do sixty. If he's doing sixty, you do eighty. . . . Don't let the crowd influence you. . . . If he gets in a rhythm, go in with a forearm and push him out of it. . . . I'm looking for at least twenty-five jabs a round. Pick him apart. That's how you dominate."

At 8:12, the final preliminary fight ended. Jermain started hitting the pads with greater intensity.

"We're bringing back a world champion," Burns said.

People in a fighter's camp believe, particularly when their fighter is young and undefeated as Taylor was. But Jermain would be facing a man who hadn't lost a fight in twelve years. In a matter of hours, win or lose, he would no longer be a rising star. Either he would be the undisputed middleweight champion of the world or just another name on Bernard Hopkins's ring record.

It was a pro-Taylor crowd. That was evident from the roar of approval that resounded when Jermain entered the arena. There were 11,992 fans in attendance. One-third of them had come from Arkansas.

Two minutes later, Hopkins made his way to the ring.

Michael Buffer introduced the fighters.

The bell for round one sounded.

One could imagine the thoughts in Jermain's mind: *I'm in the ring with a great fighter. Now is the time to find out if I'm a great fighter too.*

The early rounds belonged to Taylor. Almost always, Hopkins fought cautiously in the early stages of his fights. Jermain advanced behind his jab while Bernard slowed the pace by retreating and keeping his right hand cocked to discourage forays by the challenger. Forty seconds into round two, a chopping overhand right followed by a left hook caused the champion to fall back and downward against the ropes. Some thought it should have been called a knockdown. Jay Nady let the moment pass.

Taylor was faster. Hopkins minimized the number of encounters by moving around the ring and did his best work while punching out of clinches with sharp, punishing blows. As a fighter, Bernard was supreme on the inside. That was where he was expected to do the most damage.

Fifty seconds into round five, the fighters clashed heads and an ugly wound pierced Taylor's scalp to the bone just above the hairline. Blood flowed freely and would for much of the night. Jermain had only been cut once before in a professional fight.

"Blood was pouring from my head," he said later. "I'd never gone through anything like that before. After the head butt, it was like, 'Boy, these rounds are long.' I was just hoping I had enough blood in me to finish the fight."

Blood can undermine a fighter's confidence. And some ring judges score blood more than they should.

After eight rounds, Taylor had outlanded Hopkins by a 63-to-40 margin. But he'd expended a lot of energy chasing. In round nine, he tired, and the roles of predator and prey were reversed.

Hopkins began his assault. In round ten, a right hand hurt Jermain. More punishing blows followed. Round eleven was the same. Now Hopkins's fists were doing his talking for him. That one hurt, didn't it, Jermain?

Then came a moment that will forever define the career of each fighter. There was a minute left in round eleven. The momentum was all with Hopkins. Taylor was backed against the ropes, in trouble. Hopkins landed a big right hand. And in his darkest moment, Jermain summoned the strength to fire three hard shots with lightning speed into Bernard's body. Rather than continue the exchange, Hopkins stepped back. No one knew it at the time, but that was when Jermain Taylor established himself as a champion.

"I was dog-tired," Jermain acknowledged afterward. "No way of getting around it. I said to myself, 'Man, this is it. Either you've got it inside or you don't.'"

"Ladies and gentlemen, we have a split decision," ring announcer Michael Buffer told the crowd when the fight was over. "Jerry Roth scores the bout 116 to 112 for Hopkins."

Pat Burns patted his fighter's cheek. "Don't worry; that's just one."

"I knew the next one would be for me because that's the way they read them," Jermain said later.

"Duane Ford, 115–113 for Taylor."

"Okay, here we go," Jermain told himself.

Twelve thousand people in the arena held their breath as the final moments of the drama unfolded.

"Paul Smith, 115–113 to the winner by split decision and NEW . . ."

Years later, Jermain would look back on that moment and remember, "All I heard after that was the cheering."

There were no titles on the line when Wladimir Klitschko and Samuel Peter met in the ring for the first time. But it was a matchup with far-reaching implications for the heavyweight division.

The Road Back for Wladimir Klitschko
Wladimir Klitschko vs. Samuel Peter— September 24, 2005

Knockout power is an aphrodisiac in boxing. And the heavyweights are boxing's flagship division. Because of these realities, a lot of dreams were riding on Samuel Peter's broad shoulders when he arrived at Boardwalk Hall in Atlantic City on the night of September 24, 2005, to fight Wladimir Klitschko.

Peter was born into a middle-class family in Nigeria and is one of the two best heavyweights ever to come out of Africa. Ike Ibeabuchi is the other. Samuel was a promising soccer player, fast and strong, until an adolescent knee injury ended his hopes for turf glory. Then he turned to boxing and came to the United States in 2001 to pursue his ring career. Prior to fighting Klitschko, he had 24 wins in 24 fights with 21 knockouts.

Peter is a likable man with a ready smile. At times, it appears as though his cell phone is surgically attached to his ear.

"I'm a happy person," Samuel has said. "I grew up with a good mother and a good father. They taught me to respect my elders and be humble. They loved me and taught me about God. To be a good person gets you to heaven." As for residing in the United States, he declared, "It's a great life here. Someday, I will be buried in Nigeria, but I am happy where I am now."

Regarding the sweet science, Peter proclaimed:

★ "In boxing, I have never been knocked down and I never will be. I am a special fighter. I don't think anybody can put me down. I don't compare myself with anybody because I am special. One day, people will compare other fighters to me."

★ "I want to make money. Money motivates me. To think about fighting for five or ten million dollars makes me run day and night. But to be the first African champion, to make history for my country and all of Africa, is also important to me."

★ "Boxing to me is a game. You hit me; I hit you. To knock somebody out feels better than scoring a goal. But boxing is a sport, not a war. In a war, I would run backwards. If you want to go to war, go to Iraq."

Meanwhile, prior to fighting Peter, Klitschko was considered damaged goods. After starting his career with twenty-four consecutive victories, he'd been knocked out by Ross Puritty (a thirteen-loss journeyman). He rebounded with sixteen straight wins (all but one by knockout) and claimed the WBO heavyweight title. But even then, there were danger signs.

Klitschko had totally dominated Ray Mercer and Jameel McCline during his second streak, but appeared to bail out each time either man threw serious punches. Then he lost his title when he was knocked out in two rounds by Corrie Sanders, won comeback fights against Fabio Moli and Danell Nicholson, and was stopped in five rounds by Lamon Brewster.

The loss to Brewster was particularly troubling. Afterward, the Klitschko camp claimed that Wladimir had been drugged. "We know the result of the fight," Klitschko said. "Lamon Brewster won. But I have questions. My mind was crystal clear but my body and legs wouldn't respond. I couldn't breathe. I was fighting with myself just to move in the ring, not against my opponent. And the collapse came so fast. In the third round, it took effort to get up from my chair. It's important for me to know why. I want to find the answer to what was wrong with me."

Extensive tests overseen by Dr. Margaret Goodman (chief ringside physician for the Nevada State Athletic Commission) found no evidence that Klitschko had been drugged. And regardless of the reason for his failure against Brewster, Wladimir often looked as though he was skating on thin ice when he was in the ring. He'd shown an inability to take big punches, and there were those who thought that he no longer took little punches well either. Desultory wins over DaVarryl Williamson and Eliseo Castillo after the loss to Brewster did nothing to restore his luster.

"From nothing to everything is a very long road in boxing," Wladimir acknowledged. "But from everything to nothing is just one short step."

Klitschko–Peter was an intriguing matchup. Wladimir voiced the view that the fight was "where I will regain my stature." But the odds suggested otherwise.

Peter was a 7-to-5 betting favorite based on his punching power and Klitschko's suspect chin. Indeed, many of Samuel's partisans were counting on Wladimir's weaknesses as much as Samuel's strengths in calculating Peter's keys to victory. But others wondered how Samuel would deal with adversity if it came his way. Real adversity. Not just being outpointed, but being tired and getting hit by a big man who could punch. Dishing it out is great. But could Peter take it if his resolve were tested?

As expected, Emanuel Steward (who trained Klitschko) predicted that his man would win.

"Boxing is so desperate for excitement in the heavyweight division that people are building Samuel Peter up beyond all reason," Steward declared. "Peter is nothing more than a ten-month sensation. And in my mind, he hasn't even been that sensational in those ten months. Samuel thinks he'll overpower Wladimir, but that won't happen. When you get to a certain level, you can't win fights on power alone. You think that all it takes is one of yours to make everything go your way. But being able to punch hard is only part of what world-class boxing is about. At the highest level of the sport, you don't just knock people out. Wladimir will control Samuel for the entire fight. Getting hit by a 250-pound man who knows how to fight will be a new experience for Samuel. After two rounds of eating the kind of punches that Wladimir is hitting him with, he won't want to fight anymore."

★★★

Wearing gray sweatpants and a white T-shirt with "www.samuel-peter .com" emblazoned in green letters across the front, Samuel Peter entered his dressing room at Boardwalk Hall in Atlantic City on fight night at 8:20, lay down on a rubdown table, and closed his eyes.

One day earlier at the weigh-in, Peter's thighs had evoked images of giant oak trees. Now he seemed smaller than his 243 pounds. Samuel's wife, Enobong, came into the room and squeezed his hand. At 8:35, he signaled for someone to turn on his music. Gentle sounds filtered through the air.

Peter sat up on the rubdown table and began to sing.

"Did I tell you that I love you. Did I tell you that I want you. Did I tell you that I need you. You make me feel like heaven is here on earth."

Assistant trainer Cornelius Boza-Edwards took a scissors and started cutting loose threads from the blue sequined trunks that Samuel would wear later in the evening.

Over the next two hours, myriad people came and went. The core group (manager Ivaylo Gotzev, trainer Pops Anderson, assistant trainer Kenny Croom, and Boza-Edwards) remained.

The taking of a urine sample by an inspector for the New Jersey State Athletic Control Board and the referee's pre-fight instructions followed. From time to time, Samuel stood up and danced to the music.

At 9:05, Vitali Klitschko (Wladimir's older brother) and James Bashir (an assistant to Emanuel Steward) came in to watch Boza-Edwards tape Peter's hands. Samuel ignored them and continued to dance and sing.

"Anything that you can do, no one can do it better. Anything that you can say, no one can say it better."

Vitali was on edge. "It's easier for me to fight than to watch my brother fight," he'd acknowledged earlier in the day. "If I fight, I'm cool. If my brother fights, I'm nervous."

At 9:10, Peter sat down on a folding metal chair and the taping began. After the first roll of gauze was applied, Samuel reached for his watch and handed it to Boza-Edwards, who stretched the heavy metal band around his fighter's fist in the manner of brass knuckles.

Bashir's eyes widened.

Samuel laughed.

Boza-Edwards removed the watch.

There was no change in Vitali's expression. He was measuring the man who, in less than two hours, would seek to destroy his brother.

At 9:35, the taping was done. Peter would be called to the ring sometime between 10:20 and 11:00 depending on the length of the semifinal bout between Miguel Cotto and Ricardo Torres.

Once again, Samuel began to sing.

"It's the truth that I feel. My destiny is sealed. I know I can move any mountain. . . . Lord, when I thought it was over for me, you gave me strength and lifted my burdens. Thank you, Lord, for giving me strength to carry on."

There was no television monitor in the room. Word came that Cotto–Torres had begun. Samuel began a series of stretching exercises. Then he gloved up and hit the pads with Croom.

Over the next half hour, there were reports on the progress of Cotto–Torres: "Torres is down in round one. . . . Cotto is down in the second round."

Samuel sat on a folding metal chair and stretched out his legs. Then he stood up and began to dance, smiling at his reflection in a mirror on the wall.

"Cotto and Torres are in round five," he was told.

Kenny Croom and Samuel worked the pads again.

Cotto stopped Torres in the seventh round.

"You walk in five minutes," Team Peter was instructed.

Pops Anderson led the group in prayer.

At 10:55, Peter left his dressing room for the ring. Every fight is a journey into the unknown. The fact that he was stepping up in class made this encounter particularly unpredictable for him. For the first time in his professional career, Samuel would be facing an opponent whose tools were comparable to, if not better than, his own.

In the end, neither fighter was as flawed as the other side had hoped for. And neither lived up to the high expectations of his backers.

Peter was the aggressor for most of the bout, but it was often ineffective aggression. As a person, Samuel is straightforward and honest with little artifice about him. Unfortunately, that was also true of his ring style. He rarely feinted and often was off-balance after missing with wild looping punches. That left him wide open for counters. But since Wladimir bailed out when punches were fired and fell into a clinch when Samuel got inside, the counters rarely came.

Klitschko did his most effective work with his jab. On occasion, he landed solid right hands. When Wladimir landed, Samuel took the punches well.

In round five, a clubbing left hook followed by a right hand to the back of the head put Klitschko on the canvas. A second knockdown that was more of a push followed. At that point, it looked as though the Klitschko strategy of "jab and grab" might become "hold and fold." But for the next four rounds, Wladimir stayed on his bike, jabbing and holding when necessary, while Peter was unable to cut off the ring.

After nine rounds, Peter was visibly tired; his right eye was closing; and Steward suggested that Klitschko pick the pace up a bit to give Samuel a reason to fall. But to put an opponent away, a fighter has to move into the danger zone. So when Klitschko by his deeds said, "I'll punch with you," Samuel answered, "WHACK." And Wladimir found himself on the canvas for the third time. At that point, discretion being the better part of valor, Klitschko became elusive again.

All three judges scored the bout 114–111 for Klitschko, who outlanded Peter with his jab by a 129-to-26 margin. The "power punch" numbers were even.

Wladimir won because he was the technically more proficient boxer. And he did something that he'd been unable to do in the past. He came back from adversity to win a fight. He proved his courage if not his chin.

Samuel showed heart and the ability to take a good punch. But he was exposed as a work in progress rather than a finished fighter.

Following the loss to Klitschko, Peter won decisions over James Toney (twice) and Jameel McCline. Then he knocked out Oleg Maskaev to claim the WBC heavyweight title. But he was still a fighter who relied heavily on brute strength. In the first defense of his belt, he was knocked out by Vitali Klitschko (who was returning to the ring after a four-year absence). Vitali won every minute of every round. Showtime blow-by-blow commentator Steve Albert labeled the bout "a glorified sparring session," and expert analyst Al Bernstein said Samuel's performance was "dreadful." Eventually, Peter was relegated to opponent status, fighting at weights as high as 291 pounds and losing six of his final ten bouts between 2010 and 2019.

At the other end of the spectrum, in the years following his triumph over Peter, Wladimir Klitschko crafted a twenty-two-fight winning streak (including a tenth-round knockout in a 2010 rematch against Samuel). He collected multiple belts and was widely recognized as the class of the heavyweight division. Finally, in 2015, Wladimir was outpointed by Tyson Fury and relinquished his crown.

Anthony Ottah was brought in to lose to a young heavyweight prospect being groomed for stardom. This is the story of that fight.

The Opponent
Anthony Ottah vs. Kevin Burnett—February 16, 2006

Early on the evening of February 16, 2006, Anthony Ottah took the subway from his home in Brooklyn to Thirty-Fourth Street in Manhattan.

Ottah, forty years old at the time, was a large, muscular man with a dignified presence and honest face. He came to the United States from Nigeria in 1982 and had been married for eighteen years. He and his wife had a fifteen-year-old son and an eleven-year-old daughter.

Ottah was wearing black work pants and a blue denim jacket over a green sweatshirt. He had shaved earlier in the day. His face and scalp were smooth. At 250 pounds, there was a little extra weight on his six-foot, one-inch frame, but he was in good shape.

Ottah had fought as an amateur from 1988 until 1990 and returned to the ring a decade later. His first professional bout was a four-round loss in 2001 to a fighter who was also making his pro debut. On February 16, 2006, as he rode the subway, his record stood at one win, four losses, and one draw with no knockouts either way. He trained two or three times a week after his day job for an hour at the Kingsway Gym. "I like to box," he said. "It teaches you to respect other men. I do it because I enjoy it. It's inbred."

Ottah was what is known in the trade as an "opponent." He fought with dignity and he fought to win. He simply wasn't at a level where he could make a living doing it and never would be. On this particular night, he'd been penciled in as a "learning experience" for a young prospect named Kevin Burnett. There were fighters who Ottah could beat, but he'd been chosen for this evening with confidence that he simply wasn't good enough to beat the gifted young man who would be in front of him.

Fights like this are essential to boxing. They're part of what goes into building a young fighter. If a prospect like Burnett goes in tough too many times, there will be excess wear and tear on his body and any losses will make it harder for him to get to the big dollars. Hence, mismatches.

A mismatch is a fight in which a fighter's physical assets and skill level are so superior to that of his opponent that the outcome is a foregone conclusion. In other words, a mismatch is about watching a highly skilled, physically gifted athlete beat up another person.

Burnett was six feet, six inches tall and twenty-three years old with a 2–0 record. In 50 amateur fights, he'd registered 37 knockouts. His trainer was Don Turner, who'd worked with Evander Holyfield and Larry Holmes. There was money behind him.

When DiBella Entertainment (which was promoting the fight) suggested Ottah as an opponent, the Burnett camp asked around and got a uniform response. Ottah was a tough guy who would stand and fight, but his skills were limited. Very limited.

"That's what we want," Burnett's manager, Craig Hamilton, said. "We don't want an opponent who will run and hold and make Kevin look bad. We want a guy who will stand in front of him and fight. I know Ottah is tough and I know Ottah is coming to win. But if Kevin can't handle him, then we're very wrong about Kevin."

Ottah knew his limitations. "I'd have more of a future in this game if I was young," he said one day before the fight. "But what can I do? In life, there is always joy and there are always regrets. I hope to win this fight. Then I'll talk about more."

Meanwhile, the much-respected Jimmy Glenn, who gave Ottah a hand early in the fighter's career, acknowledged, "I don't call promoters for him anymore, but sometimes they call him. He told me a few weeks ago, 'Jimmy, I took the fight.' I try to be nice to everyone and let them down easy, so what could I say? He's a fighter at heart. There ain't no quit in him. He should have retired a few years ago, but everybody sees that George Foreman thing and thinks they can fight forever. Hopefully, he won't get hurt. And when he retires, he'll have done what he wanted to do."

Ottah was hardly a typical fighter. After coming to the United States to get an education, he graduated from the State University of New York with a degree in accounting. At the time he fought Burnett, he was an examiner for the New York State Department of Insurance. His job was to audit the books of insurance companies to make sure that they were in compliance with state law. He wasn't fighting out of desperation. He was fighting because he wanted to fight.

"I come from a fighting clan," he said. "Where I was born, in a village called Nenwe, we box as a tradition. The men box and the whole village comes to watch. From the time I was three years old, I was boxing."

Other than his health, Ottah had nothing to lose by fighting Burnett. But he didn't have much to gain either. The fight was scheduled for four rounds. His purse would be $1,000. DiBella was pleased that Ottah lived in Brooklyn. That meant he wouldn't have to pay for a hotel room and airfare to bring him in for the fight.

★★★

As Ottah was travelling alone on the subway, Kevin Burnett walked from his room at the New Yorker Hotel to the Manhattan Center next door where the fight would take place. Don Turner, Craig Hamilton, and Johnnie Ray Kinsey (his weight-training coach) were with him. Burnett, Turner, and Kinsey had come to New York from their training camp in North Carolina three days earlier. Hamilton drove in from Long Island on the day of the fight.

Burnett's management team had three participants. Hamilton did the nuts-and-bolts day-to-day work and was the expert on the business of boxing. Previously, he'd guided Michael Grant to $8 million in purses highlighted by a $3.5 million payday for fighting Lennox Lewis at Madison Square Garden. New York attorney Gary Friedman provided legal expertise. Steve Geppi (a Baltimore businessman who owned several auction houses and was one of the largest comic-book distributors in the world) was the money guy.

Pursuant to contract, Burnett received a stipend of $2,000 a month. Management also paid $1,000 a month for weight training, $1,000 a month for training camp expenses, and other boxing-related outlays such as the cost of sparring partners. All of these expenses were advances against future earnings.

In return, management would receive 30 percent of each Burnett purse of $1 million or less. The percentage would be adjusted downward on a sliding scale to as little as 15 percent on purses above that number. So far, Hamilton and company hadn't taken their share of any purse, but Burnett had been required to pay Turner his 10 percent trainer's fee. For the Ottah fight, Burnett's purse would be $800. The amount was irrelevant. It was the learning experience and the expected "W" on his record that were important.

Burnett was one of seven children from a single-parent family in Georgia. He'd started boxing at the Augusta Boxing Club when he was eight years old. Initially, Hamilton had concerns about Burnett's conditioning and eating habits. On Thanksgiving Day 2005, he weighed 338 pounds. Then Turner and Kinsey got their hands on him. Fat was being replaced by muscle. He now weighed 290 pounds with a projected goal of 265.

"Being a fighter is healthy if you do it right," Burnett said. "You have to take care of your body, exercise and eat right. I know that now."

Burnett had never been knocked down as an amateur or pro and maintained that he had never been badly hurt either. "My best weapons are my jab, my left hook, and body shots," he said the day before he fought Ottah. "I don't know my weaknesses yet. But as the competition steps up, I'll find out what they are." Then he added, "I'm in boxing to make history. I daydream about being heavyweight champion of the world and one of the greatest fighters of all time. Boxing gives me the opportunity to create my own historic legacy."

In the dressing room at the Manhattan Center, Don Turner looked around the room and smiled. "The journey has begun," he said.

★★★

Ottah arrived at the Manhattan Center at 6:30 p.m. His fight against Burnett would be the first bout of the evening, the spot generally reserved for the least-competitive matchup of the night. He had been assigned to the "opponents" dressing room with Jose Spearman, Anthony Hunter, Cliff Walker, and Christopher "Shaka" Henry, each of whom would be knocked out later in the evening in less than three full rounds.

Ottah stripped down to white briefs and white socks and did several minutes of stretching exercises alone on the floor. Then trainer Willie Dunne joined him. A New York State Athletic Commission doctor came in and checked his blood pressure. Ottah put on his protective cup. Dunne rubbed Vaseline on his legs and arms.

"Does anyone have a towel?" Dunne asked.

No one did, so the trainer left the room to find one.

Ottah took a pair of creased black trunks out of his gym bag and put them on. Dunne returned with a towel. There were more stretching exercises. Dunne taped Ottah's hands, put Vaseline on the fighter's torso and face, and wiped his hands with the newly acquired towel. Ottah gloved up and began working the pads with Dunne.

"If he's coming at you," Dunne instructed, "stand up to the man. Get one in there so he stops coming. The minute he cocks his hand—BOOM—left hook to the body. Hook to the body; then the right hand behind it. Two shots at a time. Don't go for three."

Each time Ottah jabbed, he lifted his head and brought his left hand back slowly, fatal flaws in boxing.

"Don't raise up, damn it," Dunne cautioned. "Stay low; close it up. Don't leave a lane for the guy to come back at you. Look; this guy you're fighting is soft. He's overweight; he weighs 290 pounds. This is an easy fight for you. Just don't get hit with something you don't need to get hit with. Fight smart. Keep him in the center of the ring. Put your weight behind your punches. This is an opportunity for you, man."

Don Quixote and Sancho Panza tilting at windmills.

At precisely 8:00 p.m., Ottah entered the ring. To those in attendance, he wasn't an educated man, a husband, or father. He was an opponent. He looked lonely, like a bull being led to slaughter. A minute later, Kevin Burnett stood opposite him. Referee Tony Chiarantano gave the fighters their final instructions. On paper, it was an easy fight for Burnett. In the ring, it would be hard.

Seconds into round one, Ottah landed an overhand right flush on Burnett's cheek, then another. They didn't do much damage because throwing punches is an art that Ottah hasn't fully mastered. But they sent a message: "I'm here to fight." Burnett began stalking but he was neglecting his jab. That enabled Ottah get off first. It was Ottah's round.

Round two was more of the same with Ottah throwing wide, looping punches. A stiff jab would have stopped him in his tracks. Or Burnett could have stepped inside and beaten him to the punch with a left hook or uppercut. But the prospect did neither, nor was he showing much in the way of head movement. He was losing form. Ottah was loading up on every punch and landing from time to time. Burnett scored with an overhand right that stopped Ottah momentarily. Then Ottah came forward again, anxious to trade. Again, it was his round.

A trainer and management team can bring a fighter only so far. In the end, the fighter has to get in the ring and do things for himself. "You're down two rounds," Don Turner told his charge. "There's two rounds left. Get it together now."

Burnett came out more aggressively in round three. Finally, he was effectively working his jab. Ottah was tiring. He was a forty-year-old man who had only three hours a week to train. His hands were dropping lower and lower, his punches coming in ever-widening arcs. Burnett landed several hooks to the head and body followed by an uppercut, the best punch by either man in the fight. Clearly, it was Burnett's round.

Round four. The prospect's pedigree was showing. Jab, jab, body shot, hook to the jaw. "My best asset as a fighter," Ottah had said one day earlier, "is my ability to ride out the punches when I'm hit." Now he was in trouble. It was time for Burnett to pour it on, knock him down, hurt him, make it a 10–8 round to win the fight. Gut-check time for both men. Ottah landed an overhand right. He was going to fight till the end.

And then Burnett did something that a fighter should never do if he's intent on becoming great. With thirty seconds left and victory within reach, he made a silent compact with his opponent. He backed off and, by his conduct, told Ottah, "I'm not pressing the action anymore, and you shouldn't either."

Ottah had gotten 100 percent out of what he had. For every second of the fight, he'd pushed himself to the limit and done everything he was capable of doing. Burnett fell short of that standard. Burnett won the round, but it wasn't enough. The decision of the judges was a draw.

After the fight, Ottah took a quick shower, dressed without drying himself fully, and picked up his paycheck. He had earned every penny of it. "This is a game where you have to prove yourself every time out," he said. When he spoke, he put emphasis on the word "every."

Anthony Ottah took the blows of a younger, stronger man and kept coming. He'd matched his heart and will against his foe in the same way, if not with the same skill, that Muhammad Ali and Joe Frazier did against each other. He had earned the respect that is due a professional fighter. That was a good note to end his ring career on. He never fought again.

James Toney was a superb fighter with a compelling personality who never made it to the top rung in boxing. His fight against Hasim Rahman showed why.

James Toney and What Almost Was
James Toney vs. Hasim Rahman—
March 18, 2006

There was a time when James Toney seemed destined for ring greatness.

Toney was born on August 24, 1968. At age fourteen, he began fighting as an amateur. Then he turned to football, playing quarterback and free safety in high school. He received scholarship offers from the University of Michigan and Western Michigan University. "But I wasn't a team player," James recalls. "And I wasn't good at taking orders. So I went back to boxing."

Toney graduated from high school in 1987 and turned pro as a fighter one year later. He'd played football at 205 pounds, but slimmed down to 160 for the start of his ring career. At five feet, nine inches tall, he fought like a pit bull and seemed almost impervious to pain. He was tough and skilled, took a good punch, and was at his best working inside as a counterpuncher who broke opponents down and beat them up.

"Smash-mouth boxing is what I do best," James said. "I'm not afraid to get hit."

And give Toney credit. He meant it when he said, "I'll fight anyone, anywhere, anytime. If you're bigger and badder than me, let me see it. Prove it to me. Fight me."

"James Toney would take up smoking cigarettes if it meant he could fight cancer," John Wright wrote.

The only blemish on Toney's record in his first twenty-six fights was a draw against Sanderline Williams. Then, on May 10, 1991, he journeyed to Davenport, Iowa, the hometown of IBF middleweight champion Michael Nunn, and stopped the previously undefeated Nunn in eleven rounds. He successfully defended his IBF title six times, after which he moved up in weight and knocked out Iran Barkley to claim the IBF super-middleweight crown.

By late 1994, Toney was undefeated in forty-six fights and near the top of most pound-for-pound lists. The bubble burst when he fought Roy Jones and was dominated over the course of twelve long rounds. Toney attributed the defeat to his having to lose forty-four pounds in the two months preceding the fight in order to make weight. But ballooning past two hundred pounds was his own fault. And in his next outing, he was outquicked and outworked by Montell Griffin in a battle for the IBF light-heavyweight title. In 1996, James lost to Griffin again. Six months later, he came out on the short end of a decision against Drake Thadzi.

"Lack of motivation hurt me," Toney admits. "I didn't train right. I didn't run for eight years. After the Barkley fight, I was never really in shape."

Toney resurrected his career in 2003 with a hard-fought decision over Vassiliy Jirov to claim the IBF cruiserweight crown. Then he stopped Evander Holyfield in nine rounds. That earned Toney his second "Fighter of the Year" designation from the Boxing Writers Association of America, the first having come in 1991. In 2005, he won a twelve-round decision over John Ruiz in a WBA heavyweight title fight. But his pre-fight urine sample tested positive for nandrolone (an illegal steroid). The verdict was changed to "no decision." James was stripped of the WBA belt and suspended for ninety days, and Ruiz was reinstated as champion. Ten months later—on March 18, 2006—Toney reached for the brass ring again, this time fighting Hasim Rahman in Atlantic City for the WBC heavyweight title.

Five years earlier, Rahman had become THE heavyweight champion of the world by knocking out Lennox Lewis in the fifth round. After beating Lewis, Hasim had the opportunity to fight Mike Tyson with Cedric Kushner (who'd brought him to the top) as his promoter. Rahman would have made more money for that one fight than he made in his entire ring career. But he chose to jettison Kushner in favor of Don King and a duffel bag filled with cash. In his next outing, fighting for King, Hasim lost a rematch against Lewis.

Then, in August 2005, Rahman won a desultory twelve-round decision over Monte Barrett to become the "interim" WBC champion. Soon after that, Vitali Klitschko retired and Hasim was given the WBC crown by fiat of the sanctioning body's executive board. Much of the maneuvering critical to this outcome was orchestrated by King. But once Rahman was enthroned, he jumped ship again and signed with Bob Arum.

Meanwhile, Dan Goossen had spent the previous three-and-a-half years rebuilding Toney as a contender. But in order to get the Ruiz fight, he'd been forced to cede a piece of his promotional interest in Toney to King. Hence, King was rooting for Toney in Rahman–Toney. And Arum, by virtue of his association with Rahman, was the lead promoter.

The promotion received a boost of sorts in late January when Toney and Rahman got into a shoving match at the WBC's "Night of Champions" in Cancún, Mexico.

"He scratched me on my lip like a little bitch," Toney reported. "He's a fucking pussy. Everyone is saying Hasim Rahman is bigger than me and stronger than me. Man, you can be big all you want to. He's lacking in the one area which really counts. That's the heart. If you chip at a rock long enough, it falls apart."

Rahman, of course, responded in kind, saying, "James Toney's not smart enough to make me angry. I'm not mad to the point where I'm going to go in there and do something foolish. I just don't like him. He talks too much and he needs to be shut up. I'm going to humble him. I don't see any problem. I'm not being cocky. I'm not being overconfident. I'm just going to expose James for the fraud that he is. He don't belong in the ring with me."

Meanwhile, Toney was a 9-to-5 betting favorite and his camp was confident. James had beaten Holyfield and Ruiz while Rahman had lost to both of them.

"Let's be honest," Freddie Roach (Toney's trainer at the time) said. "Rahman looked good for one fight in his life. He knocked out Lennox Lewis. What has he done since? Who has he beaten? He's lost every big fight he's had since then. Rahman is big and he has a good jab and a strong right hand, but James will deal with that. James doesn't get hit with right hands. He's the best defensive fighter out there. Heavyweights can't hit him."

Then came the weigh-in. And Toney's partisans were a bit shaken.

Weight had been an issue for James throughout his ring career. Before knocking out Michael Nunn to claim the IBF middleweight crown, he'd weighed in at 157 pounds (his lightest fighting weight ever). But over time, when it came to food, his discipline had eroded. Whether he was fighting as a super-middleweight, light-heavyweight, or cruiserweight, he'd had trouble making weight.

"When I left the cruiserweight division [to fight at heavyweight]," Toney proclaimed, "I said, 'Hallelujah!' I'm at my natural body weight now. I feel good. This is the way I am."

But questions about Toney's weight remained. And in private, he admitted, "I looked at myself in the mirror in Cancún, 275 pounds. It was like, 'Damn; I think I'm having a baby.'" Then he'd added, "People say I look like a Buddha. But this Buddha will kick your ass."

Weighing in to fight Rahman, Toney tipped the scale at 237 pounds—the fifth fight in a row in which he'd upped his own personal fight-weight high. Rolls of fat jiggled around his waist. One writer in attendance suggested that his weight be announced in kilograms so it wouldn't sound as bad.

Then Rahman stepped on the scale. In the past, conditioning had also been an issue for Hasim. He'd weighed in as high as 259 pounds. Now he seemed to be in the best shape of his life, 238 pounds.

"Look at him," Rahman said of Toney. "He's fat and soft. He's still a middleweight; all his weight is around his middle. The only stretching exercises James has done are at meals when he stretched his stomach."

Muscles don't show a fighter's heart and will to win. But the fact remained that Rahman had never looked better while Toney was a thirty-seven-year-old fighter carrying the wear and tear of seventy-six professional fights. Coming in at 237 pounds, he wasn't giving himself the best chance to win.

★★★

Toney entered his dressing room at Boardwalk Hall on fight night two hours before the bell for round one was scheduled to ring. There was a chill in the room. James bent over and adjusted a portable heater on the floor to "high."

A ring doctor came in, checked Toney's blood pressure, and asked a series of pro forma questions.

"Have you had any injuries in the past three months?"

"No."

"Are you on any medications?"

"No."

"Have you been suspended for medical reasons?"

"I had that steroid thing, but that's all."

The doctor left.

James stood up, took off his dark-blue warm-up jacket, and began a series of stretching exercises. At one point, he bent over to touch his toes but came up six inches short.

Most fighters get tense and irritable as a fight approaches. Toney's mood improves as fight time nears. One day earlier, he had gone to the airport to pick up his sister. His mood was jovial as he'd laughed and talked animatedly with passengers in the baggage claim area. Now, in the nervous hours before fight time, he seemed like a kid looking forward to playing in a pickup football game.

"This is the best sport in the world," James told the members of his team who'd gathered in the dressing room around him.

A stream of consciousness followed.

"Ain't nothing like boxing. . . . I feel good. I'm ready to pop off. . . . Outside the ring, I get excited. In the ring, I'm calm. If you get excited, you make mistakes. The ring is a calm place. . . . Great fighters don't need a plan before a fight starts. They do what they have to do and adjust as the fight goes on. My plan is that I'm James Toney. . . . I live for this shit. I was born to do this. . . . They love me in Detroit. They love me in New York. They love me in Las Vegas."

James stood up, waved his arms, and shouted, "Pterodactyl! Caw! Caw! Caw!"

Then, suddenly, the lights went out.

There was silence in the dressing room followed by a cheerful voice: "That's why they call me James 'Lights Out' Toney."

A maintenance man was summoned.

"You got a heater, two 500-watt TV lamps, all the other lights. And everything's running from the same circuit," the group was told.

The dressing room was starting to get cold again. The only light still working was in the adjacent bathroom.

James put his warm-up jacket back on.

A technician came in, ran the cord from one of the TV lights to a different outlet, and put duct tape over the cord so no one would trip over it. Twelve minutes after the lights went out, they were on again.

At nine o'clock, James sat on a chair in a corner of the room and turned his attention to an undercard fight on the television monitor. Fifteen minutes later, Don King entered with an unlit cigar in his mouth.

"There he is," King boomed. "James 'Lights Out' Toney is getting ready to kick some ass. It's ass-kicking time."

Suddenly, the room seemed very small.

"Friends, Americans, countrymen," King intoned. "We're going to bury that motherfucker Hasim Rahman tonight. There will be no mercy. James 'Lights Out' Toney will put the lights out all over Rahmanville."

Freddie Roach began taping Toney's hands.

Larry Hazzard (chairman of the New Jersey State Athletic Control Board) came in with referee Eddie Cotton and WBC supervisor Rex Walker. Cotton gave the pre-fight instructions.

After the officials left, King resumed his oration.

"William Cullen Bryant told us, 'The truth crushed to earth will rise again.' The shield of righteousness and the sword of truth are in James Toney's hands, and he shall smite Hasim Rahman. Ain't no room for traitors. Kick that motherfucking traitor's ass. James Toney and the Lord, working together, shall smite that ugly motherfucker down."

At 9:35, the taping was done. Toney shadow-boxed for several minutes, then put on his protective cup and trunks.

"How do you like your cabbage?" King roared. "Raw, raw, raw. How do you like your sugar? Sweet, sweet, sweet. How do you like Rahman? Dead, dead, dead."

James took off his T-shirt.

Roach rubbed baby oil on the fighter's back, shoulders, chest, and arms.

There was more shadow-boxing.

At ten o'clock, Roach gloved Toney up. Then they began working the pads together.

"Nice," the trainer told him. "Beautiful. . . . That's it; take him to school. . . . He's got a slow jab; you'll see it coming. Beat it over the top all night long."

The padwork increased in intensity with James's punches coming faster and harder.

"How long? Not long," King cried out. "Truth and justice shall prevail tonight."

Then it was time. Toney left for the ring. The rest of his team followed.

As the dressing room emptied out, King sat still with an American flag in his hand.

"This is a tough game," he said softly. Then he yawned.

★★★

It was a good fight. Rahman came out hard, going to the body and setting a fast pace. He didn't use his reach. Rather, he was fighting on the inside (Toney's fight) to beat James, intent on outhustling and outmuscling his foe, relying on superior conditioning and strength to win.

It was trench warfare in the early rounds. After the third stanza, the crowd gave both men a standing ovation. Then Rahman began working his jab. In round five, Hasim suffered a cut above his left eye from an accidental head butt, but it didn't change the flow of the fight.

Toney's balance seemed to be off, possibly because of the excess weight he was carrying. At times, his balance problems made it look as though Rahman was moving him with punches more than was actually the case.

The pace slowed late in the fight with both men pounding away at anything they could hit. Fighting off the ropes, Toney landed the cleaner shots. But Rahman kept the pressure on and took the blows when James hit him flush.

According to CompuBox, Rahman had a 279-to-263 edge in total punches landed while Toney led 215 to 159 in power punches. Judges Tom Kaczmarek and Nobuaki Uratani scored the bout even at 114–114. John Stewart had it 117–111 for Rahman. Interestingly, Hasim won the last round on all three scorecards to salvage his title with the draw. James was presumed to be the mentally tougher of the two fighters. But in the final three minutes, Rahman was the one who gutted it out.

After the fight, Toney returned to his dressing room and embraced Roach.

"Sorry, Freddie," he said.

"You got nothing to be sorry about," Roach responded. "You won that fight. Sometimes, when a guy is countering off the ropes, the judges don't understand what's going on."

Toney went into the bathroom, took a shower, and returned.

"Anybody got cold water?" he asked.

Someone handed him a bottle of cold water. A cell phone was placed in his hand. Floyd Mayweather Jr. was on the line.

"How you doin', James?"

"I'm fine, man. How are you?"

"Real good," Mayweather told him.

"What are you gonna do to Zab Judah?"

"Kill him. Murder in the first degree."

When the conversation was over, Toney began to dress. A white shirt, charcoal-gray suit, black shoes. Then he sat down in a chair and smiled as his wife, Angie, knotted his blue-and-gold tie.

"I tired down the end," James told her. "But all the cleaner harder shots were mine. Don't matter what the judges say. I'm still the best heavyweight in the world." He stood up. "Now that I'm in a suit, I feel good."

The American Revolution began in Boston. More than two centuries later, Ricky Hatton journeyed to "Beantown" to restore order and battle Luis Collazo for the WBA welterweight crown.

Ricky Hatton Stakes His Claim in America

Ricky Hatton vs. Luis Collazo— May 13, 2006

British boxing enjoyed a renaissance at the start of the new millennium. Lennox Lewis was the preeminent heavyweight in the world. Naseem Hamed made his mark with a string of knockout victories. And Joe Calzaghe proved to be a special fighter. But no Brit stirred passions more than Ricky Hatton.

As a boy, Hatton loved Bruce Lee films. He took up kickboxing at age eight but was short and stocky with stubby legs—not good for a kickboxer. Thus, when Ricky was ten, his father took him to the Louvolite Boxing Club, where his tutelage in conventional fisticuffs began.

Fast-forward seven years.

"I had my own gym," Billy Graham, who would train Hatton for most of the fighter's pro career, later recalled. "And I kept hearing about this fighter, Richard Hatton. He was an amateur, and I was getting conflicting reports. Some said he was fantastic. Some said he was just a strong kid. There are lots of kids at seventeen who are strong for their age and can punch but never amount to much. Then, one day, I got a phone call saying he was coming to spar at my gym. He was looking at different gyms to see where he wanted to be. I had more fighters than I wanted but I was curious about him. I let him spar. And what he did, he should not have been able to do at that age. It made my hair stand on end. This kid was the best seventeen-year-old I'd ever seen. He could punch. But more important, his balance and anticipation were extraordinary for his age. I told him to have a look around the other gyms, that any trainer in the world would want him and I hoped he'd pick me."

Hatton turned pro under Graham's tutelage in 1997. Sky TV began calling him "Ricky" and the name caught on. He won the lightly regarded World Boxing Union 140-pound title in 2001 and successfully defended it sixteen times. He was a crowd-pleasing, nonstop-action fighter who proclaimed, "I fight like a lunatic. I'm very aggressive in the ring. It's very un-British, the way I fight."

Hatton was regarded in some circles as a paper champion until June 4, 2005, when he challenged Kostya Tszyu for the IBF crown. Tszyu was "the man" at 140 pounds, having knocked out Zab Judah in a title-unification bout and beaten the likes of Julio César Chávez, Sharmba Mitchell, Rafael Rueles, and Jesse James Leija. Hatton put a beating on Tszyu, who failed to come out for the twelfth round. It was one of the biggest wins ever for a British boxer. Five months later, Ricky solidified his standing with a ninth-round knockout of Carlos Maussa in an IBF–WBA title-unification bout. That brought his record to 40 wins in 40 fights with 30 knockouts.

Hatton was massively popular in England. But he wanted to be recognized as a great fighter around the world. "I had to come to the United States to prove myself," he said later. "I had fought for so long in England that a lot of people thought I was a protected fighter."

Those wishes coincided nicely with business developments in America. HBO had long been recognized as the most powerful force in boxing, but a string of entertaining matchups on Showtime (including Hatton–Tszyu) had turned heads. That led HBO to offer Ricky a lucrative three-fight contract with an option in HBO's favor for a fourth bout.

The choice of an opponent was problematic. Naoufel Ben Rabah (the mandatory IBF challenger for Hatton's 140-pound title) was unacceptable to HBO. Sky TV vetoed Vivian Harris. Juan Lazcano was agreed upon, then injured a hand in training and pulled out. Carlos Baldomir opted to face Arturo Gatti. José Luis Castillo and Diego Corrales decided to fight each other. Kostya Tszyu wasn't interested in a rematch. Finally, the powers that be settled on WBA 147-pound champion Luis Collazo.

Collazo had crafted a 26–1 (13 KOs) ring record. He'd won the WBA 147-pound title by decision over José Antonio Rivera one year earlier and successfully defended it by knockout over Miguel Ángel González. In addition to going up in weight, Hatton would be fighting a southpaw for the first time since 2002. Technically, he was the challenger. The two men would be fighting for Collazo's title. But make no mistake: Ricky was the one defending what he had.

The fight was scheduled for May 13, 2006, at TD Banknorth Garden Arena in Boston. In later years, the close-knit team around Hatton would be torn asunder. But on this occasion, Team Hatton was united.

The charter members were Ray Hatton (who served as his son's business manager), Carol Hatton (affectionately referred to in her son's circle as "the boss"), Matthew Hatton (Ricky's brother), Jennifer Dooley (Ricky's girlfriend), and Billy Graham. Also on hand were cutman Mick Williamson, Kerry Kayes (Ricky's strength coach and nutritionist), Paul Speak (a Manchester police officer who had become a close friend), and Alan Stevenson (another friend).

"We're a very close group," Hatton said of the people around him. "It's not just a bunch of guys on a payroll. We're family and friends."

Two years earlier, at age twenty-five, Ricky had moved out of his parents' house and into a home of his own. It was a 32-second walk from his parents' front door. He'd actually timed it.

"Usually, it's bollocks when people say that someone successful is still the boy next door," Graham noted. "But Ricky is happiest when he's with people he grew up with. He has the same friends he went to school with. He goes to the same places he always went to. He's a regular guy."

On the morning of the fight, Hatton had breakfast in the hotel restaurant with the members of his team. He laughed, joked, and welcomed anyone who came by to chat. At one point, a middle-aged couple left an adjacent table and the man's cell phone dropped to the floor. Ricky rose from his chair, picked it up, and called after the man to give the phone back to him.

As a matter of habit, Hatton's pre-fight breakfast consisted of eggs, bacon, sausage, orange juice, and toast. On the afternoon of a fight, he liked McDonald's cheeseburgers and French fries. "He's not fighting on what he eats on the day of a fight," Ray Hatton explained. "He's fighting on all the good food he's eaten in the weeks coming up to the fight. What he eats on fight day is comfort food for him."

When breakfast was done, instead of going to his room, Hatton relocated to the hotel lobby.

Ray and Carol Hatton had always told their son, "It costs nothing to be nice." Heeding that advice, Ricky is in the habit of offering a kind word to everyone he meets. He's unpretentious and approachable, talks easily with fans, and is never at a loss for words. Instead of being a matinee idol, he's "one of us."

Hatton sat on a sofa in the hotel lobby until 4:00 p.m., playing cards and chatting with members of his camp, friends, fans, and anyone else who came by. In essence, the hotel lobby had become his living room. Hours before one of the biggest fights of his life, there were no barriers, physical or otherwise, between him and the rest of the world.

There was little talk about the fight to come. Earlier in the month, Ricky had observed, "From what I can see, Collazo has fast hands. He's a slick boxer who is always on the move. Being a southpaw, he's just that little extra awkward and more tricky than most fighters I've fought. He's a little taller than me. But when I moved up to welterweight, I expected to see much bigger fighters. Collazo didn't seem huge or physically imposing to me when we met. I actually felt bigger than him, even though it's me that's moving up in weight."

Now Hatton's comments regarding his opponent were limited to thinking back to the final pre-fight press conference when Collazo announced that he had a present for him.

"I expected he'd give me a dress or some nonsense like that," Ricky recalled.

Instead, referencing Hatton's penchant for drinking copious amounts of beer between fights, Collazo had given him a six-pack of Guinness. Ricky responded with the thought that they might be adversaries at the moment but, after the fight, they could share the Guinness. Collazo said he didn't drink and would opt for a cup of tea instead.

"That was music to my ears," Hatton told those gathered around him in the hotel lobby. "I thought, 'Now I'll get to drink it all myself.'"

Billy Graham was asked how fighting away from Manchester might affect Ricky. Hatton was used to entering a sold-out arena with the crowd going wild. Every punch he landed elicited a roar that spurred him on and was heard by the judges. Ricky's entrance music was of particular note. The Manchester City anthem—a jazzed-up version of "Blue Moon"—had a unique sound when twenty-two thousand rabid fans sang it in unison. Would a lesser entrance and less partisan crowd matter?

"Not at all," Graham answered. "Ricky has enormous confidence and belief in himself."

Then Graham thought back to a moment eight years earlier. Naseem Hamed had come to America to fight Wayne McCullough, and Hatton was on the undercard.

"Naz was mouthing off as he was known to do," Graham recalled. "Ricky looked at him and said to me, 'I'm just as confident as him, you know.'"

★★★

Hatton arrived at TD Banknorth Garden Arena on fight night at 8:20 p.m. His brother, Matthew, was midway through an eight-round preliminary bout against a club fighter named Jose Medina. Standing in the rear of the arena, Ricky watched, uttering instructions that couldn't be heard more than an arm's length away.

"Finish the round strong. Hook. That's it. Hook again. Don't be waiting on him; he'll steal the round. Put the punches together. Come on, Matthew. Work. Bang him. That's it. That's it."

The decision was announced. 78–74 Medina; 78–73 Hatton; 77–74 Hatton.

Ricky thrust a clenched fist above his head, turned, and walked to his dressing room—a small enclosure with a rubdown table, two wood benches, a half-dozen folding chairs, and several large British flags taped to the walls. Rock music began to play. He emptied the contents of his gym bag onto one of the benches.

Matthew came in and the brothers embraced.

"Big night, your first fight in America," Ricky told him. "I'm proud of you."

Hatton likes a loud dressing room with a party atmosphere. As time passed, a stream of friends, camp members, and others came by. People stood against the walls, chatting with one another. His parents weren't there.

"Carol and I never go in the dressing room before a fight," Ray Hatton has said. "It's not a place for mums and dads. All we'd do is say stupid things like, 'Look after yourself, son.' What else is he going to do?"

The center of the room belonged to Ricky, who was in nonstop motion, walking, shuffling, singing, skipping, punching.

At nine o'clock, referee John Zablocki came in to give the fighter his pre-fight instructions.

There was a reason that twenty-five years had passed since the last major fight in Boston. Boston isn't a big fight town. And the Massachusetts State Athletic Commission isn't known for competence.

One day before the fight, commission chairman Nick Manzello was insisting that Hatton–Collazo be contested with ten-ounce gloves despite the widely accepted requirement that eight-ounce gloves be used in 147-pound championship bouts. Finally, he relented.

On fight night, Hatton's pre-fight preparation in his dressing room was interrupted four times by commission officials who wanted to pose for photographs with him or get his autograph. One official requested that he sign two boxing gloves. A fighter doesn't want someone from the governing athletic commission to be angry with him. So in each instance, Ricky complied. When it was time to begin taping his hands, there was a delay because no one from the commission was present.

Zablocki, like the judges assigned to the fight, was from Massachusetts. When he was done with his instructions, he asked if there were any questions.

"We just want a fair shake if Ricky gets cut," Graham said. "We've got a great cutman. Will you give us that chance?"

"I know Ricky fights through cuts," Zablocki told him. "I'll give him and the cutman every opportunity."

Zablocki left. Ricky began warming up again, circling, throwing punches, stopping only to turn the volume of the music higher to a near-deafening decibel level. Graham and the others shouted to each other to be heard above the din.

A second from Collazo's camp came in to watch Graham tape Ricky's hands. Then Ricky pulled on his trunks. Blue, silver, and black, adorned with two British flags and elaborate white fringe. The trunks made the pope's ceremonial garments look drab.

"John L. Sullivan never wore anything like these," Ricky noted.

At ten o'clock, Hatton gloved up and began hitting the pads with Graham. Then a switch inside his head flipped and a ferocious look crossed his face. A loud grunt accompanied each punch. He was no longer nice Ricky, the boy next door. He had become Freddy Krueger, who no one would want living in their neighborhood.

Record rains had fallen on Boston for three days, which limited the size of the crowd. Those in attendance were overwhelmingly pro-Hatton.

The assumption in Ricky's camp was that the early rounds would be difficult for him but that over time he would break Collazo down. In reality, the converse was true. Ten seconds into round one, Hatton decked the champion with a sharp left hook. That was followed by damaging body blows through the first two rounds. Then Collazo began using his height and speed more effectively. The first half of the fight was all action with the only blood coming from a cut high on Collazo's forehead resulting from an accidental clash of heads. After that, the pace slowed.

Hatton was never a one-punch knockout artist. He wore opponents down with constant pressure and an accumulation of blows. But against a natural welterweight, those tactics weren't as effective as they'd been in the past.

Also, Hatton was an inside fighter. "In close," he would say, "you've got to hold a bit and move the other guy's arms around to get your punches in. It's an art to make room for your shots." But there were times when Zablocki broke the fighters when he could have told them to punch out. And midway through the fight, a second accidental head butt began the process of closing Ricky's left eye.

Collazo was the one who finished strong, staggering Hatton with a series of blows midway through the final round. It was a close fight. Ricky outlanded his foe 259 to 213 with a 254-to-167 differential in power punches. The judges' verdict was unanimous: 115–112, 115–112, 114–113 for Hatton.

In his dressing room after the fight, Ricky sat heavily on a chair and held an icepack to his left eye. The eye was almost closed, and the skin around both eyes was black, blue, pink, purple, and swollen.

"Are you all right?" his mother asked.

"Of course, I'm all right." Ricky smiled and countered with a question of his own. "I don't make things easy, do I?"

Without waiting for an answer, he went on.

"I fought Kostya Tszyu. That was a tough fight. Then I fought Maussa.

That was a tough fight. And after that, like a fucking lunatic, I go up in weight and fight another champion. Did the fans get value for money?"

They certainly did, he was told.

"This was my toughest fight," Ricky continued. "I felt that I was stronger than Collazo, but the difference in strength wasn't as great as when I fight at 140. I asked myself several times during the fight, 'I can still make ten stone; what am I doing this for?' I rose to the occasion against Kostya Tszyu, and Collazo did the same tonight. He's a good fighter. He's tricky and he has a style that's hard for me. He took the body shots well. I know they hurt him, but he took them well. The last round, he shook me but I had my faculties about me the whole time. It was just a matter of riding out the storm. People remember fights like this. I don't want too many of them, but it's important to win a few like tonight."

Ricky stood up and started toward the shower, then added a final thought.

"Show me a fighter who has an easy night every time, and I'll show my ass in Woolworth's window."

John Duddy never won a world title. But the popular Irish middleweight ennobled boxing.

The Night John Duddy Was Great
John Duddy vs. Yori Boy Campas—
September 29, 2006

On September 29, 2006, John Duddy fought Yori Boy Campas at The Theater at Madison Square Garden. Duddy was never a great fighter in the traditional sense. But that night, he was great.

A native of County Derry, Ireland, Duddy lived and trained in New York. "I feel at home in America," he said. "But I'm a guest here. My home will always be in Ireland. I'm not Irish-American. I'm an Irishman who's living now in New York."

Duddy was gracious and charming with a thick Irish brogue. He wasn't just media friendly; he was friendly to everyone. He looked like a fighter from an old-time movie. In other words, he didn't look like a fighter. His face was too pretty. His body lacked the clear muscle definition that characterizes many of today's elite athletes. But his charisma and action style made him popular in the Irish American community.

Duddy was also linked to a seminal moment in Irish history. On Sunday, January 30, 1972 (a day known as "Bloody Sunday"), fourteen unarmed demonstrators were shot to death by British soldiers during a civil rights march in Northern Ireland. The march had been organized by Derry MP Ivan Cooper to protest a policy of internment without trial that the British government had introduced on August 9, 1971. One of the dead was seventeen-year-old John Francis Duddy.

He was my uncle," John said. "That's my history, and there's nothing I can do about it. His name was John Francis Duddy, and my name is John Francis Duddy. He was a fighter and I'm a fighter, but I didn't become a fighter because he was a fighter. My father never talked at length about my uncle when I was growing up. It wasn't a political home. We were taught to treat people with respect regardless of race, creed, or color. My uncle's death was a tragedy but it happened years before I was born."

Duddy was an atypical prizefighter. There was no wellspring of anger, no history of parental abuse. He'd never slept on the streets or gone hungry as a child.

His interest in the sweet science began with his father; a club fighter who posted a 3–4 record in the early 1980s. "He took me to the gym," John recalled. "I started training for the fun of it when I was five and had my first fight at seven. My father allowed me to do it, but he also encouraged me to play other sports and do other things. He always made it clear that I could stop if I wanted to."

Duddy had 130 amateur fights and won 100 of them. In March 2003, he came to America. "That was my dream," he said. "I'd been to America a few times as an amateur and knew this was the place to be." Soon, he was training at the legendary Gleason's Gym. He turned pro with a first-round knockout of Tarek Rached on September 19, 2003. Eighteen months later in what was expected to be the first big test of his pro career, he scored a first-round knockout of 16–0 Lenord Pierre to run his record to 9–0 with 9 KOs.

Duddy had significant flaws as a fighter. Too often, he stood upright and was disinclined to bend at the knees, which left him susceptible to left hooks. He didn't move his head enough. When in retreat, he tended to move straight back. And his free-swinging style left him open to counterpunches.

But the ride continued. On March 16, 2006 (the night before St. Patrick's Day), Duddy scored a first-round knockout over Shelby Pudwill. The fight took place at The Theater (a 4,955-seat venue adjacent to the main arena in Madison Square Garden). It was only the second time in history that The Theater sold out for a fight.

By September 2006, Duddy was undefeated with 15 knockouts in 17 bouts. Within the boxing industry, he'd become a much-talked-about phenomenon. Acclaimed sports artist LeRoy Neiman observed, "He has everything that the crowd favorites of the 1940s and '50s had. Good looks, charisma, an exciting style. There's some real dazzle to him." Jack McGowan wrote in the *Belfast Telegraph*, "Duddy is riding a magic carousel. He's impulsive, high-spirited, and a risk-taker; Irish-handsome and Irish exciting."

"I'm pleased with where I am right now," Duddy said. "A year ago,

I felt like an amateur in a professional sport. I'm a lot more comfortable being a professional boxer now, and I've damn sure left my amateur days behind. It's like a dream, really. I'm fighting guys now that I used to watch on television."

One of those guys was Luis Ramón "Yori Boy" Campas.

Campas was thirty-five years old with the wear and tear of ninety-six professional fights on his body. But he'd been to the mountaintop and was a former world champion with a record coming in against Duddy of 88 wins against only 8 defeats with 72 knockouts. Five of those eight losses had come in championship bouts against the likes of Félix Trinidad and Oscar De La Hoya. John wouldn't beat Campas by just showing up.

Duddy entered his dressing room at Madison Square Garden on fight night wearing pine-green sweatpants and a black T-shirt. It was 7:30 p.m., three and a half hours before fight time.

John liked quiet in the hours before a fight. Wordlessly, he sat on a folding metal chair and took a sip from a bottle of water. Sometimes as the minutes passed, he clasped his hands, then separated them and ground a clenched fist into the palm of his other hand. At times, he rotated his head and shoulders slightly. His eyes were closed. He talked to no one.

For the next two hours, he sat that way, focusing his thoughts on the violent world that was growing ever larger in his mind. Soon, only the man standing across the ring from him—the man who would try to beat him senseless—would matter.

"I hate the waiting," John once said of the hours before a fight. "I want to get it started. I don't want to get it over with, but I want to get it started. There's a difference."

At 9:30, trainer Harry Keitt began taping Duddy's hands. There was virtually no conversation between them. Occasionally, Keitt asked, "How does that feel?" Each time, John answered, "Good."

At 9:45, the taping was done.

"Let's get dressed," Keitt said.

Duddy put on gold-trimmed Kelly-green trunks and began to loosen up in the center of the room. As he moved, Keitt talked to him softly in the manner of a hypnotist.

"Back him up. Break him down. He's too short, too slow, and too damn old. Break him down. Nice and smooth. Turn your punches over. Put him on his back. Break him down."

At 9:55, Duddy sat down on the folding metal chair again, closed his eyes, and rotated his head in differentiating arcs. No one spoke.

At 10:20, he gloved up, then went to an adjacent room to hit the warm-up pads with assistant trainer Orlando Carrasquillo.

"Speed and power," Keitt intoned. "Break him down. Nice and smooth. Break him down."

Then it was time.

Great fights don't require great fighters. They require good fighters with great courage and heart. Duddy–Campas was a great fight.

In round one, Duddy seemed faster, younger, bigger, and stronger. He was the aggressor and won the round. Then everything changed.

Defensively, as earlier noted, Duddy was a flawed fighter. Campas was aware of those flaws. And in round two, he took advantage of them. John was rocked by punches from all angles. A right hand opened a horrible gash above his left eye. Another right wobbled him at the bell.

From that point on, Duddy–Campas was a brutal, bloody war. Cutman George Mitchell struggled valiantly to stem the blood that was flowing from above Duddy's left eye. But every round, as soon as the bell rang, Campas rained punches on the eye again. John was taking a beating.

In round five, a head butt opened up another ugly gash, this one above Duddy's right eye. Round after round, the fighters stood their ground, punching hard and punching back harder when hit. Both men were hit flush more often than a fighter should be hit. Each man seemed impervious to pain.

In round six, it appeared as though Duddy was on the verge of succumbing to exhaustion. His legs seemed rubbery and his stance widened. In round seven, Campas continued his assault. Blood streamed over John's swollen face. He was getting beaten up.

Then, in round eight, the tide turned. Duddy staggered Campas with a big right hand and rocked him again at the bell. In rounds nine, ten, and eleven, he poured it on. Like Duddy earlier in the fight, Campas refused to fall. In round twelve, incredibly, Yori Boy staged a rally of his own.

This observer gave Duddy the nod by a 115–114 margin. The judges confirmed his triumph with a more generous 117–111, 116–112, 115–113 decision.

Duddy had done the hardest thing to do in sports. He was being beaten up by a professional fighter. He'd had every opportunity to quit. But he came back to turn the tide and win.

After the bout, Duddy returned to his dressing room. His face was discolored and swollen. Gaping cuts that would require twenty-four stitches to close protruded above his eyes. He'd taken more punishment in the preceding hour than in all his previous fights combined.

"I'm under no illusions," John said. "It was a great fight for the crowd; like one of those old fight movies that goes back and forth, back and forth, ding-dong, ding-dong. But for me, it wasn't so good. I got hit a lot. I have a lot to learn and a lot of work to do."

But his eyes sparkled with excitement and he seemed exhilarated by it all.

"This is what boxing is all about," he said. "This was more than I've ever experienced. It was one of the best personal experiences I've had in my life. The cuts were bad. In the past, I've had nicks and scrapes; never a cut like this. But if you panic in a fight, you don't belong in a boxing ring. So I asked myself, 'Are you going to run or are you going to stand and fight?' I'd never been in a position like that before, where my back was against the wall and I was fighting an opponent who took everything I threw at him and hit just as hard as I did. That's the first time I was ever really asked in the ring, 'Do you want to be a professional fighter?' And the answer was 'yes, I do.'"

Nikolai Valuev was fighting for more than a "W" on his ring record when he journeyed to Chicago to defend his WBA heavyweight title against Monte Barrett.

Nikolai Valuev's Quest for Acceptance
Nikolai Valuev vs. Monte Barrett—
October 7, 2006

Nikolai Valuev was born in Leningrad (now St. Petersburg) on August 21, 1973. A massive man of biblical proportions, he stands seven feet, two inches tall and weighs over 300 pounds. His size is accentuated by a protruding forehead with large bumps (frontal bossing) that are a normal part of his brow but look as though they were raised by blows. Everything in his life has been shadowed by his size.

Valuev came from a working-class family. Both of his parents were five feet, five inches tall. But his grandmother told him that his great-great-grandfather was "a giant of a man" named Vasily and a direct descendant of the Tartars (a Mongolian tribe that overran parts of Asia and Europe in the thirteenth century).

At age thirteen, Valuev was sent to a boarding school that specialized in sports. Soon, he was playing on a team that won a junior-level national basketball championship. Then his interests broadened to include track and field. At age nineteen, he won a national junior title in the discus and was invited to attend the Institute of Sport in Leningrad with an eye toward competing in the 1996 Olympics. At the institute, he caught the attention of a boxing trainer named Oleg Shalaev.

Valuev was twenty when he took up boxing.

"At first, it was very hard for me," he later recalled. "Most boxers begin at a much younger age, and everything was new to me. I had never thrown a punch in my life. Punching the heavy bag, shadow-boxing, sparring, even skipping rope was a challenge."

In late 1993, Valuev turned pro. Because of his size, he was marketed as a "special attraction" on fight cards in Japan, Korea, Australia, England, Russia, Belarus, Ukraine, and the Czech Republic. In 2003, he signed a promotional agreement with Wilfried Sauerland. That led to improved training (with Manuel Gabrielian) and better sparring partners.

Valuev's first twelve fights under the Sauerland banner were contested in Germany. Over time, the level of opposition improved. Victories over Paolo Vidoz, Gerald Nobles, Attila Levin, Clifford Etienne, and Larry Donald followed. On December 17, 2005, Valuev won a majority decision over John Ruiz to claim the WBA heavyweight title. Then came a three-round annihilation of Owen Beck that brought his ring record to 45 wins in 45 fights. Had he been a foot shorter and a hundred pounds lighter, he wouldn't have been much as a fighter. But the same could be said about Shaquille O'Neal as a basketball player.

Valuev entered the ring by stepping over the ropes, not through them. Between rounds, he sat on a custom-made stool. He was labeled "The Beast from the East" and "The Russian Monster" but disliked the nicknames. "My parents called me Nikolai," he said. "My surname is Valuev. I am Nikolai Valuev. For me, no other name exists. Everything else is for the kindergarten."

Valuev was also explicit in saying that he did not define himself by his size. He wanted his place in the world to be more like that of everybody else, to not be gawked at as a giant. He thought of himself as an athlete, not just a boxer. And that was secondary to his identity as a husband, father, and friend.

"I like loyalty," Valuev said in a conversation with this writer. "I like it when people say what they mean and stand by it. I hate injustice. I want my family to be provided for well and to have a good place in this world."

The words flowed.

"I am not a machine," Valuev continued, the gravitas of his remarks etched on his face. "I am not a piece of meat. I am not a circus show. I am a normal human being. I have human feelings. I have a beautiful family. I have many friends. I like good music, classical music. I read books. People sometimes do not treat me like a human being because of my size. They make a sensation. I try to not take it personally because they do not know me as a person. But there are times when it hurts me inside."

Nikolai's wife Galina and their son Grishna represent safe harbor for Valuev.

He met Galina in 1999 and was sufficiently enamored to begin writing poetry for her. "The poems are personal," he explained. "They were written for Galina, and I don't discuss them. All I will tell you is that she didn't throw them back at me. She still has all of the poems."

Then, in February 2006, Valuev's image took a hit when he was accused of assaulting a sixty-one-year-old parking attendant named Yuri Sergaev outside the Spartak Ice Palace in St. Petersburg. According to the attendant, Galina had parked illegally in a space reserved for buses and he told her to move her car. She then telephoned Nikolai, who came to the arena, dragged the attendant to a ventilation shed, and beat him. Valuev countered that his wife called him in tears and said that, as she was taking Grishna to the ice rink, Sergaev yelled at her and mocked her. He then rushed to Spartak to defend her.

"He insulted my wife," Valuev explained. "I grabbed him by the collar to bring him to his senses. I did not hit this man. There was a lot of ice in the parking lot. He slipped and fell. I sincerely regret the conflict but you have to understand: I acted like any normal man in my position would, whether he was the world champion or a simple engineer."

Sergaev was treated for a concussion and facial bruises. One got the impression that few things were more upsetting to Valuev than anything that might bring unhappiness to his wife and son.

On October 7, 2006, Valuev defended his IBF title for the second time against Monte Barrett in Chicago.

Valuev had fought twice before in the United States. On May 31, 1997, he'd knocked out Terrell Nelson in two rounds. Four years later, he disposed of George Linberger in one stanza. Both of those bouts were in Atlantic City. The second was notable because it was co-promoted by Don Elbaum, who hosted a pre-fight press conference at the Russian Tea Room in New York. "Blini and caviar will be served," the media advisory promised. At least there were blini.

This time, Don King was the promoter of record. The fight marked Valuev's debut on HBO. To emphasize his height, the network fashioned a promotional campaign featuring vertical wallscapes instead of the customary horizontal billboards. Meanwhile, at the kickoff press conference in New York, the hyperbolae were flying.

"He's the eighth wonder of the world," King proclaimed. "He's the jolly red giant. King Kong. He picked up the Empire State Building. He's faster than a speeding bullet. He can leap over the Sears Tower in a single bound. Is he a bird? Is he a plane? He's Super Nikolai Valuev."

Valuev sat stoically through it all. When the press conference was over, Alan Hopper (King's director of public relations) complimented the fighter on the stylish pinstripe suit he was wearing and told him, "The media will like that. It's a sign of respect for them and the sport."

"Thank you," Valuev responded. "But I don't wear the suit and tie for them. I wear it because I respect myself."

That was followed by a further bit of insight shared with this writer.

"I'm not a child," Valuev said. "I know for sure that I get everything now because people want something from me. As soon as they don't need me anymore, all appearances will vanish. That's like beautiful packaging for a bad-tasting candy."

Barrett was all but overlooked in the hubbub. He was thirty-five years old, had fought only twice in the preceding thirty-one months, and hadn't been in the ring since losing to Hasim Rahman fourteen months earlier. His purse for fighting Valuev would be $175,000.

"Boxing isn't a sport for me," Barrett told reporters. "It's a business."

In the past, Barrett had experienced difficulty coping with big men like Wladimir Klitschko and Lance Whitaker. Moreover, Valuev had gone twelve rounds on six occasions, winning each time.

"There will be times when Monte has to fight with him and not just box," James Bashir (Barrett's trainer) said two days before the fight. "But we'll pick our spots." As for Valuev's height, Bashir said optimistically, "Hit him in the body and, all of a sudden, he'll be six-seven."

Still, there was a 106-pound weight differential to deal with. Valuev would tip the scales at 328 pounds to Barrett's 222. And Bashir was unhappy with the fact that the Illinois Boxing Commission had okayed an eighteen-foot ring rather than the traditional twenty. "Trust me; those two feet make a difference," he said. Then, the night before the fight, Team Barrett went to the arena, measured the ring, and found that it had shrunk to sixteen feet, nine inches. They threatened to call the fight off, and the eighteen-foot ring was restored.

There was an almost preternatural calm in Valuev's dressing room before the fight. An hour before the bout, his hands taped, Nikolai paced back and forth. There was no music. No one talked. Roars from the crowd filtered into the room as Tomasz Adamek and Paul Briggs battled furiously in a light-heavyweight title encounter inside the arena.

Valuev kept moving . . . pacing . . . stretching . . . shadow-boxing. At one point, he bent over at the waist and touched his palms flat against the floor with ease despite wearing braces on both knees.

Manuel Gabrielian gloved him up.

Valuev resumed warming up, more intensely now with the trainer issuing instructions. The few times that Nikolai spoke, it had to do with an equipment adjustment or request for water. His shoes were retied. His protective cup was repositioned beneath his trunks. Each sequence of hitting the pads was more intense than the one before.

After working with Gabrielian for thirty minutes, Valuev sat on a chair in quiet repose. In that moment, he looked more vulnerable than fierce. The playing field in the battle ahead would be more level than most fans understood. Size is just one factor in boxing. Nikolai would have to overcome Barrett's natural advantage in speed, reflexes, and coordination. He would be called upon to endure physical pain. And if he were felled by the smaller man, he would become an object of derision.

The warm-up began anew. At 10:15, Valuev threw his final punches. Readying to leave the dressing room, he stepped on an HBO cable that had been stretched across the floor, felt the weight of his body at an awkward angle on his ankle, and uttered a word in Russian that sounded as though it had four letters. The ring walk followed.

Valuev was flawed and beatable as a fighter. But he was never easy to beat.

On the downside, he was habitually slow to set his feet and punch with leverage. His repertoire was limited. He telegraphed everything he threw. And he didn't use his size as well as he could have on the inside. When an opponent tied him up, Nikolai should have leaned on him with all of his weight. But he didn't. That might have been because he feared having a point taken away by the referee. Or he might not have wanted to be mocked for his size. Whatever the reason, it diminished his effectiveness as a fighter.

The other side of the coin was that Valuev's style allowed him to fight within his limitations. Outstretched, his left hand kept opponents at bay.

It was hard to land over or around it. His jab, when used effectively, piled up points. And given his size, he could counter with a right hand over an opponent's jab. He had good stamina and paced himself well. His work rate was constant throughout a fight. He took a good punch and, when hit, punched back. Also, when he was able to set his feet at proper distance, his blows had concussive force.

In other words; Valuev was predictable. Opponents knew in advance what he was going to do in the ring. Okay; now try to stop it.

It was clear from the opening bell that Barrett had come to fight. In the early going, he set a fast pace, stayed in the center of the ring, and got off first, landing stiff jabs and overhand rights. He also managed to keep Valuev turning, which denied Nikolai the time he needed to set his feet and punch with leverage. But it's hard to maintain form against a seven-foot, two-inch, 328-pound giant who keeps moving forward. As the bout progressed, Barrett wore down. That allowed Valuev to dictate the pace, and his size became a decided advantage.

Valuev's arsenal consisted largely of jab–right hand, jab–right hand with an occasional uppercut. But it was enough. In round eight, a chopping right hand that was more of a cuff put Barrett down. Monte was skating on thin ice.

In round eleven, the ice cracked. Barrett was sufficiently exhausted that Valuev was able to set his feet and put his weight behind his punches. A roundhouse right that would have hurt anyone landed flush and sent Monte to the canvas. He rose, badly hurt, and was felled again, this time by an uppercut. At that point, James Bashir jumped into the ring and stopped the carnage.

"People might criticize Valuev but they can't beat him," Don King proclaimed at the post-fight victory party. "No one says that Nikolai is Muhammad Ali, but he's improving all the time. I'm elated and my heart rejoices when I think about the possibilities and potentialities of Nikolai Valuev. All roads lead to the giant."

After beating Barrett, Valuev successfully defended his title by stoppage over Jameel McCline. Then, on April 14, 2007, he lost a majority decision to Ruslan Chagaev. Victories over Jean-François Bergeron, Siarhei Liakhovich, John Ruiz (in a rematch for the newly vacated WBA title), and Evander Holyfield followed. In the last fight of his ring career, on November 7, 2009, he was outpointed by David Haye.

Then, plagued by chronic physical problems, including two bad knees (both of which had been operated on), Valuev retired from boxing. His final record showed 50 wins against 2 losses with 34 knockouts. He was never knocked down as an amateur or pro and left a legacy of having always conducted himself in the athletic arena with dignity and personal grace. As a coda to his ring career, in 2011, he was elected to the Russian Parliament.

Boxing's historical record, like most history, centers on kings, not foot soldiers. But boxing is about more than great champions. Journeymen and young fighters with optimism are an important part of the sport.

First Bout at 3:05 p.m.
Hector Beltran vs. Ernest Johnson—May 5, 2007

On May 5, 2007, Oscar De La Hoya and Floyd Mayweather met in the ring at the MGM Grand Hotel and Casino in Las Vegas after the most extensive marketing campaign in the history of boxing. More than 60 percent of the seats in the sold-out MGM Grand Garden Arena carried a price tag of $2,000 or more. There were more than 800 requests for media credentials.

Five hours earlier, two unknown fighters fought in an eight-round lightweight bout on the same square of illuminated canvas.

Ernest Johnson was a twenty-seven-year-old African American from Chula Vista, California. His father was a boxing trainer. His mother worked for GMAC in foreclosures and loans.

Growing up, Johnson played sports year-round. He began boxing at age thirteen, compiled a 68–11 amateur record, and was good enough to be invited to the 2000 Olympic trials. But boxing was sandwiched in between track (400 meters was his specialty), football (he started in high school as a wide receiver), and baseball (pitcher and centerfield). Ernest also wrestled at 125 pounds, fashioned a 101–19 record, and was offered a wrestling scholarship to California State University in Fullerton. But he turned it down to pursue a career in boxing.

"I decided to take boxing seriously when I got out of high school," Johnson explained. "You can't make a living wrestling."

To make ends meet financially, Johnson was managing a gym and working as a personal trainer for fifteen to twenty hours a week. "I want to go back to school someday," he said. "Get into physical therapy and maybe open my own gym."

Johnson's best weapons as a fighter were his speed and his jab. Prior to May 5, 2007, his record stood at 16 wins against 2 losses with 7 knock-outs. But only three of his victories had come against opponents with a winning ledger. And on the two occasions when he stepped up in class, he'd lost unanimous ten-round decisions.

"The first loss," Ernest said, "I took the fight on six days' notice and it was close. The second one, I overtrained because of the first loss. I had no snap on my punches and my shoulder was bothering me because of tendonitis and a slight muscle tear."

After his second defeat (in November 2004), Johnson took twenty-six months off for physical therapy and to let his shoulder heal. His fight on the undercard of De La Hoya vs. Mayweather would be his second since the layoff.

Johnson had been in a big-fight atmosphere before. Six years earlier, he'd made his pro debut on the undercard of Floyd Mayweather vs. Diego Corrales. Not long after that, he ran into Mayweather at a supermarket in Las Vegas.

"I introduced myself and he was nice," Ernest remembered. "Just to be part of something like this is huge. You never know who might see you or put you on another card. This is a stepping stone that I hope will lead to something bigger."

On the afternoon of May 5, Johnson arrived at the MGM Grand Garden Arena at 1:45 p.m. He and four other fighters had been assigned to dressing room #2. Ernest was wearing black sweatpants, a black T-shirt, black warm-up pants, and a black Everlast ski cap. His father, Ernest Johnson Sr., was with him.

There were six rectangular tables in the room. One for Nevada State Athletic Commission officials and one for each fighter's camp. John O'Donnell and John Murray (two Brits with undefeated records who were scheduled to fight in the second and third bouts) were already there. Johnson sat on a chair and adjusted the earpiece on his MP3 player, then scanned the display window to decide what to listen to next.

A commission inspector came into the room.

"Should we go ahead and wrap?" Ernest Johnson Sr. asked.

"Yes."

Johnson began taping his son's hands. Eric Gomez (the matchmaker for Golden Boy Promotions) entered. "You're the first fight," he told the

Johnsons. "Be ready to go at three o'clock." Then Gomez turned to the inspector. "Walk him out at three o'clock sharp."

At 2:15, the taping was done. Around the room, other fighters were being primed for battle. Johnson found a small square of unoccupied space and shadow-boxed for several minutes.

Referee Vic Drakulich came in and gave Ernest his pre-fight instructions.

The fighter began hitting warm-up pads with his father.

It was 2:55 p.m.

"Get your robe on, Johnson," the inspector ordered.

At three o'clock sharp, Ernest left the dressing room and was escorted through a brightly lit corridor to the arena floor. There was no ring-walk music. When he stepped into the ring, he looked across the enclosure and saw a young man named Hector Beltran.

Beltran was born in Mexico and came to the United States with his family at age two. His stepfather was a truck driver. His mother worked for a catering service. A long, ugly scar ran across his abdomen.

"I was a miracle baby," Hector explained. "When I was two months old, the doctor told my mom there was only a small chance I'd live. My organs were all tangled up, so they did the surgery. I'm here, so I'd say it came out pretty good."

Beltran began boxing at age twelve.

"I was riding my bike past a gym," he remembered. "The door was open, so I stopped and looked in. The coach asked if I wanted to come inside, but I rode away. The next week, the same thing happened, only this time I went in. It was something to do and it kept me out of trouble."

A year later, Beltran had his first amateur fight. "I was nervous," he recalled. "But a few days before, I had a puppy three months old that was stolen. Just before the bell rang, my coach told me, 'See that guy across the ring. Pretend like he's the guy that stole your puppy.' That got me going."

Beltran graduated from high school and took a job as an inventory clerk in shipping and receiving for the Winn Meat Company in Dallas. His record as he stood across from Johnson was 10–1 with 9 knockouts, but the numbers were deceiving. The fighters he'd beaten were, for the most part, "professional losers." In his only bout against an opponent with a winning record, Hector had lost a six-round split decision.

"The fight I lost," Beltran said, "my son, Hector Jr., was born six days before it. And two days after he was born, I broke up with my girlfriend. My head wasn't into boxing. I only sparred one day for that fight."

The loss was followed by two knockout victories, but Beltran was inactive for seventeen months after that. Then, in late April, he was offered the opportunity to fight Johnson on the De La Hoya–Mayweather undercard.

"This caught me off guard," Hector acknowledged one day before the fight. "I took some time off from boxing to get my life in order, and I have responsibilities to my son. It's hard to work nine-to-five, share custody of my boy, and be in the gym, all at the same time. I've only sparred for a week for this fight. But I'm a much better fighter than what I get credit for. I'm young [twenty-two years old]. I have good power and mental toughness. This is a break-out opportunity for me."

"By the way," Beltran added. "My puppy that was stolen; it was a pit bull. I don't want anyone thinking it was a poodle."

The first time that Johnson and Beltran saw each other was on Friday afternoon at two o'clock when they reported for their pre-fight physicals in Studio 1 at the MGM Grand Garden Arena. They sat side by side, filling out forms at a Nevada State Athletic Commission table and barely glancing at each other. Both men are likable, soft-spoken, and polite, but they didn't speak.

"It's a little awkward," Johnson said afterward. "You know you're going to fight this guy tomorrow, so you kind of size him up. Anyone who says he doesn't is lying."

What did he think of Beltran?

"They say he's a puncher, but I've never seen him fight or watched tapes. He's taller than I thought. I was expecting a shorter fighter."

After their physical examinations, each man weighed in at 137 pounds. The highlight of the day for Beltran was that he got to shake hands with De La Hoya when Oscar came in for his own physical.

"Oscar is my hero," Hector said. "I grew up watching him fight, and I admire the way he has control of his whole life. When we shook hands, he seemed real nice."

On the afternoon of the fight, Beltran entered dressing room #4 at 1:20 p.m. A "participant" credential hung from a chain around his neck. Trainer Dennis Rodarte and assistant trainer Pablo Cortez were with him.

The dressing room was empty. Hector sat on a straight-backed chair and texted a friend. Then he lay down on the carpeted floor, put a rolled-up towel beneath his head, and stared at the ceiling. Several minutes later, he crossed his arms across his chest, turned his head to the side, and closed his eyes.

Each of the five fighters assigned to dressing room #4 was an underdog. The fights had been made for their opponents to win.

At two o'clock, Hector stood up, took a pair of worn red boxing shoes out of a red gym bag, and put them on. The room was beginning to fill up with other undercard fighters and their cornermen.

Rodarte taped Beltran's hands. When he was done, Hector put on his red velvet trunks and gloved up.

At 2:35, Eric Gomez entered the room. "We walk at three," he told Rodarte. "You've got twenty-five minutes."

Beltran went into the adjacent shower room and began hitting warm-up pads with Cortez. After he fought, Hector would take a shower. From that point on, the shower room floor would be wet and useless to the other fighters for warm-up purposes.

Rodarte put Vaseline on Beltran's face.

Ring announcer Lupe Contreras came into the dressing room and asked Hector how he'd like to be introduced.

"Handsome."

"Handsome Hector Beltran?"

"Yes, sir."

"Out of Dallas?"

"Right."

The doors to the arena had yet to open when Beltran and Johnson made their way to the ring.

There were no paying spectators in the stands. The only people present were HBO technicians, ushers, Nevada State Athletic Commission personnel, and a few others with jobs to do.

Contreras took the microphone.

"Ladies and gentlemen," he intoned. "Welcome to the MGM Grand Garden Arena for one of the most anticipated nights in the history of boxing."

Beltran was introduced first: "In the blue corner, fighting out of Dallas, Texas, Handsome Hector Beltran."

Johnson's introduction followed. At precisely 3:05 p.m., the bell for round one rang. The doors were now open. There were fourteen paying customers in the stands.

Beltran came out firing power shots early in round one while Johnson tried to establish his jab. Hector won the round on each judge's scorecard. Then things fell into a pattern. At the start of each round, Beltran was an effective aggressor, but he would tire, at which point Johnson fired back. Ernest should have forced Hector to work harder. By not pushing him, he allowed Beltran to rest when he needed to.

Each man's corner shouted encouragement throughout the fight. The crowd was silent because there was no crowd. Beltran was the harder puncher. Occasionally, he turned southpaw, looking for different angles. After round six, Rodarte put a big gob of Vaseline on Hector's cheek, possibly hoping that Drakulich would order him to wipe it off, thereby giving his fighter an extra ten seconds of rest. But the referee let it go.

Round seven belonged to Johnson. Then Beltran dug deep and rallied to win the final stanza. The decision of the judges was a draw.

In his dressing room afterward, Johnson was disappointed. "His switching back and forth [from an orthodox to a southpaw stance] caught me off guard," Ernest admitted. "I didn't know he did that. And I was anticipating his getting tired, but he did and then he didn't."

In dressing room #4, Beltran was in a happier mood. "I know I should stay in the gym more," he acknowledged. "But when you don't get a fight for a while, you don't train like you should. This was good. It's something to build on."

A commission inspector approached with pen and paper in hand. "Hector, do you want to sign for your check?"

A smile crossed Beltran's face.

"Yeah, I do want that."

Across the room, Lorenzo Bethea, a junior-welterweight from Atlantic City, was readying for battle. Bethea had lost four of his six most recent fights and in a matter of minutes would enter the ring to face John Murray (who was undefeated in twenty bouts and being groomed for stardom). An hour later, Bethea would be in an ambulance on his way to the hospital with bleeding in his brain.

Meanwhile, upstairs, a mass of humanity had entered the MGM

Grand Hotel and Casino. The passageway leading from the hotel registration desk to the casino floor was like a New York City subway platform at rush hour. Every gaming table was full. Bettors were lining up to walk into the sports book and move within view of the odds boards and giant television screens. The big fight was four hours away. The MGM Grand was the place to be.

Bernard Hopkins loved fighting but acknowledged that there was a downside to being a professional boxer: "You do get hit," he noted.

The Executioner
Bernard Hopkins vs. Winky Wright— July 21, 2007

Bernard Hopkins was unique as a fighter in that he will be remembered more for what he accomplished in the ring when he was old than when he was young. That became clear on July 21, 2007, when at age forty-two, he defeated Ronald "Winky" Wright at the Mandalay Bay Resort and Casino in Las Vegas.

Boxing fans are familiar with the Hopkins saga. At age seventeen, he was sentenced to five to twelve years in prison for multiple street crimes. "I don't blame the judge," he said later. "I'd been in court thirty times in two years. What else was he supposed to do?"

For fifty-six months, Hopkins was one of three thousand inmates in Graterford State Penitentiary in Pennsylvania. When he was released just shy of his twenty-third birthday, he had meager vocational skills and little margin for error. Then he turned to boxing and lost his first pro fight. He sat out the next sixteen months, returned to the ring in 1990, and was defeated only once over the next fifteen years. That was by Roy Jones in a 1993 IBF middleweight title bout when Bernard didn't take the risks he needed to take and was outboxed over twelve rounds. Then Jones went up in weight and, in 1995, Hopkins captured the IBF middleweight crown with a seventh-round knockout of Segundo Mercado. Ultimately, he made twenty consecutive title defenses. When he beat Félix Trinidad in a 2001 title-unification bout at Madison Square Garden, he achieved superstar status.

The Trinidad fight was the first time that Hopkins's age weighed against him in pre-fight predictions. Bernard was thirty-six; Félix was twenty-eight. But Hopkins dominated from start to finish and knocked out his previously undefeated opponent in the twelfth round. Bernard's second signature victory—a ninth-round knockout of Oscar De La Hoya—came three years later.

But in 2005, at age forty, Hopkins faltered against Jermain Taylor. He came into the Taylor fight with a 20–1–1 record in world-championship contests and the third-longest championship reign in boxing history (ten years, eighty-two days). But Taylor outfought him en route to a split-decision triumph and did it again by unanimous decision five months later.

At that point, a lot of people thought Hopkins was done as a fighter. After all, most boxers fade badly when accosted by Father Time. Sugar Ray Robinson was 37–15–4 after his thirty-fifth birthday. Marvin Hagler and Carlos Monzon were retired at age thirty-five.

Then, confounding his critics, Hopkins went up in weight and, at age forty-one, seized the light-heavyweight crown with a dominant performance against Antonio Tarver. That redefined his legacy.

Hopkins could be smart and foolish, diplomatic and brusque, funny and mean, charming and cruel. At times, he was wise. He didn't like being wrong and rarely admitted it when he was. Among the thoughts he uttered were:

* ★ "In the ring, I'm a dangerous guy. I destroy careers. I ruin other people's dreams."
* ★ "There's a time to be humble and a time for war. Boxing is war. It ain't no joke. It ain't no show. You have to think violent. I'm not shy when it comes to inflicting pain on people."
* ★ "Nothing is fair, what fighters do. You hit behind the head? It's not legal but it happens. There's no such thing as a dirty fighter to me. It's just an opportunity. Don't cry and complain to the referee, We're not in church; we're fighting. If you want to not get a bruise, then go play golf."
* ★ "In the ring, there's a chance you can die or become a vegetable. I would rather it be him than me."

But a mean streak only helps a fighter if he has the skills to go with it. Hopkins had the tools of a great fighter. He had remarkable genetic gifts. But the key to his success was his work ethic. He was always in shape and rarely walked around at more than a few pounds above his fighting weight.

"Bernard gives more of himself than any fighter I've ever known," Naazim Richardson, who trained Hopkins in his later years, said. "Most fighters, if they tried to do what Bernard does, they'd break. There are very few human beings who can give what Bernard gives, mentally or physically. Sometimes you have to tell him to back off and slow down. I've never seen a fighter get up mentally fight after fight like Bernard does. Each time he steps in the ring, it's like his first championship fight. Every trainer who ever lived would like to work with a fighter like Bernard Hopkins."

Boxing is about who executes best in the fractions of a second when an opening is there. The outcome of a fight is determined by which fighter does what has to be done in those fleeting slivers of time. Forget about the costume mask and executioner's hood that Hopkins sometimes wore to the ring. He was a smart, conservative boxer who adhered to the view that every move mattered.

"I'm not a guy who comes to blast you out of there," Bernard said. "I've never considered myself a one-punch knockout artist. I'm more of a technician. I take my time. I dissect. Eventually, I'll beat you up."

"Bernard is not a football player," Richardson noted. "Bernard is not a basketball player. Bernard is a fighter. He's one of the few out there today who has truly learned the craft of boxing."

Hopkins–Wright was a crossroads fight for both men.

Wright was the antithesis of Hopkins. His public persona was easygoing. He didn't stir passions. He just quietly did his job and hadn't lost over the previous seven and a half years, a span that included two victories over Shane Mosley and another over Félix Trinidad.

Age matters in boxing. Wright opened as a 6-to-5 betting favorite, in large part because of Hopkins's forty-two years, although, as Bernard pointed out, "Winky is thirty-five; he ain't no spring chicken either."

"We're going to force this fight," said Dan Birmingham (who had trained Wright since Winky's amateur days). "We're going to set a fast hard pace. You look at Winky's past fights; he's landed punches every five to ten seconds on every opponent, and Bernard's not going to be any exception. We're coming right at him. We're going to start this fight hard and we're going to finish this fight hard right up until the last second. We're going to make Bernard fight. And if they think they're going to wear us down, then I'm glad they're thinking that way because it's not going to happen."

"I know how to win," Wright added. "I'm gonna kill the boogey-man. People don't have to be scared no more. The boogey-man will be gone."

Hopkins, of course, had a contrary view.

"There is no puzzle in a boxing ring that I can't solve," Bernard said. "This fight is based on who can figure out the puzzle and make the other guy do what he don't want to do. Winky is like a turtle. He likes to go into his shell, but I've seen every style and fought every style. I know everything that Winky has, and I also know that Winky don't have as many weapons in his arsenal as I do. I'm going to get the turtle to stick his head out of his shell and then I'm going to knock it off. I'm undefeated against southpaws; ten and oh with nine knockouts. There's nothing Winky can do that will surprise me. Winky's going to get hit more in this fight than he's been hit in any fight in his life. Winky thinks he's better than me. I know I'm better than him. I'll beat him and beat him until that drop of water where you didn't fix the ceiling tears the floor up."

There was also the matter of size. The contract weight for the fight was 170 pounds. At six feet, one inch, Hopkins was three inches taller than Wright. His most recent fight (against Tarver) had been at 175 pounds. By contrast, Winky had never fought above 160.

"Do you know what it took with this body for me to make 160 pounds all those years?" Hopkins asked rhetorically. "I went through torture for thirteen years to make 160 pounds. I've got a new body now, and it's like driving a new car."

Boxing needs competitive fights between elite fighters. Hopkins–Wright was that kind of matchup. Both men were in the top five on virtually everyone's pound-for-pound list. Neither man had ever been knocked out. Their encounter was for the *Ring Magazine* light-heavyweight championship belt, which was a bit disingenuous given the 170-pound contract weight. But as Bernard observed, "One of the great things about fighting for the *Ring* belt is that there are no sanctioning fees."

★★★

Bernard Hopkins entered dressing room #4 at the MGM Grand Garden Arena at 5:55 on Saturday night. A rush of "smart" money had raised the odds to 9-to-5 in Wright's favor.

Hopkins was wearing blue jeans and a black-and-gold hooded shirt with a navy-blue do-rag on his head. Sitting in a cushioned chair, he put his feet up on a folding chair in front of him and smiled.

"I slept all afternoon," he said. "Weighed myself in the hotel right before I left; 184 pounds tonight."

For most of the next two hours, Hopkins chatted amiably with those around him. He was remarkably relaxed with a kind word for everyone who was part of his team.

Freddie Roach had assumed the role of lead trainer for the fight because Naazim Richardson had been hospitalized for five weeks after suffering a stroke. But Naazim was in the dressing room too, having taken solid steps toward recovery. His speech was good and he was moving well although there was still some weakness on his left side.

"How you feel, Naazim?" Hopkins asked.

"Blessed to be here with my warrior."

Bernard turned to cutman Leon Tabbs.

"Leon, my man. I ain't needed you yet, but it's good to know you're here."

"I'm ready, champ."

The dialogue continued with others.

"How's your wife? How's your kids?"

There was a fifty-inch flat-screen television at the far end of the room. Michael Katsidis was in an undercard fight against Czar Amonsot that was developing into a bloody brawl.

Hopkins took off his jeans and shoes and pulled on a pair of royal-blue boxing trunks. Then he sat down again and stretched out his legs. Richardson covered his chest and legs with towels.

Bernard leaned back and closed his eyes.

"That's a time when all sorts of whispers cross my mind," he said later. "So I shut out the world and think about my mom."

No one talked. The only voices heard were those of Bob Sheridan and Dave Bontempo on the international television feed. Bernard opened his eyes periodically to watch the action on the screen unfold.

Everything in the dressing room was methodical, measured, and calm. Bernard took a sip from a bottle of water. "No sense using up energy now," he said. "I can turn it on and off. Watch me when the time comes."

At seven o'clock, assistant trainer John David Jackson went next door to watch Wright's hands being wrapped.

With a member of Winky's team present, Roach began taping Hopkins's hands.

Katsidis–Amonsot ended and the semifinal bout between Óscar Larios and Jorge Linares began.

At 7:20, the taping was done. Bernard lay down on a towel on the floor and began a series of stretching exercises, his first physical activity since entering the dressing room.

Referee Robert Byrd came in and gave the fighter his pre-fight instructions. After Byrd left, Hopkins stretched some more and began shadow-boxing.

At 7:45, Bernard gloved up and began working the pads with Roach.

"Somebody cut a towel and put it over my head," he said after five minutes of work. "I'm sweating like a motherfucker."

At eight o'clock, the padwork stopped and the room fell silent. There was a prayer in Arabic, ending with "Allahu Akbar" ("God is great").

More padwork with Roach.

"How much time?" Hopkins asked. "What are we working with?"

Richardson looked at the television monitor. "Ninth round," he answered.

"Naazim," Bernard said, still hitting the pads. "They couldn't keep you in no bed."

"This ain't your first time down this path," Richardson responded. "Just be you, soldier. Nobody ever made you fight at their pace. You control."

Linares stopped Larios in the tenth round.

Hopkins finished hitting the pads with Roach, sat down on a folding metal chair, and stretched his legs out on the floor. Then he opened his mouth and, with his tongue, pushed out a bridge of false teeth.

"It's all mental," he said. "That's what great fighters are made of. But the psychological stuff means nothing if you can't fight."

Hopkins stood up. Now there was a street-alley sneer on his lips. His eyes were mean.

The Executioner was ready to kill.

It was a good fight; two extremely talented professionals, both of whom had come to win. In the early going, they traded rounds. Wright showed his jab, and Hopkins was Hopkins. He boxed and mauled, taking what was given to him and more. Regardless of age, he still had a nasty right hand lead that scored when Wright stood still for a fraction of a second in front of him.

Early in round three, a clash of heads opened a hideous gash on Wright's left eyelid. It was ruled unintentional. But Bernard's head movement, more than Winky's, was the cause. Thereafter, Hopkins compounded the handicap by rubbing his head and gloves against the cut from time to time, not to mention punching at it. On several occasions, Robert Byrd warned Bernard about holding and using his head on the inside. But he never took a point away and ignored the occasional low blow.

The first six rounds saw a lot of action with Wright forcing the pace. Then the action slowed. After eight stanzas, the fight was close. But the final rounds belonged to Hopkins, who emerged victorious on the judges' scorecards by a 117–111, 117–111, 116–112 margin.

"Winky comes to fight," Bernard acknowledged in his dressing room after the bout as Leon Tabbs held an icepack to the swelling around his left eye. "Winky can be dead tired and he still does what he does. Winky don't go away when things get tough, and Winky is strong."

Remarkably, after beating Wright, Hopkins fought for another nine years. He had one last big win left in him; a unanimous decision triumph over Kelly Pavlik in 2008. But there were losses to Joe Calzaghe, Chad Dawson, and Sergey Kovalev and, at age fifty-one, a career-ending knockout defeat at the hands of Joe Smith. His final Hall of Fame ledger stands at 55 wins, 8 losses, and 2 draws, with 32 of his wins coming by way of knockout.

Kelly Pavlik climbed off the canvas to dethrone Jermain Taylor in one of the most exciting middleweight title fights ever.

The Night Kelly Pavlik Became King
Kelly Pavlik vs. Jermain Taylor—
September 29, 2007

On September 29, 2007, Kelly Pavlik challenged Jermain Taylor at Boardwalk Hall in Atlantic City for the middleweight championship of the world.

Pavlik was born in Youngstown, Ohio, in 1982. His father, Mike, was a steelworker who left the mills to take a job as an insurance agent. His mother, Debbie, was a cook at Hardee's, a fast-food restaurant chain.

Kelly compiled an amateur record of 89 wins against 9 losses. He worked odd jobs to get the money to go to tournaments. More often than he cares to remember, he was removing dirty dishes from tables in a Youngstown restaurant when his high school classmates came in for something to eat after a school dance.

Pavlik turned pro in 2000. He had a thin, muscular body and knew one way to fight—a crowd-pleasing style of go forward, punching. But a fighter's career moves slowly, and Kelly was hampered by problems with a tendon in his right hand. To supplement his income, he washed dishes and took other jobs. Until early 2007, he did occasional landscape work for ten dollars an hour to help make ends meet.

On May 19, 2007, Pavlik's life changed. He knocked out highly regarded Edison Miranda in seven rounds. That performance silenced a lot of doubters. Suddenly, Kelly was no longer a protected white kid. He was a 31–0 fighter with 28 knockouts and the mandatory challenger for middleweight champion Jermain Taylor.

Taylor had won a bronze medal at the 2000 Olympics and turned pro under the aegis of promoter Lou DiBella. Pat Burns, a former Miami cop with an extensive amateur coaching background, was brought in to train him. Under Burns's tutelage, Jermain won his first twenty-three pro fights. Then, on July 16, 2005, he eked out a narrow split decision over

Bernard Hopkins to claim the undisputed middleweight championship of the world.

There was a parade in Taylor's hometown of Little Rock, Arkansas, to celebrate his triumph. Thousands of fans attended a rally at the end of the route. "That was the best feeling I ever had," Jermain said afterward. "It was amazing that all those people came out just for me." Then came a trip to New York for a meeting with fellow Arkansan Bill Clinton. "Anywhere I go," Jermain said, "restaurants, clubs, wherever; they don't charge me. Of course, when I was broke and needed it, no one gave me anything for free."

On December 3, 2005, Taylor decisioned Hopkins in a rematch. He seemed poised for superstardom. But a corrosive factor was at work.

Taylor had grown up without a father. And a Little Rock resident named Ozell Nelson had filled the void, playing a pivotal role in Jermain's early life. He'd even taught him the rudiments of boxing. Now Nelson and Pat Burns weren't getting along.

After Taylor won his rematch against Hopkins, there was sniping that Burns had a "white slave-master mentality" and wasn't a top-notch trainer despite his having overseen Jermain's transformation from a raw amateur to middleweight champion of the world. There was a lot of money to be made off Taylor now that he was a champion, particularly if Burns's salary were to become available for redistribution. Taylor owed much of his success as a fighter to Burns. But in his mind, Nelson had saved his life. After the second Taylor–Hopkins fight, Burns was replaced by Emanuel Steward.

Steward was a legendary trainer and deservedly so. One doesn't have to debate the issue of whether he was a better trainer than Burns. It's enough to say that Burns was a better trainer for Taylor.

Steward brought Taylor to the Kronk Gym in Detroit to train and introduced him to a lifestyle that wasn't a good fit. Nelson was given an expanded role in training camp. Jermain's next three performances reflected Burns's absence. He fought without his usual fire against Winky Wright and salvaged a draw. Lackluster victories over Kassim Ouma and Cory Spinks followed. As he readied to face Pavlik, his record stood at 27–0–1 with 17 knockouts. But he was a vulnerable champion.

A logical case could be made for victory by either fighter. Taylor was undefeated in seven fights against present or former world champions. He would have an edge in handspeed over Pavlik. Also, Kelly didn't move his head enough and had a tendency to bring his left hand back low after throwing his jab. Against Miranda, Kelly had showed he could take a punch. But could he take jab after jab and combinations?

Moreover, Jermain had fought through adversity. He'd suffered a bad scalp wound in his first fight against Hopkins. His left eye had been shut by Winky Wright. Each time, he'd emerged with the crown. His will was strong. He'd gone twelve rounds seven times. By contrast, Pavlik had gone nine rounds once. Kelly had never heard the ring announcer say "round ten . . . round eleven . . . round twelve."

But the case for a Pavlik victory was equally strong. Kelly had a solid chin and power in both hands. He was expected to hit Taylor harder than Jermain had ever been hit.

Meanwhile, Pavlik's hometown of Youngstown was squarely behind him. Once, Youngstown had been at the center of steel production in the United States. But the local economy had soured in the 1970s. Steel mills closed; factories shut down. The city had never recovered.

Now Youngstown had a hero to root for, a reason to feel good about itself. And the entire state of Ohio embraced Kelly. One day before Taylor–Pavlik, the boardwalk in Atlantic City was a sea of scarlet, gray, and white (the uniform colors for Ohio State). Interest in the fight was so intense that General Motors planned to shut down the late shift at its plant in Lordstown (near Youngstown) on Saturday night because so many of its workers planned to stay home and watch the fight.

Pavlik entered his dressing room in Boardwalk Hall on fight night at 8:34 p.m. He was wearing a gray warm-up suit with a scarlet stripe down each leg and white piping. Mike Pavlik, trainer Jack Loew, manager Cameron Duncan, Michael Cox (a Youngstown policeman), Jack's son (John), and Kelly's oldest brother (Mike Jr.) were with him. Cutman Miguel Diaz, who had worked Kelly's corner since his first pro fight, was already there.

Loew was the only trainer that Pavlik had ever had. When Kelly was nine, he began learning the rudiments of boxing under Jack's tutelage at the Southside Boxing Club—a converted pizza joint in Youngstown. Loew was also the owner and sole employee of a company called The

Driveway Kings. He sealed asphalt driveways for a living. One week before Taylor–Pavlik, he was sealing driveways in the morning before going to the gym.

As Pavlik settled in the dressing room, the preliminary fights were underway. In the first bout of the evening, Ray Smith (one of Taylor's sparring partners from Little Rock) had been knocked out by Richard Pierson (a Pavlik sparring partner). Then heavyweight Terry Smith (also from Little Rock) lost a six-round decision to Robert Hawkins.

"I got good news for you," Diaz told Kelly. "Both of Jermain's Taylor's guys lost."

The dressing room had seen better days. The industrial carpet was worn and the vinyl-topped rubdown table was scarred with discolored tape covering multiple gashes.

Referee Steve Smoger entered and gave Pavlik his final pre-fight instructions. Dr. Sherry Wulkan of the New Jersey State Athletic Control Board administered a final pre-fight physical exam. When they were done, Kelly yawned. Then he began texting friends.

"Oklahoma [one of the top college football teams in the nation] got beat pretty good today," Jack Loew said.

"Texas too," Mike Pavlik added.

Mike pointed toward a television monitor by the door. "Too bad we can't get Ohio State on that thing."

Kelly stopped texting long enough to pull up some college football scores. "Ohio State is losing to Minnesota," he said.

"What?" his father uttered in disbelief.

Kelly smiled. "Just kidding. The Buckeyes are up 14–0; 7:22 left in the second quarter."

He put down his cell phone and stretched out his legs on a folding chair in front of him.

Larry Merchant of HBO came in to conduct a pre-fight interview.

"I've waited for this for seven years," Pavlik told him. "I just want to get in there and let my hands go. He'll have to keep up with me."

At 9:41, Kelly lay down on the carpet and began a series of stretching exercises. Ten minutes later, he stood up. "Time to put my soldier gear on," he said.

Shoes first. Then his trunks—gray with red, white, and blue trim.

When a fighter gets to the championship level, his dressing room reflects his preferences. Pavlik preferred low key and quiet. The conversation around the room was casual, what one might expect to hear in the gym before a sparring session.

Loew began wrapping Kelly's hands. Throughout training, the muscles in the fighter's back had been tighter than he would have liked. Now, as Loew wrapped, Mike Pavlik massaged his son's back and shoulders.

Mike had been a constant presence in Atlantic City. Broad-shouldered with a shaved head, he looked as though he could bench-press the Rock of Gibraltar. He was enjoying the journey and, at the same time, looking after his son.

The odds had been virtually even in the days leading up to the fight with the "smart" money on Taylor and the Youngstown money on Pavlik. In the past twenty-four hours, the professional money had come in, making Jermain an 8-to-5 favorite.

At 10:17, the taping was done.

"How are we doing?" Mike Pavlik asked.

"I'm very very confident," Loew told him. "Nothing to do for this boy anymore but let him fight."

Kelly gloved up and began hitting the pads with his trainer.

"Stay behind the jab," Loew instructed. "Jab, right. . . . Jab, right."

Each time, the follow right was a bit off target.

"Stay behind the jab and relax. . . . There. That's it. Double jab. . . . Now let it go."

The punches began landing with explosive power.

When the padwork was done, Kelly alternated between pacing back and forth and shadow-boxing.

Miguel Diaz put Vaseline on Kelly's face.

The fighter hit the pads with Loew one last time.

"That's it. . . . Wow. . . . Nice and easy. . . . Push him back with that big long jab. Double it up. . . . There you go. Back him up and you win."

An HBO production coordinator came into the room.

"Two minutes and you walk."

Kelly stood up and moved toward the door.

There had been no music, no one shouting "You da man!" Just quiet confidence and calm.

Michael Cox checked his cell phone one last time. "The [Ohio State] Buckeyes won 30 to 7," he announced.

Mike Pavlik put an arm on Kelly's shoulder.

"All that work, all those years; it comes together now," he told his son. "You were born to be here tonight."

Youngstown was in the house. That was clear as the fighters made their way to the ring. The crowd made it sound as though the bout was being fought in Ohio. There was a thunderous roar for Pavlik and loud boos for Taylor.

Taylor came out aggressively in round one, going right after Pavlik. He was quicker than the challenger and his hands were faster. All three judges gave him the round. When the stanza was over, Jack Loew told Kelly, "Control the pace. Be patient. Stay behind the jab. It's a basic fight."

Round two began with more of the same. "I was surprised," Pavlik said later. "I thought he'd try to box me more, but he came to fight. He has handspeed and he can punch."

Definitely, he can punch. Midway through round two, Taylor timed a right hand over a sloppy Pavlik jab. The blow landed high on the challenger's head. Pavlik staggered backward, and the champion followed with a fifteen-punch barrage that put Kelly down.

"I was scared to death," Mike Pavlik admitted later. "That's the worst feeling I've ever had in my life. I wouldn't have cared if the referee had stopped it. To be honest, I was hoping it was over."

"The first thing that went through my mind," Kelly said in his dressing room after the fight, "was, 'Oh, shit.' But I heard the count. I was aware at all times. I told myself, 'Get up; get through this.'"

Pavlik rose at the count of two, but there were 88 seconds left in the round. "I was shaky," he admitted. "That right hand hurt. I've been knocked down before but there was never a buzz. It had always been a balance thing. This time, there was a tingle and my legs weren't so good. I did what I could to survive. He hit me with some more hard shots, but I got through the round. Some guys quit when they get knocked down, and some get back up."

There comes a time when a fighter has to dig deep within himself by himself. In the corner after round two, Kelly managed a weak smile. "I'm okay," he told Loew. But he was bleeding from the nose and mouth.

"Stay on that double fucking jab," Loew ordered. "There's a lot of time left. You have ten more rounds to do your job."

Then, incredibly, Pavlik won round three. The punches that Taylor had thrown in the second round seemed to have taken more out of the champion than the challenger. Jermain paced himself in the stanza rather than following up on his advantage. Pavlik threw ninety-nine punches over the three-minute period, earning the nod on each judge's scorecard.

The die was cast. Taylor was faster. He was ahead on points throughout the bout. But inexorably, Pavlik was walking him down with nonstop aggression behind a strong double jab. More and more often, the champion found himself having to punch his way out of a corner. When the fight moved inside and one of the challenger's hands was tied up, Kelly fought with the other hand rather than clinch. He made Jermain fight every second of every round.

"Jermain has a chin," Pavlik acknowledged afterward. "I hit him with some punches, flush, right on the button early, and he didn't budge. But then he started to wear down. In the fifth round, I thought I hurt him a bit against the ropes. But he came back with a right hand that came close to putting me in trouble again, so I reminded myself to be careful. In the seventh round, I hit him with another good right hand and his reaction was different. I saw his shoulders sag. There was that little buckle in his knees and I knew I had him."

When the right hand that Pavlik was referring to landed, Taylor backed into a corner again. Kelly followed with a barrage of punches.

"Jermain went limp," referee Steve Smoger said later. "He was totally gone, helpless."

Smoger stepped between the fighters. Two minutes and 14 seconds into round seven, Kelly Pavlik was the new middleweight champion of the world. Taylor was ahead at the time of the stoppage 59–54, 58–55, 58–55 on the judges' scorecards.

When Pavlik returned to Youngstown after the victory, a caravan of police cars and fire trucks met his SUV at the Ohio border to escort him home. And the perks kept coming. Kelly was even the subject of a resolution passed by the United States House of Representatives, praising him for his commitment and continuing loyalty to the Youngstown community.

But all good things come to an end. And in boxing, they tend to end sooner rather than later. Pavlik won a clear-cut decision in a rematch against Taylor. Then, after a successful title defense against Gary Lockett, he went up in weight and was outpointed by Bernard Hopkins. He returned to 160 pounds with knockout victories over Marco Antonio Rubio and Miguel Angel Espino. But on April 17, 2010, he lost his crown by decision to Sergio Martínez. Problems with alcohol and several stints in rehab followed. He retired from the ring in 2012 with a 40–2 (34 KOs) ledger.

"The main thing," Kelly said later, looking back on it all, "is I won the world title. That's something nobody can ever take from me."

One of the things that made Ricky Hatton so appealing was that he was a fan of the fans.

A Look Back at Ground Zero for Mayweather–Hatton
Floyd Mayweather vs. Ricky Hatton— December 8, 2007

"People watch me because I'm an exciting fighter," Ricky Hatton once said. "But I think they watch me too because they look on me as a mate. I don't expect people to roll out a red carpet when I walk down the street. There are no bodyguards. I don't want VIP treatment. I'm just a normal kid doing very well at what he does. I like my food. I'll go to the pub for a few pints and to throw darts. The best thing about being a fighter is when people come up to me and say, 'Ricky, you're a world champion and you're just like me.' What the fans think means a lot to me. There's no point in being a great fighter if people think you're a dickhead."

Most ordinary people want to be treated like stars. Hatton is a star who wants to be treated like ordinary people. That was on display during the first week of December 2007, when Ricky challenged Floyd Mayweather Jr. at the MGM Grand in Las Vegas.

Mayweather had become The Man in boxing seven months earlier by virtue of a split-decision victory over Oscar De La Hoya. Hatton was undefeated with 43 victories in 43 fights and 31 knockouts. Two years earlier, he'd stopped Kostya Tszyu in eleven rounds to seize the IBF 140-pound crown. Then Ricky went up in weight to claim the WBA welterweight title by decision over Luis Collazo.

Mayweather was a clear betting favorite over Hatton. Age wasn't a factor. Floyd was thirty; Ricky was twenty-nine. But weight was. This would be only Hatton's second fight at 147 pounds.

"I've studied the tapes," Ricky said prior to the bout. "Floyd is very very good at what he does. He's got fantastic handspeed. He's got a wonderful defense, and he likes to take the steam out of his opponents by making them miss. He's a very versatile fighter. He has so many tricks;

you have to deny him the time and space to do his thing. But it's very pleasing for me that the fight where Floyd was at his least comfortable was the first fight against José Luis Castillo, who was able to bully him to the ropes a lot. I don't think Castillo is physically as strong as me, as quick as me, or has footwork as good as me. I move in very, very quickly on my opponents and stick to them like glue. I've got the style to give Floyd absolute nightmares. His handspeed will concern me if I'm on the outside, but it won't bother me when I'm on his chest. I will constantly be in his face and give him no chance to rest.

"I don't think Mayweather realizes I'm as good as I am," Hatton continued. "He just sees the obvious. Strong kid with a big heart who keeps coming forward. But there's a lot more to me than that. There's a lot of thought to what I do; if you watch carefully how quick I move in on my opponents, how I change the angles. It's only when fighters actually get in there with me that they realize there's a method to the madness."

And there was one more factor to be considered. The Hatton camp wanted (and needed) a referee who would let Ricky fight on the inside and not prematurely separate the combatants.

There was a buzz in Las Vegas during fight week. An estimated eighteen thousand Hatton fans had flown in from England, bringing energy to the Strip that hadn't been seen since Oscar De La Hoya vs. Félix Trinidad in 1999. The Ricky Hatton theme song sounded again and again:

> There's only one Ricky Hatton
> One Ricky Hatton
> Walking along
> Singing a song
> Walking in a Hatton Wonderland

On fight night, Hatton entered dressing room #4 at the MGM Grand Garden Arena at 5:45 p.m. A piece of paper taped to the door read, "Blue Corner—Ricky Hatton." Beneath that, someone had scrawled in a blue marker pen, "Ready by 7:55 p.m."

The dressing room was hot and stuffy. A British flag was taped to the wall. A large blue-plastic tub filled with ice and several dozen bottles of water stood by the door. Three pint bottles of Guinness had been thrown into the mix for a post-fight celebration.

Minutes earlier, Matthew Hatton (Ricky's brother) had completed an eight-round fight against Frankie Santos of Puerto Rico. He had yet to return to the dressing room.

"Matthew won," Ricky was told.

"Knockout or decision?"

"80–72, 80–72, 79–73."

Ricky smiled. "That's a good start on the evening."

Matthew and his cornermen (trainer Billy Graham, nutritionist Kerry Keyes, and cutman Mick Williamson, all of whom would work Ricky's corner later in the night) came through the door. "We got that one out of the way," Graham said. "One down and one to go."

Ricky fingered a rolled-up piece of tape and shot it toward a garbage can in the manner of a basketball point guard. The tape missed its target. "Not my sport," he said. He walked over, picked the tape off the floor, and dropped it in the trash.

A Sky TV crew came in to conduct a brief interview for British television. They were followed by Larry Merchant of HBO.

"Just leave me alone and let me do what I have to do," Hatton said to no one in particular after the television crews were gone. "I'm trying to make sense when I talk, but my mind's not on doing interviews now."

Then Hatton set about connecting the wires on an audio system he'd brought with him and positioned the speakers where he wanted them. For a moment, he looked like a young man moving into a new apartment.

At 6:35, music began to blare. For the next two hours, it would be very loud in the dressing room. Except for the time spent having his hands taped, Ricky would be on his feet, constantly moving like a hyperactive child, pacing and shadow-boxing with increasing intensity to the music.

A television monitor at the far end of the room showed Edner Cherry knocking out Wes Ferguson with a picture-perfect left hook in the first pay-per-view bout of the evening. "I wouldn't mind landing one of them in a bit," Hatton offered. "Please give me one of them tonight."

Billy Graham looked across the room at cutman Mick Williamson and said quietly, "I'm afraid we're going to need him tonight. I'm a realist. I think Ricky will win, but he gets cut. He gets bad cuts, and Floyd throws those fast slashing punches."

As time passed, Sugar Ray Leonard, Shane Mosley, and Marco Antonio Barrera entered to wish Ricky luck. The music kept changing, from rap to acid rock to something akin to an Irish jig. At seven o'clock, Hatton changed tracks again and the raspy voice of Mick Jagger was heard.

"I can't get no satisfaction . . ."

Ricky picked up the pace of his shadow-boxing and sang aloud.

"I can't get no satisfaction . . . Cause I try and I try and I try and I try."

Soon everyone in the room was singing.

"I can't get no . . . I can't get no . . . When I'm drivin' in my car, and the man comes on the radio . . ."

Floyd Mayweather's image appeared on the television monitor.

"I'm coming for you, fucker," Ricky growled.

David Beckham entered the room. He and Hatton had met earlier in the year and been texting back and forth ever since. "I can't believe that someone like David Beckham texts me," Ricky had said several months earlier. The fighter had attended a Los Angeles Galaxy soccer game as Beckham's guest. Now the favor was being returned.

Beckham stood by the door, maintaining a distance; one world-class athlete respecting the mental preparation required of another. At 7:15, for the first time in ninety minutes, Hatton sat and Billy Graham began taping his hands. Only then did Beckham walk over and clasp Ricky on the shoulder.

Recording star Tom Jones (who would sing "God Save the Queen" later in the evening) came in. Ricky looked up. "Is Elvis coming too?" he queried.

At 7:24, referee Joe Cortez entered the room to give Hatton his pre-fight instructions. Five months earlier, Cortez had refereed Ricky's fight against José Luis Castillo without incident. Now Cortez ran through the usual litany and closed with, "Any questions?"

"Ricky is an inside fighter," Graham said. "He fights clean but he's an aggressive fighter."

"I'll let the fight take its course," Cortez promised.

The referee left. Graham finished taping Hatton's hands. David Beckham and Tom Jones slipped out the door. Kerry Kayes helped Ricky on with his trunks—teal and silver with black trim and black fringe.

The television monitor showed Jeff Lacy and Peter Manfredo facing off for round one in the final preliminary bout of the evening. It was expected to be a short fight. Hatton gloved up and began working the pads with Graham.

At eight o'clock, Lacy and Manfredo were still in the ring. It was only round five.

Ricky paced a bit. . . . There was more padwork with Graham.

8:12 . . . Lacy and Manfredo began round eight.

8:20 . . . Aggravation was etched on Ricky's face. He had expected to be in the ring by now.

At 8:23, Lacy–Manfredo ended.

In the main arena, Tom Jones sang "God Save the Queen" followed by Tyrese's rendition of "The Star-Spangled Banner."

Finally, Team Hatton left the dressing room.

As Ricky came into view, there were thunderous cheers from the crowd.

The fighters were introduced and the bell for round one sounded.

As expected, Hatton moved forward from the start with Mayweather potshotting from the outside. The crowd roared with every blow that Ricky landed, but Floyd's hands were significantly faster. Mayweather's speed was a problem for Ricky. And the conduct of referee Joe Cortez made the challenge more daunting.

To get inside, Hatton had to navigate his way past Mayweather's fists and also Floyd's left elbow. Once inside, he was frequently fouled. Mayweather was allowed to go low; hold; and use his head, forearms, and elbows as offensive weapons. Often, Ricky maneuvered into position to work effectively and Cortez broke the fighters even though Hatton was still punching. By breaking them prematurely again and again, the referee denied Ricky the chance to impose his physical strength and forced him to fight much of the battle at long range. That, in turn, exposed him to Floyd's potshots as he tried to work his way back in again.

In the first round, Cortez broke the fighters eleven times, many of them when one or both men had an arm free and was punching. From there, it got worse; thirteen times in round two and fourteen in round three.

A live underdog waits for the moment when the favorite makes a mistake that will undermine his superiority. In Mayweather–Hatton, it never came. In round three, Floyd opened an ugly gash above Ricky's right eye. Still, Hatton persevered. In round five, he did his best work of the night, winning the stanza on the cards of all three judges. Significantly, Cortez broke the fighters only four times in round five.

Round six began with another Hatton offensive. Then, fifty seconds into the stanza, Mayweather appeared to turn his back as a defensive maneuver with his head going through the ropes. Ricky threw a punch and missed, and Cortez took a point away from Hatton.

"When the referee took a point away, I lost my composure a bit," Ricky said afterward. "I thought I was doing all right. I was two rounds down probably, but coming on nicely. Then the point got taken away, and I felt it wasn't going to be a level playing field. So I began trying to force things and took more risks and left myself open more than I should have."

Mayweather ran the table thereafter. In round eight, he began putting his punches together, landing hard clean shots to the head and body. Round nine was more of the same. But Hatton kept coming and his fans' ardor never dimmed. The crowd sang "There's only one Ricky Hatton" again and again with a fervor that increased as their hero's troubles grew, as though they were trying to will him to victory.

In round ten, Mayweather closed the show. Hatton launched a left hook from too far away. As Ricky's arm went in motion, Floyd countered with a highlight-reel blow. Rather than wait for the punch to miss, he threw second and landed first with a lightning left hook of his own. Hatton never saw the punch coming. He went down and got up, but he knew he'd been hit. Then Mayweather landed several more blows, and Cortez appropriately stopped the fight.

Six thousand miles is a long way to travel for a broken heart.

In the dressing room after the fight, Hatton sat on a chair and bowed his head.

Carol Hatton walked over to her son, leaned down, and hugged him. "You did us proud," she said.

Ricky's father and brother joined them.

"I really thought I was going to win," Ricky told them.

Ray Leonard came in to offer condolences.

Billy Graham stood off to the side.

"I still think Ricky can beat Floyd," the trainer said. "But he didn't, so that's it. I give Floyd credit. He finished the fight. He brought the curtain down, didn't he?"

A security guard opened the door. "Brad Pitt and Angelina Jolie would like to come in. Is it all right?"

Before Ricky could answer, the women in the room, who now also included Jennifer Dooley (then Ricky's girlfriend) and Jenna Coyne (Matthew's fiancée) answered in the affirmative.

The celebrity couple entered. Brad Pitt walked over to the fighter. "There's still only one Ricky Hatton," he said.

Ray Leonard went in search of a photographer who would take a photo of him with Pitt and Jolie.

Eventually the well-wishers filtered out and Ricky was left with his core team.

"The referee did me no favors tonight," he said, reflecting on the previous hour. "I can't complain about Floyd. It's a rough business. You do what you can get away with, and Floyd was good on the inside. I'm not exactly Mother Theresa in the ring myself. If I can get a sly one in there, I'll do it. But the referee let Floyd foul the living daylights out of me. And when I was in position to do damage, he forced me out to long range again. Let's be honest. The referee was poor tonight."

Then Hatton lay down on the rubdown table, motionless with his hands crossed across his chest. Dr. Frank Ryan closed the wound above his right eye with one deep stitch on the inside and seven on the outside. One could only begin to imagine the echoes that were reverberating in Ricky's mind. The three bottles of Guinness lay in the ice, untouched.

Speaking of his hometown, Kelly Pavlik once said, "In Youngstown, when you're on top, you're on top. But when you let them down, you're the worst person in town. It's funny how that works. You don't want to become the bad guy in the city for failing at something. But at the same time, it's pretty neat to be that guy, to be in that situation."

Boxing Is a Cruel Teacher
Kelly Pavlik vs. Bernard Hopkins—
October 18, 2008

On October 18, 2008, Kelly Pavlik entered the ring at Boardwalk Hall in Atlantic City intent upon scoring a decisive victory over Bernard Hopkins. He didn't have to knock Hopkins out. But he was committed to fashioning a triumph that left no doubt as to which man was the better fighter. "I want everybody to know that I beat Hopkins," Pavlik said. "And I want Bernard to know that I beat him too."

Pavlik was born and raised in Youngstown, Ohio. In 2008, the national economy was experiencing what Youngstown had endured for three decades. Since 1980, as jobs vanished, the city's population had dropped from 115,000 to 80,000. It had the lowest median income in the United States among cities with 65,000 people or more.

Pavlik had stayed close to his roots. He and his wife lived with their twenty-two-month-old daughter in Boardman, a community adjacent to Youngstown. And Kelly was the proverbial local boy made good. On September 29, 2007, he'd dethroned Jermain Taylor to become middleweight champion of the world.

After Pavlik beat Taylor, Youngstown and the surrounding environs embraced their new hero. Kelly threw out the ceremonial first pitch before Game 4 of the American League Championship series between the Cleveland Indians and the Boston Red Sox, sat beside the legendary Jim Brown after presiding over the coin toss at a Cleveland Browns football game, and addressed the Ohio State Buckeyes before they took to the gridiron to play archrival Michigan. "These are teams I've rooted for my whole life," Kelly said. "It was awesome."

Yet through it all, Pavlik maintained a self-effacing sense of humor. When a reporter asked, "Do you think that you can take the place of Oscar De La Hoya [as the face of boxing] after De La Hoya retires?" Kelly answered, "It would be nice. But I've got a couple of things against me. First of all, there's my looks."

Indeed, Pavlik's appeal was such that his promoter, Bob Arum (an ardent supporter of Hillary Clinton), prevailed upon him to endorse the New York senator in the 2008 Democratic presidential primary in Ohio.

"I was at home and the telephone rang," Kelly later recounted. "I picked it up, said 'Hello,' and someone said, 'Hi, this is Hillary Clinton.' I'm like, 'Sure. Right. Uh-huh.' She's trying to convince me it's really her, and I'm wondering which of my friends is jerking me around."

A local Chevrolet dealer gave Pavlik an SUV in exchange for some autograph sessions and a local commercial. There was a $100,000 endorsement deal with Affliction, a fledgling clothing company. For a fighter who'd been doing landscape work for ten dollars an hour a year earlier, it was a sweet turnaround. But after a while, the bloom started coming off the rose.

"I'm a simple guy," Pavlik acknowledged. "I don't like flash and the limelight too much. I like to do things around the house and spend time with my daughter, and there's been a lot of times lately when I haven't had any 'me' time. You're supposed to go to the gym. Bust your butt. Go home. Fight. But I'm also supposed to be a role model. And do this charity. And please, visit this dying kid in the hospital; it would mean so much to him. And the next day, it's an old man who's dying or I go see children with mental disabilities. I don't have time to do everything people want me to do. And if you don't do everything that everyone else wants you to do, all of a sudden you're an asshole."

A victory by decision in a rematch against Jermain Taylor and a knockout of Gary Lockett raised Pavlik's record to 34–0. The question then became, who would he fight next? HBO approved Arthur Abraham, Paul Williams, and Winky Wright as opponents, but none of those fights could be made. Arum offered Kelly a million dollars plus an upside to fight Marco Antonio Rubio on an independently produced pay-per-view card. But Pavlik's purse had been $2.5 million for the Lockett fight and he wanted to stay at that level.

Thus, Team Pavlik looked to opponents in higher weight divisions. Pavlik vs. Bernard Hopkins at a catchweight of 170 pounds followed. "Nobody has beaten up Hopkins," Arum explained. "If Kelly can knock Hopkins out or beat the hell out of him, he'll be on top of the world."

Each fighter was guaranteed a $3 million purse. And Kelly's 160-pound title wouldn't be at risk.

"I respect Kelly Pavlik," Hopkins told the media at the kickoff press conference. "I have nothing bad to say about Kelly Pavlik. Kelly Pavlik became middleweight champion of the world the right way. He earned it."

"I want my legacy to be as great as Bernard's," Pavlik said in response.

The media was less kind. Eric Raskin of ESPN.com declared, "Paying to watch Hopkins fight is like paying to watch a pitcher hold a runner on first." Steve Kim of Maxboxing.com wrote, "The problem in selling this fight is the specter of seeing Hopkins do what he does best, which is to take away his opponent's preferred offensive weapon and suck the life and action out of any fight he's involved in."

In other words, the world expected a boring fight. And the near-unanimous assumption among the media was that Pavlik would win. Kelly's assignment wasn't just to beat Hopkins. Jermain Taylor and Joe Calzaghe had already done that. It was to beat Hopkins decisively, thereby establishing himself as boxing's newest superstar.

That was a tough assignment. Pavlik was a middleweight. Within that realm, size and strength were his biggest advantage. But against Hopkins (who'd gone up in weight to dominate Antonio Tarver at 175 pounds after losing to Taylor), Kelly would be forfeiting that edge. A crucial element of his fight plan would be to wear down Bernard with constant pressure. But in boxing, it's hard to wear down a bigger foe.

And more significantly, Hopkins would be the smartest, most skilled opponent that Pavlik had faced. "You know how I fight," Kelly told fans at a rally in Youngstown. "You know my style. Nothing's gonna change."

That was the problem. Hopkins knew exactly how Kelly fought. "This kid is so fundamental," Bernard told his trainer, Naazim Richardson, at the start of training camp. "If I can't beat him, I should retire."

Later, Hopkins added, "I got the book on Pavlik. Comes straight forward. Jab. Good right hand. Determined. Lots of heart. Slow. Not a skilled boxer. The last time I fought in Atlantic City was two years ago against Antonio Tarver. I was a 3-to-1 underdog and Antonio was going to knock me out. Do you all remember that? I'm not like any of those other guys that Pavlik beat. This fight is going to be two construction workers fighting on a pier when both of them is hungry but one of them is more skilled than the other. That's my kind of fight."

"Kelly has been in there before against athletes who boxed a bit," Richardson told the media during fight week. "Bernard is all about fighting, and there's a difference between a great athlete and a great fighter. Kelly has a shotgun for a right hand. But if you take away the shotgun, he ain't got nothing. Bernard might not have a shotgun, but he's got a switchblade, a razor blade, and a dagger. Bernard can't play basketball. Bernard can't rap. But Bernard can fight his ass off."

That said, the image of Hopkins sucking air and stalling for time in the late rounds of his most recent outing against Joe Calzaghe convinced many that Pavlik was a lock. Kelly's greatest perceived advantage was the age differential between the fighters. Bernard was forty-three; Kelly was twenty-six.

"There comes a day when every old dog has to be put down," Jack Loew, Pavlik's trainer, said. "This will be a good fight for six or seven rounds. But a fighter can back up and take shots for just so long. One way or another, whether it's the referee or a towel from the corner or Bernard himself, this fight will end early. I think Kelly will stop him in the late rounds."

As for the possibility of Hopkins seeking an edge by engaging in illegal tactics, Loew warned, "Don't be surprised if we put Bernard's nuts in this throat before he touches us low. We're just as rough as he is on the inside."

Joe Scalzo of the *Youngstown Vindicator* summed things up when he wrote, "Pavlik gets asked about his weight; Hopkins gets asked about his age. Pavlik gets asked about winning by knockout; Hopkins gets asked about losing his recent fights by controversial decisions. Pavlik gets asked about his next fight. Hopkins gets asked, 'When's your last fight?' Not surprisingly, Pavlik is a 4–1 favorite."

Indeed, rather than debate the outcome of the contest, some insiders openly wondered what would happen when (not if) Hopkins found himself in trouble. Would he (a) fight like a warrior to the point of going out on his shield; (b) foul to gain an edge and, failing that, be disqualified; or (c) feign an injury and quit?

But Top Rank matchmaker Bruce Trampler sounded a cautionary note. When a conversation turned to big-money fights that lay ahead for Pavlik after he beat Hopkins, Trampler noted, "Before all that happens, 'A,' Kelly has to win the fight, and, 'B,' Kelly has to win the fight."

★★★

Team Pavlik arrived in Kelly's dressing room at Boardwalk Hall on fight night at 8:45 p.m. Several minutes later, Dr. Domenic Coletta of the New Jersey State Athletic Control Board came into the room to administer the final pre-fight physical examination. Everything went according to form until Coletta asked, "Are you on any medication?"

"Yes, sir."

"What for?"

"Bronchitis," Kelly answered

That was a serious departure from the norm.

"Did you have a fever?"

"Not today."

"Before today?"

"A hundred and one degrees."

"What have you been taking?"

Mike Pavlik (Kelly's father) handed a sheet of paper to the doctor. "Here's what they gave Kelly."

Coletta scanned the list. Mucinex, penicillin (one shot on Wednesday night), and ciprofloxacin (500 mg twice a day through the day of the fight).

"How do you feel now?"

"Okay."

Coletta finished his work and left. Over the next ten minutes, Mike and Jack Loew exchanged bad jokes. Then Mike turned pensive.

"This has been an incredible journey and I'm glad to be part of it," he said. "But when it's over, I won't miss it. When your kids are little, you say, 'When they're older, I won't worry about them.' But you always worry. Little kids, little problems. Big kids, big problems."

Arturo Gatti came into the dressing room to wish Kelly well. In previous years, Gatti had been the standard-bearer for boxing in Atlantic City. Pavlik hoped to become his successor.

Kelly began doing stretching exercises on the floor.

On a television monitor in a corner of the room, middleweight prospect Danny Jacobs could be seen disposing of a badly overmatched Tyrone Watson in the first round.

HBO production coordinator Tami Cotel entered and asked Kelly to weigh in on the "unofficial" HBO scale. Kelly complied. One day earlier, Hopkins had officially weighed in at 170 pounds and Pavlik at 169. But those numbers were deceiving. Now, Kelly (wearing a track suit but no shoes) weighed 176 pounds. Minutes earlier, wearing sneakers, Hopkins had tipped the scale at 185. Bernard would have a considerable weight advantage.

The second pay-per-view fight of the evening (Marco Antonio Rubio vs. Enrique Ornelas) began.

Referee Benjy Esteves came in and gave Kelly his pre-fight instructions. "Are there any questions?" Esteves asked at the end.

There were none.

"The Hopkins corner said they were concerned about rough tactics from Kelly," the referee added.

That elicited a collective laugh from Team Pavlik.

"All right; just keep it clean," Esteves cautioned.

Rubio emerged with a split-decision triumph over Ornelas.

John Loew (Jack's son) went down the hall to watch John David Jackson tape Hopkins's hands.

Kelly took off his track suit, put on black ring trunks, and laced up his shoes.

At 10:20, Jack Loew told the control board inspector, "Tell the Hopkins people I'm starting to wrap. If they want somebody here, fine. But I'm starting."

Steven Luevano against Billy Dib (the final preliminary bout) began.

Naazim Richardson entered the room and watched as Loew taped Kelly's hands. When the job was done, Kelly moved to the center of the room and began shadow-boxing. More stretching exercises followed.

At eleven o'clock, Loew gloved Kelly up.

Fighter and trainer began working the pads. It was Kelly's first strenu-
ous exercise of the night.

"Double jab," Loew instructed. "That's it. Chin down. Aggressive
but patient."

Kelly began to cough.

"Stick to the game plan. Nice and easy. . . . Double the jab. That's
it. . . . Punish him. Hard to the body. . . . If you hit him on the belt and
he turns to the referee to bitch, jump on his ass."

Each time Loew took a break, Kelly went into the adjacent bathroom,
coughed, and spat out phlegm. The third time he did it, Mike Pavlik
turned away in a corner of the room, pressed both fists against the wall,
and took a deep breath. A very deep breath. "Christ," he murmured.

There was a near-capacity crowd in Boardwalk Hall. Pavlik entered
the ring first to a roar of approval. Hopkins, wearing a hood and black
executioner's mask, followed.

At the start of a fight, a boxing ring is like a chessboard with an
infinite number of possible moves to be played. Bernard didn't play with
Kelly, but there were times when it looked as though he was. He did
everything right and fought more aggressively than he had in a long time.

The first two rounds set the pattern for the fight. Hopkins was faster.
He moved in and out at will. Working off the absence of a left hook in
Pavlik's arsenal, he circled to the right to avoid Kelly's right hand. Kelly's
jab wasn't landing, which made his right hand largely ineffectual.

The best that could be said for Pavlik's performance after two rounds
was that he was one point ahead of where Joe Calzaghe had been at a
similar juncture in his fight against Hopkins (when Joe was knocked
down in round one and lost round two as well). The questions now were
(1) could Kelly make adjustments as Calzaghe had done and (2) could
Bernard keep it up for twelve rounds. The answers were "no" and "yes."

Pavlik simply couldn't get untracked. There were times when it
looked as though he was fighting in slow motion. Hopkins was in control from beginning to end. He found the holes in Kelly's defense and
exploited them with sharp precision punching. He was too big and too
good. He outboxed Pavlik and he outfought him. He asked questions all
night long and Kelly had no answers.

By round eight, it was clear that Pavlik needed a knockout to win.

But Bernard is hard to play catch-up against and no one had ever knocked him out. In round nine, his punches opened an ugly slice on the outside of Kelly's right eyelid. Finally, in round ten, Pavlik maneuvered Hopkins into a corner and landed a right hand flush. Nothing happened.

"That's when I knew the fight was over," Naazim Richardson said afterward.

Hopkins outlanded Pavlik 172-to-108 with a 148-to-55 edge in power punches. Contrary to all expectations, he also threw more punches than Kelly in nine of the twelve rounds. Referee Benjy Esteves deducted a point from Pavlik for hitting behind the head in round eight and from Hopkins for holding in round nine. The judges scored it 119–106, 118–108, and 117–109. Hopkins fought a superb fight. No over-forty fighter had ever looked better.

"This was the best performance of my career," Bernard said when it was over. "Better than Tarver, better than Trinidad, better than Oscar, better than my twenty-one defenses. It outdoes everything I accomplished. I am extremely happy tonight."

Meanwhile, as Hopkins celebrated his victory, a markedly different scene was unfolding in Pavlik's dressing room.

"I felt weak," Kelly told the members of his team gathered around him. "I didn't have anything on my punches. I couldn't get off; it just wasn't there. He beat me to the punch all night long."

Kelly's wife, Samantha, moved to his side.

"Jermain Taylor is faster than Hopkins. And against Jermain, I never had that problem. The way I fought tonight, anybody could kick my ass."

Tears welled up in Kelly's eyes. He sat on a chair and began to cry. Samantha knelt at his knees and tried to console him.

"You didn't lose this fight," Mike Pavlik told his son. "The loss was my fault. I should have pulled it when you got bronchitis."

Kelly shrugged. "I lost it."

Domenic Coletta came in and administered a brief post-fight physical examination. Then it was time to decide what to do about the cut on Kelly's eyelid. "We can do stitches now or a butterfly now and stitches in the morning," the physician advised.

"Let's get it over with tonight," Mike Pavlik said.

"I'll call ahead to the hospital," Coletta offered. "They'll have some-one ready to stitch it up."

At 1:00 a.m., Kelly left the dressing room with his father and a para-medic at his side. As they walked to a waiting ambulance, Kelly was approached by several fans who wanted him to stop and pose with them for photos. Each time, he complied.

"Good fight," one of the fans said.

"Actually, it wasn't so good," Kelly responded.

Kelly and his father got in the back of the ambulance with the para-medic. At 1:10 a.m., they arrived at the emergency room entrance to the Atlantic City Regional Medical Center. Kelly walked through the reception area into a small square room with a linoleum tile floor and hospital-green curtain drawn across the door. After he lay down on the bed, a nurse came in to check his blood pressure and temperature.

A second nurse followed.

"How much do you weigh?"

"One hundred seventy-two pounds."

"How tall are you?"

"Six-two and a half."

"Date of birth?"

"Four, five, eighty-two."

Address . . . telephone number . . . Social Security number. . . .

"Do you have a headache now?"

"No."

At 1:20, Dr. Eric Wolk entered the room, introduced himself, and examined the cut.

"I'm not a plastic surgeon," Wolk said. "But I can do this. I'd tell you if I couldn't."

Kelly nodded. "That's okay. I trust you."

"It's a very linear laceration. It will close up nicely."

"My grandmother was a nurse. She sewed me up lots of times when I was a kid."

Wolk filled a syringe with anesthesia.

"We're going to numb it first. Then we'll irrigate it. After that, we'll close it up."

At 1:30 a.m., the needle went in.

"Is anything else bothering you?" Wolk asked.

"Just my feelings."

Mike Pavlik patted his son's leg. "This is my fault," he said. "Every instinct, every intuition I had told me I should have pulled the fight when you got bronchitis."

Wolk crafted seven stitches.

"Can I take a shower when I get back to my room?" Kelly asked.

"No problem. Just don't rub the eye."

Kelly stood up. "Thanks, doc. I appreciate it."

"Feel better," Wolk said.

Kelly took a deep breath. "I've lost once," he told his father. "Hopkins is a legend and he's lost five times."

Father and son embraced.

"I don't care about the loss," Mike said. "All I care about is that you're all right."

At 2:00 a.m., Kelly and Mike Pavlik walked out of the hospital into the chill night air. In five hours, the sun would rise over the Atlantic Ocean. Kelly's face would be bruised and swollen. It would hurt to know that he'd lost an important fight. But he'd fought with honor. He'd finished on his feet. And he was still middleweight champion of the world, even though it didn't feel like it at the moment.

The losses that a great fighter suffers at the end of his career become unimportant from a historical perspective. Sugar Ray Robinson was close to perfection as a welterweight. But as he moved up in age and weight, he traded wins and losses with Randy Turpin, Carmen Basilio, and Gene Fullmer before suffering unavenged defeats at the hands of club fighters like Ferd Hernandez and Memo Ayon. When Roy Jones stepped into the ring at Madison Square Garden to fight Joe Calzaghe, he wasn't "Roy Jones" anymore.

The Legend Grows Old
Roy Jones vs. Joe Calzaghe—
November 8, 2008

The main arena at Madison Square Garden is a nice place to make history. On November 8, 2008, Joe Calzaghe and Roy Jones Jr. did just that, although the results were far more gratifying to Joe.

Calzaghe is soft-spoken with an almost gentle manner about him. At first glance, it's hard to imagine him in a boxing ring. He conjures up images of a guitarist in a British rock band more than a professional fighter who was undefeated over the course of a fifteen-year career. But while Joe doesn't look like a fighter, he fought like one.

Calzaghe turned pro in 1993 and won the World Boxing Organization 168-pound crown with a twelve-round decision over Chris Eubank in 1997. He made twenty-one successful title defenses and finished his career with a 46–0 (32 KOs) mark. His first two signature victories were a twelve-round shutout of Jeff Lacy in 2006 and a dominant decision over Mikkel Kessler in 2007. But he was a footnote in pound-for-pound conversations during the years that Bernard Hopkins was a human soundbite machine and Roy Jones reigned as boxing's pound-for-pound king.

That changed when Calzaghe went up to 175 pounds to challenge Hopkins and Jones in consecutive fights.

Hopkins–Calzaghe came first. They met in the ring at the Thomas & Mack Center in Las Vegas on April 19, 2008. The promotion was marked by ill will underscored by Bernard's ill-chosen words, "I would never let a white boy beat me." But Calzaghe gave as good as he got in the verbal pyrotechnics leading up to the fight:

★ "Hopkins tries to get into opponents' heads. I've seen him do it in the past. But believe me, he's barking up the wrong tree with me. It may work against a twenty-two-year-old kid who's in awe, but not against me."

★ "I'm quite tired, really, of all his talk. And that's all it is; talk. He's a St. Bernard, all bark and no bite. All of his blathering sounds like he's trying to convince himself he can beat me."

★ "Look at my face. It tells you, doesn't it? I always seem to come out right. His nose is flat across his face. So much for a great defense. He must have walked into a lamp-post to get a nose like that."

★ "He thinks he can intimidate me because he's been to prison for robbery. So what? So you burgled somebody, you brave boy. That makes you a thug, not a fighter. It makes you an idiot."

Then came the fight. It started poorly for Calzaghe. One minute into the first stanza, Hopkins landed a short sharp right hand and Joe went down for only the third time in his career. He rose quickly ("It was a flash knockdown; I wasn't hurt"). But it was an inauspicious start. At round's end, Calzaghe was down by two points.

Round two was more of the same. Hopkins dictated the pace, fought hard in spurts, and got off first. The lead right was his money punch. Calzaghe was unable to penetrate Bernard's defense.

Then the tide turned. Calzaghe's southpaw stance, quick hands, and sense of anticipation started giving Hopkins trouble. Joe kept coming forward, making Bernard fight at a fast pace and increase his work rate beyond a level that the forty-three-year-old Hopkins could sustain. Joe was physically stronger than Bernard had expected. And his chin held up.

Judge Adalaide Byrd scored the fight 114–113 for Hopkins. Chuck Giampa (116–111) and Ted Gimza (115–112) saw things more clearly, giving the victory to Calzaghe.

That set the stage for Calzaghe vs. Jones.

Once upon a time, Roy Jones was mentioned in the same breath as Sugar Ray Robinson. When Jones was in his prime, his performances had the look of an action hero in a video game.

Jones won his first world championship by outclassing Hopkins for the International Boxing Federation middleweight crown in 1993. Ten years later, he defeated WBA titlist John Ruiz to become the first former middleweight champion since Bob Fitzsimmons in 1897 to capture a piece of the heavyweight crown.

But like a modern-day Icarus (whose father fashioned wings from wax and feathers so they could escape from exile on the island of Crete), Jones flew too high and too close to the sun. The Ruiz fight was his greatest triumph, but it also held the seeds of his destruction.

Jones had put on twenty pounds of muscle to fight in the heavyweight division. When he moved back to 175 pounds, his body was slow to readjust. He showed grit and heart in a victory over Antonio Tarver. Then he was knocked out by Tarver and Glen Johnson and lost to Tarver a second time. Still, he kept fighting and resurrected his career with victories over Prince Badi Ajamu, Anthony Hanshaw, and Félix Trinidad. At age thirty-nine, reaching for the brass ring one more time, Jones signed to fight Calzaghe.

"The Battle of the Superpowers" (as the bout was styled) marked the intersecting arcs that defined the careers of two great fighters. The fondness and mutual respect that they had for each other was evident from the start of the promotion. At the September 16 kickoff press conference in New York, one could all but hear the lyrics to "Mutual Admiration Society" wafting through the air.

"I've watched Roy Jones Jr. his whole career," Calzaghe told the media. "I've been a Roy Jones fan for a long time."

Jones responded in kind, saying, "Joe is an outstanding person and a great fighter."

Indeed, at the close of the press conference when the fighters posed for the ritual staredown, the stare lasted for about a second. Then Roy's eyes twinkled; his mouth curled upward, and Joe's face broke into a broad smile.

As for who would win, Jones's greatness had been founded upon speed and reflexes. In the past, he'd always been quicker than his opponent. But so had Calzaghe. And now Roy was getting old. He could no longer do the same things in the ring that he'd done before. Indeed, Alton Merkerson (who coached Jones at the 1988 Seoul Olympics and had trained him for most of his pro career) acknowledged, "Calzaghe's hands are as fast as Roy's and he'll throw a lot more punches."

Thus, the Jones camp was relying on the belief that Roy's punching power was superior to Calzaghe's. "Roy has more snap on his punches," Merkerson said. "And his punches are more effective."

"I know that the quality of my punches will overcome his quantity," Jones added. "I would never be able to match the punch output that Joe will throw. But this is pro boxing, so I don't have to match his output. I am definitely the stronger puncher."

In response, Calzaghe confidently declared, "Roy Jones is still Roy Jones. He still has speed. He still has power. I'm not underestimating this guy. But I'm not really concerned with what Roy Jones brings to the table. I'm concerned with what Joe Calzaghe brings to the table. If I bring my 'A' game, then it's game over."

As fight night approached, Calzaghe was a 5-to-2 betting favorite. The feeling among boxing insiders was that Roy might "be Roy" for fifteen seconds a round. But Joe could concede those fifteen seconds and win the other two minutes, forty-five seconds of each stanza.

★★★

Roy Jones entered his dressing room at Madison Square Garden on fight night at 9:18 p.m. and settled in front of a television monitor to watch the first pay-per-view bout of the evening, Dmitriy Salita vs. Derrick Campas. A few minutes later, Daniel Edouard (who'd won an eight-round decision in an earlier preliminary bout) knocked on the door and asked if he could come in.

Permission granted.

"I just wanted to meet you," Edouard told Jones. "I've watched you fight ever since I started boxing. You're an icon. It's an honor to shake your hand."

"Thank you, man. I appreciate it."

Roy checked his cell phone for messages and chatted with members of his team.

The room was hot. Throughout his career, Jones had rarely warmed up before fights in the conventional manner. Rather, he preferred to sit in an almost sauna-like atmosphere, warming his body and conserving energy. He seldom stretched, shadow-boxed, or hit pads in his dressing room before a bout.

Salita—Campas ended. Roy drank a half bottle of orange juice and took a pair of high-topped orange-and-black Adidas shoes out of his gym bag. The shoes were new. The manufacturer's cardboard and tissue packing were still in them.

McGhee Wright (Jones's business advisor) came into the room. They talked briefly. Roy went back to checking his cell phone messages, then took two sets of tassels from a clear plastic bag and tied them around the tops of his shoes. His mood was quiet, almost somber. He seemed detached from the storm ahead.

At 10:15, referee Hubert Earl came in and gave Jones the ritual pre-fight instructions. After he left, Roy took a small container of Vaseline and greased up his own face, then put on a pair of orange trunks with black trim. Alton Merkerson taped his hands. Billy Lewis (a longtime friend) led the group in prayer. Merkerson gloved Roy up.

At 10:58, in a departure from his normal pre-fight routine, Jones moved to the center of the room with assistant trainer Alfie Smith and began hitting the pads, throwing three, four, and five-punch combinations with fifteen seconds in between each burst.

There were cries of encouragement from around the room.

"They don't believe. We got to make some believers."

Jones joined in the commentary: "Old man fighting here."

Burst of punches.

From the chorus: "Ooooooh!"

Jones: "I am an old man, but this old man is gonna bite him."

Burst of punches. . . .

Chorus: "Yeah! It's showtime at the Apollo."

Jones: "Feels good to be back."

Chorus: "That boy is fast."

Alfie Smith flicked out his left hand, and the edge of his pad caught Roy directly in the right eye.

Jones turned away and grimaced in pain.

Everything stopped.

Merkerson took a towel and wiped Roy's face.

Then the action resumed, coming in five-, six-, and seven-punch combinations.

Jones: "It ain't over. I'm bringing it back."

Burst of punches.

Chorus: "Oooooh! The magic is back."

Jones: "Don't want to cool off now."

Burst of punches.

Chorus: "It's a Roy Jones night."

The padwork lasted for a full half hour.

"It's whatever Roy feels," Merkerson said when the work was over. "He hasn't done it like this before. He just feels like doing it now."

The worlds of Roy Jones and Joe Calzaghe were hurtling toward one another, about to collide.

The fight started well for Jones. With 48 seconds left in round one, he formally introduced himself to Calzaghe with a jab followed by a quick right hand. The latter glanced off Joe's cheek and ear onto his shoulder and put him down. Calzaghe rose and charged straight back at Roy. But when he returned to his corner at the end of the round, blood was flowing from the bridge of his nose.

"I really didn't see the punch coming," Joe said later of the knockdown. "Roy stunned me. But I didn't panic. I composed myself, got back up, and started to fight again. Anyone can fall on the floor. How you recover is what matters."

Round two was fairly even with an edge to Calzaghe (who landed far more punches although Jones's were the sharper blows). Thereafter, Joe beat Roy at his own game. He did to Jones what Roy used to do to other fighters, dominating with speed, calculated aggression, showmanship, and flair. His stamina was remarkable. When they traded, it was Calzaghe throwing four and five punches to Jones's one. "I always felt I was a step ahead of Roy," he said afterward. "I knew what Roy was going to do before he did it."

There's sadness in watching a fighter who was great when he was young grow old. Jones was fighting off the memory of what he used to do. But he couldn't do it anymore. His reflexes had slowed. His legs were old. As the rounds passed, the right hand lead was his most effective punch. But Calzaghe had a good chin. When the blows landed, he took them well. And he made Jones fight for three minutes of every round. Too often, Roy retreated to the ropes, raising his gloves to eye level in a defensive posture. When a fighter positions his hands as "earmuffs," he sends a message to his opponent: "Hit me."

The middle rounds were target practice for Calzaghe. In round seven, a sharp right hook opened an ugly gash on Jones's left eyelid. It was the first time ever that Roy had been cut in a fight. "I couldn't see out of my left eye," he said later. "It was swollen up and the blood was coming in."

"The cut looked a lot worse than it was," Barry Jordan (chief medical officer for the New York State Athletic Commission) said after the fight. "It's just that, for whatever reason, Roy's corner couldn't stop the bleeding between rounds."

Meanwhile, Calzaghe kept coming forward, relentlessly forcing the pace, never giving Jones a moment's rest. His quiet manner outside the ring belied the fact that he was a mean tough son of a bitch in it. He didn't just win rounds, he won them big—outworking, outboxing, and out-fighting Roy.

Long before the bout was over, Jones looked like a beaten fighter. It was clear that he needed a knockout to win. But Roy hadn't knocked out an opponent since Clinton Woods six years earlier. And Calzaghe had never lost, let alone failed to go the distance.

The late rounds were like watching Muhammad Ali against Larry Holmes or Sugar Ray Leonard against Terry Norris. The only weapon left in Roy's arsenal was his heart.

"I thought of stopping it," Merkerson said later. "But in a fight of this magnitude, that's hard to do. And Roy wanted to keep fighting."

Each judge scored the bout 118–109, giving Calzaghe all but the first round.

It's too bad they didn't fight when Jones was younger.

After Calzaghe beat Bernard Hopkins, he'd told the media, "I've been boxing for twenty-six years. That's a long time. I'd like this to be my last year. The money's great, but what I really want is to retire without having tasted defeat. It's easy to have one fight too many."

Then, in the days leading up to Calzaghe–Jones, Joe had declared, "I just feel like I don't want to fight anymore after this fight. It's difficult to stay motivated as you get older. Physically, I feel just as good as I felt five years ago. But mentally, it's more difficult to fight. To win my last fight in Madison Square Garden against one of the greatest fighters ever would be the perfect ending for me."

Some observers pointed to Calzaghe–Jones as proof that Joe should continue fighting. After all, he'd looked superb. But the best argument for retirement had been right in front of Calzaghe on November 8. Roy Jones had shown him what happens when a great fighter stays on too long.

To his credit, Calzaghe did retire after fighting Jones and stayed retired. Sadly, Roy fought on for ten more years. During that time, he had eighteen fights and was knocked out by Danny Green, Denis Lebedev, and Enzo Maccarinelli. On November 28, 2020, he was back in the spotlight one last time, engaging in an eight-round exhibition against Mike Tyson.

Meanwhile, as Calzaghe basked in the glow of victory at the press conference following his victory over Jones, a very different scene was unfolding in Roy's dressing room.

Jones sat in a far corner of the room on a folding metal chair with his head down. His twin sons (DeShaun and DeAndre, age seventeen) were fighting back tears. His youngest son (Roy Jones III, age eight) stood to the side with tears streaming down his face. Raegan Jones, her hair beaded, as cute as a four-year-old can be, moved to her father's side and put her arms around him.

"I'm a big girl, daddy," Raegan said. "I don't cry."

Roy smiled and gave her a hug.

Alton Merkerson pressed an Enswell against Roy's swollen left eye.

"I forgot my game plan," Roy said. "I was on track pretty good. Then, after the first round, I started loading up, trying to knock him out instead of moving in and out like we planned."

Maybe. Or maybe Roy went for the knockout because he realized early in the fight that the best chance he had was a puncher's chance.

Bernard Hopkins came into the room. Roy rose to greet him.

"Are you all right?" Hopkins asked.

"Doing fine."

The two men hugged.

"It's all about respect," Roy said. "You got yours, man."

"You too, baby."

Bernard left.

There were scattered conversations around the room.

"Calzaghe's a good fighter," Merkerson said. "He was ready and he came to fight. He has some of the abilities that Roy had. He has good upper-body movement. He's hard to hit. He's a good counterpuncher. He can get off first and his punches are sharp. He measures distance and speed and how fast you punch and what you do when he punches extremely well. He knows what's coming the same way Roy used to know."

Jones stood up, took off his shoes and robe, and sat down on the chair again. He looked much older than he'd looked several hours earlier. His face was battered and swollen with a mixture of sadness and pride in his eyes. It was the face of a fighter.

Paulie Malignaggi fought for eight more years after losing to Ricky Hatton. But his loss to the Mancunian put a damper on his dreams.

The End of a Dream
Paulie Malignaggi vs. Ricky Hatton—
November 22, 2008

On November 22, 2008, Paulie Malignaggi fought Ricky Hatton at the MGM Grand Garden Arena in Las Vegas. Entering the ring, Malignaggi knew that the hopes and dreams and hard work of twenty-eight years would be distilled into a handful of three-minute segments. Everything in his life had led up to this moment. Everything in his future would be influenced by it.

Malignaggi had turned pro at age twenty on July 7, 2001. "I had my dreams," he said later. "Nobody starts boxing to be a club fighter. I thought of boxing as a way to carve my name in history and show people that I was on this planet."

"I'm not just going to be a champion," Paulie told his promoter, Lou DiBella, before his first pro fight. "I'm going to the Hall of Fame."

Later, Malignaggi elaborated on that theme, saying, "My speed discourages everyone I fight. I've got handspeed and footspeed, but my best weapon is my brain. I know exactly where I am in the ring at all times. I'm always thinking in there, setting my opponent up and keeping him from setting me up."

But Malignaggi had an Achilles heel—a notable a lack of power that would limit him to 7 knockout wins in 44 career fights. In a way, that made his ring accomplishments all the more impressive. Often, when he went into battle, his opponent was armed with a machete while Paulie was carrying a pocketknife. He built his victories by adding up the points, round by round by round.

And Malignaggi labored under a second disadvantage as well. He was plagued by hands that HBO boxing analyst Larry Merchant called "as brittle as uncooked spaghetti." They were broken multiple times, necessitating numerous surgeries.

Still, by 2006, Paulie was undefeated in twenty-one fights and challenged Miguel Cotto at Madison Square Garden on the eve of the Puerto Rican Day Parade. "It was," he said later, "like fighting the devil in hell."

In round one, Malignaggi suffered a bad cut from a head butt. In round two, he was knocked down. He left the ring that night with the first loss of his career and broken bones in his face that took six months to heal. But he fought valiantly, went the distance, and won four rounds (five on one judge's scorecard).

Fifty-three weeks later, Malignaggi shut out Lovemore N'dou with a masterful performance over twelve rounds to claim the IBF 140-pound crown. That was his shining moment in boxing. Successful title defenses against Herman Ngoudjo and N'dou followed. But by his own admission, Paulie looked ordinary each time.

Then Malignaggi got another shot at stardom, this time against Ricky Hatton.

Prior to facing Paulie, Hatton had a career record of 44 wins with 31 knockouts against a single loss. Until 2005, he'd been widely thought of as a "protected" fighter. Then he stopped Kostya Tszyu in eleven rounds to annex the IBF junior-welterweight title. Victories over Carlos Maussa, Luis Collazo, Juan Urango, and José Luis Castillo solidified his claim to being a legitimate world champion.

In December 2007, Hatton reached for the stars. He signed to fight Floyd Mayweather Jr. But when fight night came, he was forced to battle both boxing's pound-for-pound king and the one-sided refereeing of Joe Cortez. Mayweather knocked him out in the tenth round.

Five months later, Ricky returned to the ring with a unanimous decision victory over Juan Lazcano. Hatton–Malignaggi followed.

"Every year, I start out hoping that this will be the year I make it big," Malignaggi said after the bout contracts were signed. "So far, it hasn't happened. The Cotto fight could have done it, but I came up short. Beating Ricky Hatton can get me to where I want to be. This fight can get me recognized as the best junior-welterweight in the world. This fight can make me a star."

Hatton–Malignaggi was Paulie's first fight in Las Vegas. His face was on room keys at the MGM Grand. The world press was there.

Malignaggi was long on confidence during fight week. Although the odds were 12-to-5 in Hatton's favor, he didn't think of himself as an underdog. Ricky planned to pressure Paulie, but Paulie intended to frustrate his foe.

"Speed kills," Lou DiBella opined. "And speed particularly kills Ricky. It's not punchers that give Ricky trouble; it's speed. Look at his fights against Floyd Mayweather Jr. and Luis Collazo."

"Don't compare Hatton with Cotto," Paulie added, "because they're not on the same level. Ricky is an average fighter. In England, he was pampered against club-fighter opponents. He's been very ordinary over here. I think he's regressed, or maybe he was never that good to begin with.

"Hatton has flaws that I can take advantage of," Malignaggi continued. "I've seen them all through his career. When you're fast, you can hit anybody. I'm fast, and Ricky isn't a good defensive fighter. My A-game is better than Ricky Hatton's A-game. It's going to be a very frustrating night for Ricky. He'll be catching a lot."

"Paulie thinks he's a good talker," Hatton responded. "But he tends to come out with a lot of bull. You're not going to see Ricky Hatton doing the Ali Shuffle. But you will see more head movement and a few other things that I know how to do and haven't done as often as I should lately. And you'll also see what I always do—constant pressure and body punching."

There was a question as to whether Hatton could work effectively under the aegis of his new trainer, Floyd Mayweather Sr. In late July, Billy Graham (who'd trained Ricky for every one of his professional fights) had been fired. There was a school of thought that Hatton would miss Graham both in the gym and in his corner on fight night. And more significantly, there was the issue of Ricky's lifestyle. If Malignaggi's underlying weakness was his hands, Hatton's was the abuse of his body between fights.

Ricky was a drinker—a heavy drinker. He was also a ravenous eater and typically gained forty to fifty pounds between fights. He often made light of the situation. On a teleconference call after training camp began, he'd told the media, "I've been stepping out at five-thirty in the morning to run for five miles, which is a big change from the usual routine of getting in at five-thirty in the morning after a night on the town."

But in recent fights, Hatton had tended to fade in the championship rounds. Collazo, Mayweather, and Lazcano all hurt him late. And conditioning became even more of an issue when nutritionist and conditioning coach Kerry Kayes quit Team Hatton in protest over Graham's dismissal.

Thus, the question: What had a hedonistic lifestyle coupled with the aggressive practice of a brutal sport taken out of Hatton? Ricky was thirty. Malignaggi was twenty-eight. But because of Hatton's lifestyle, he was thought of as a much older fighter. Would this be the fight when Ricky was suddenly too old to do what he did well?

★★★

Malignaggi liked to get to the arena early when he fought and give himself time to settle in. He wasn't scheduled to be in the ring until 8:00 p.m. on fight night but arrived at his dressing room at five o'clock preparatory to doing battle against Hatton.

Team Malignaggi was with him. Trainer Buddy McGirt, assistant trainer Orlando Carrasquillo, cutman Danny Milano, Umberto Malignaggi (Paulie's brother), Pete Sferazza (a close friend), attorney John Hornewer, and Anthony Catanzaro (who mentored Paulie outside the ring).

While the others engaged in quiet conversation, Paulie sat on a chair and listened to music through a pair of headphones. It was impossible for the members of his team to know precisely what doubts and fears were running through his mind. But one thing was certain. He knew the taste of defeat. Its sour residue had been in his mouth since losing to Cotto two years earlier. He never wanted to taste it again.

Over the next few hours, Malignaggi stretched, put on his shoes and trunks, had his hands taped, shadow-boxed, and listened to referee Kenny Bayless's pre-fight instructions.

At seven o'clock, he went into an adjacent room with Carrasquillo to warm up and hit the pads. McGirt stayed in the main dressing area to watch James Kirkland vs. Brian Vera (HBO's first televised fight of the evening) on a television monitor.

At 7:15, Sylvester Stallone and Chuck Zito entered the dressing room and made their way to Malignaggi and Carrasquillo.

"You look good, man," Stallone told Paulie. "Better than I ever looked."

"I'm ready. The plan is to bust him up."

"Have a good one."

In less than a minute, Stallone and Zito were gone. For the next half hour, Malignaggi alternated between hitting the pads with Carrasquillo and sitting on the arm of a worn paisley-covered sofa with his head down. More than any of the people around him, he was processing the reality of how dangerous and contingent the next hour would be.

As more than a few boxing insiders had speculated might happen, a fighter got old in the ring during Hatton–Malignaggi. But that fighter wasn't Ricky. It was Paulie.

Malignaggi had a slight edge in round one as a consequence of superior footwork and his jab. But he wasn't particularly effective with either, which was a precursor of things to come. He let Hatton get into a rhythm early and never got into a rhythm of his own.

In round two, Ricky became more aggressive and, with a half-minute left in the stanza, stunned Paulie with a chopping right hand. Thereafter, Malignaggi seemed to abandon his game plan in favor of an almost impatient battle. He fought like a fighter with a puncher's chance instead of a boxer whose only road to victory lay in putting together punch after punch to win point after point, round after round. And he didn't have a puncher's chance because he wasn't a puncher.

Hatton was physically stronger. Malignaggi's primary defense was movement. He didn't have the power to keep Ricky off. When he landed, Hatton simply walked through the punches to get inside. At times, Paulie seemed frozen, unable to punch or get out of the way of Ricky's punches. Contrary to all expectations, he allowed Hatton to get off first for much of the night.

"My neck felt like it had a stinger," Paulie said afterward. "Like there was a hundred pounds on it. I couldn't move the way I usually move. One time, I ducked and it felt like I was stuck. I guess that's what Ricky does to you. But the referee did a good job. I've been in fights where the referee was a spectator. Kenny Bayless did his job right."

Hatton took advantage of what Bayless gave him. On occasion, he jammed an elbow into Malignaggi's throat or raked a glove across Paulie's face. But overall, he fought a clean fight.

In the middle rounds, Ricky stepped up the pace, going to the body with telling effect. By round nine, Paulie was struggling to survive.

During round ten, Lou DiBella went to Malignaggi's corner and told McGirt, "He's not doing anything. Maybe it should be stopped." McGirt said no. But he did tell Paulie between rounds that, if he kept taking punches without throwing back, he'd stop the fight.

In round eleven, Malignaggi took a hard body shot and DiBella returned to the corner. "If you don't stop it, I will," he told the trainer.

Seconds later, McGirt waved the white towel of surrender. Each judge had given Paulie one round.

After the fight, Paulie sat for a long time on the sofa in his dressing room. The back of his robe was pulled up and forward over his head, completely covering his face.

Finally, he lowered the robe.

"They shouldn't have stopped the fight," he said.

There was a distraught look on his face.

"You were getting hit," he was told.

"But I wasn't taking big shots. I wasn't hurting that bad. There was less than two rounds left. How bad could it have been? This will bother me forever."

"You were behind on points and you weren't going to knock him out."

"He wasn't going to knock me out either. Losing is bad. Having it on my record that I got stopped is worse."

"No one wanted to see you get hurt."

"Against Cotto, I got hurt worse. Against Cotto, I could have understood someone stopping it, although I'm glad they didn't. Tonight . . . oh, man; no way it should have been stopped."

The door to the dressing room opened and Ricky Hatton came in. Paulie rose and the fighters embraced.

"It was a good fight, mate," Hatton said. "You weren't that far behind me. Most of the time, you were causing me murder."

There were more compliments. Then Hatton left.

Paulie kicked a towel that was on the floor. "The most important fight of my life and I didn't finish. I'm better than being stopped."

"You didn't get stopped. Someone else stopped it."

"Yeah, but that's not what the record book will say. The record book will say 'TKO by 11.' It goes down in history now: Paulie Malignaggi got stopped."

"You fought a good fight."

"No, I didn't. I fought like I was forty years old. I saw openings, but my mind and hands wouldn't connect."

"Did your hands give you trouble?"

"My hands are fine. How could I hurt my hands? I didn't hit him all night."

Fighters who rely on speed and reflexes as their edge over opponents peak young. That was true of Malignaggi, who never fought with the skill set or fire of his youth again. Still, there would be more fights and one more moment of glory.

On April 29, 2012, in Ukraine, Paulie scored a ninth-round knockout of Vyacheslav Senchenko to claim the WBA 147-pound title. But that win was sandwiched between losses to Juan Díaz (avenged in Paulie's next fight), Amir Khan (a knockout defeat), and Adrien Broner (by disputed decision), and KO losses to Shawn Porter, Danny Garcia, and Sam Eggington. Finally, at the end, there was an ill-conceived June 22, 2019, bareknuckle fight that resulted in a unanimous-decision loss to Artem Lobov.

Malignaggi's final ring record (not counting the Lobov fight) was 36 wins, 8 losses, 7 KOs, and 5 KOs by. The fighter who inflicted the most physical damage on him was Miguel Cotto. But in many ways, Hatton–Malignaggi hurt more.

"That fight cost me my dreams," Paulie said years later. "If I beat Hatton, I become a star. I might even have made it to the Hall of Fame. The way I fought that night will bother me till the day I die. It was like God gave me a gift when they made that fight and I fucked it up."

When Ricky Hatton fought Manny Pacquiao, he had the unenviable task of facing a fighter for the ages who was at his peak.

Manny Pacquiao at the Summit
Manny Pacquiao vs. Ricky Hatton— May 2, 2009

There was a three-fight stretch when Manny Pacquiao drew comparisons with the greatest fighters who ever lived. On December 6, 2008, he bludgeoned Oscar De La Hoya into submission over eight brutal rounds. Eleven months later, he destroyed Miguel Cotto en route to a twelfth-round stoppage. But it was in between these outings—on May 2, 2009, in Las Vegas—that Pacquiao solidified his claim to greatness with an electrifying annihilation of Ricky Hatton.

Outside the ring, Pacquiao has a gentle quality. He speaks so softly that one often has to lean close to hear what he's saying. Despite his accomplishments and celebrity status, there's a humility about him. He signs autographs, poses endlessly for photographs, and gives away money. A lot of money. Perhaps more than he should.

The Philippines, with 106 million people, is the thirteenth-most populous nation on the planet. Another 10 million Filipino expatriates live in other countries. Pacquiao was—and still is—the most idolized Filipino ever. His story is one that his countrymen and countrywomen identify with.

Pacquiao has lived in a world surrounded by need. He ran away from home as a child, reportedly because his father ate a stray dog that Manny wanted to keep. Thereafter, he slept on the streets, often in a cardboard box. He began boxing for money at age fourteen and, prior to fighting Hatton, had earned the right to call himself the best flyweight, super-bantamweight, super-featherweight, and super-lightweight in the world.

"Pacman" had crafted a 5–1–1 record against Marco Antonio Barrera, Erik Morales, and Juan Manuel Marquez. Beating De La Hoya elevated him from hero to icon. Hundreds of thousands of fans lined the streets of General Santos City for his victory parade.

"The people where I live are not bad people," Pacquiao said. "They are only poor. If I can help, it is my duty. I know what they're feeling. I remember, as a little boy, I ate one meal a day and sometimes slept in the street. I'm not shy to tell of my life because I want to give inspiration and show how Manny Pacquiao went from nothing to something. It is an honor to me that the people feel about me the way they do. I know that millions of people are praying for me, and that gives me strength. It inspires me to fight hard, stay strong, and remember all of the people of my country trying to achieve better for themselves. I do my best to bring happiness and a feeling of honor to all the people in the Philippines. My fight is not only for me but for my country."

Ricky Hatton wasn't as iconic a figure as Pacquiao. But like Manny, he'd stayed close to his roots. His "one of us" persona had made him a hero in his home city of Manchester and beyond. "In boxing, the glory is your own," he said. "But I'm also doing it for Manchester, and I'm doing it for England."

Hatton, at his best in the ring, pressured opponents until they broke. Prior to facing Pacquiao, he'd won 45 of 46 bouts. His most notable victory was an eleventh-round stoppage of Kostya Tszyu in 2005. His sole defeat came at the hands of Floyd Mayweather in a fight in which referee Joe Cortez appeared to tilt the playing field in Mayweather's favor.

"It wasn't a humbling experience because I'm humble to begin with," Hatton said of the loss. "But it was devastating."

After losing to Mayweather, Ricky had rebounded to decision Juan Lazcano and knock out Paulie Malignaggi. That set the stage for Pacquiao–Hatton.

The boxing world converged on the MGM Grand Hotel and Casino in Las Vegas for fight week. There was a nice buzz. The bout had been sold out since mid-April. Tickets were selling at a premium. A lot of people in the media were there, not just because their jobs required it but because they wanted to be there.

By eleven o'clock on Friday morning (the day before the fight), several thousand Brits were waiting outside the MGM Grand Garden Arena in anticipation of the three o'clock weigh-in. The arena was configured to accommodate six thousand people for the afternoon. By 2:00 p.m., every non-media seat was filled and another thousand fans were unable to gain admittance.

The Ricky Hatton Band was in full swing with "Walking in a Hatton Wonderland" and "God Save the Queen" being sung again and again.

Pacquiao weighed in at 138 pounds; Hatton at 140 (the contract weight). By the time they stepped into the ring twenty-nine hours later, Manny had gained ten pounds; Ricky, twelve.

Pacquiao was a 5-to-2 betting favorite. Most "boxing people" were picking Manny to win. However, there was often a "but."

"But I wouldn't be surprised if it turns out that Ricky is too big and strong for Manny."

After all, Hatton, had never weighed in for a fight at less than 138 pounds. Pacquiao began his career at 106 pounds and had fought above 130 pounds on only two occasions. Manny, it was thought, had never faced an opponent who brought as much size, strength, and pressure to bear as Ricky would bring. Hatton—Ricky's partisans believed—could employ basic boxing skills and overpower Pacquiao the way he'd overpowered Kostya Tszyu four years earlier.

Hatton, of course, voiced similar sentiments, declaring:

* "I'm bigger; I'm stronger. Pacquiao may have fought at 147 pounds [against De La Hoya]. But trust me—this is a new weight division for him. I have always stated that no one in the world can beat me at 140 pounds, and I stand by that statement. At 140 pounds, I'm too strong and too big for anyone."
* "Pacquiao is a slick, fast, effective boxer. But if you look at the defeat by Erik Morales in 2005 and the close fights he had with Juan Manuel Márquez, he doesn't like sustained pressure. I am a fighter that is constantly in your face, constantly throwing punches."
* "It's a very very tough fight. But to say I'm confident would be an understatement. I've never felt more certain of victory than I do right now. I know his strengths and his weaknesses, but I also know what I am capable of doing. There's no doubt in my mind who is going to win the fight. I've never been more confident. If people want to re-mortgage and put a few quid on me, they should."

"I don't predict before my fights," Pacquiao said when asked how he thought the bout would end. "Ricky Hatton is a good fighter. I know that he is a little bigger than me and a strong fighter, but I am faster. I just want to do my best and give a good fight."

Freddie Roach was less reticent. Roach had trained Pacquiao for eight years, during which the Filipino (who'd once relied almost exclusively on speed and a powerful left hand) had evolved into a complete practitioner of the art of boxing.

"I've watched tapes of Hatton's last twenty fights," Roach declared. "We know his strengths and his weaknesses. Ricky is a world-class fighter, but he doesn't have the ability to adjust. He fights the same way over and over again. And his balance is poor. When he has you on the ropes and sets his feet, he can throw a good hook to the body. But in the center of the ring, he's not a puncher. Manny has to stay off the ropes. If he does that, his speed and power will be too much for Ricky. He'll walk him into some shots and knock him out. Manny is a much better fighter than Ricky."

When fight night came, Roach was the first member of Team Pacquiao to enter dressing room #3 at the MGM Grand Garden Arena. He arrived at 5:45 p.m. and began organizing the tools of his trade (tape, towels, and various pieces of boxing equipment) on a long table opposite the door. Fifteen minutes later, Pacquiao arrived with twenty people in tow, among them his wife (Jinkee), his mother-in-law and sister-in-law, and assistant trainer Buboy Fernandez.

Pacquiao sat on a rubdown table. After several minutes of conversation, he took off his sneakers and socks and began putting protective pads on his toes, covering blisters that hadn't healed.

More friends and girlfriends of friends filtered into the room. Thirty-eight people were there. "It is easier if you have friends around, laughing," Manny has said. "Always, there should be laughing."

Now there was just quiet conversation.

The first pay-per-view fight of the evening came on a flat-screen television in a corner of the room. The voice of HBO commentator Jim Lampley filled the air. Without the television, the room would have been as quiet as a library. It was hard to believe that thirty-eight people made so little noise.

At 6:25 p.m., Roach moved to the center of the room and told the gathering, "In five minutes, anyone who doesn't belong here has to leave."

Five minutes later, a half-dozen women (including Jinkee) and a few others left. Twenty-eight people remained.

Pacquiao put on his socks and laced up his shoes. Larry Merchant came in for the ritual pre-fight HBO interview. Once Merchant left, Roach again moved to the center of the room.

"Please—if you don't belong here, leave."

No one moved.

Two members of the Las Vegas Metropolitan Police Department were summoned and cleared the room of unauthorized personnel.

Lee Beard (Hatton's assistant trainer) came in to watch Pacquiao's hands being wrapped. For the most part, remarkably, Manny performed the chore himself, singing softly as he worked. When need be, cutman Miguel Diaz assisted the fighter as Roach looked on.

The television, which was turned off when Merchant came in to conduct his interview, hadn't been turned on again. The hum of the air-ventilation system was the loudest noise in the room.

Manny finished taping his left hand, held it up, smiled at his handi-work, and began applying gauze to his right hand.

The television was turned back on. Danny Jacobs was midway through an eight-round whitewash of an overmatched Michael Walker.

"Can we change to the basketball game?" Manny inquired. "Chicago Bulls and Boston."

The answer, after tinkering with the television set, was "no." Pacquiao shrugged and continued wrapping his hands. When he was done, he stood up, slapped his fists together, and cried out, "Let's get ready to rumble!" Then he shadow-boxed briefly in the center of the room.

At 7:30, a twelve-person prayer group led by a Filipino priest entered. There was a brief prayer.

Referee Kenny Bayless gave Manny his pre-fight instructions.

Pacquiao resumed shadow-boxing and loosening up.

At eight o'clock, Manny put on a pair of white boxing trunks with black trim; then a red, white, and blue robe.

Roach gloved Pacquiao up.

The room was cleared again. Now only Manny, his cornermen, and a commission inspector (and this writer) were present.

At 8:10, serious padwork with Roach began. Unlike most fighters in the dressing room before a fight, Pacquiao works with his robe on. Periodically, it slipped open and Buboy Fernandez retied it.

The padwork grew more intense. Pacquiao's fists were a combination of blinding speed and power, culminating in a flurry of punches that seemed to explode on the pads.

"Oooo! See ya," Roach said approvingly.

"And if he goes like this," Manny added (imitating Hatton coming in), "I go BOOM!" At which point, he launched a slow-motion counter right hook aimed at Roach's jaw.

Then Manny smiled the smile of an athlete who was primed and ready to play a game. He was completely relaxed, as though he believed he was protected by a higher power. Or maybe he was simply confident in knowing that he was the best fighter in the world.

The fight began as expected, with Hatton moving forward and Pacquiao, in his southpaw stance, circling out of harm's way. Thirty seconds after the opening bell, a sharp counter right hook shook Ricky. That was followed by more hooks and straight left hands punctuated by a sharp counter hook at the two-minute mark that sent Hatton tumbling face-first to the canvas. He rose at the count of eight, was pummeled around the ring, and decked again for another eight-count with nine seconds left in the round.

That left Hatton's fans with the fragile hope that Pacquiao–Hatton would somehow be like Pacquiao–Marquez I (where Marquez was decked three times in the opening stanza but rallied to salvage a draw). However, Pacquiao was a much better fighter in 2009 than he was in 2004. And Marquez makes adjustments well on the fly, whereas Ricky doesn't.

In round two, Hatton came back for more and Pacquiao with his fists said, "I'll give it to you." Speed alone might not kill, but speed plus power does. Ricky fought as well as he could, which kept him on his feet until the 2:52 mark when a straight left hand landed flush on the jaw and deposited him unconscious on the canvas.

It was a knockout that will appear on highlight reels forever and a career-defining demolition. Hatton has a pretty good chin, and Pacquiao reduced it to English china.

After the fight, Pacquiao returned to his dressing room and embraced a throng of admirers (Denzel Washington among them). There was a group prayer. Manny signed his ring stool, various fight-night credentials, and other memorabilia.

Then a member of Team Pacquiao handed Manny a smartphone and announced, "It's David Díaz [a previous Pacquiao knockout victim]."

"Hello, my friend," Pacquiao said, beginning the conversation.

"I'm so happy," Díaz told him. "On all the advertisements for the fight, they've been showing me on television, lying face down on the canvas. Now they've got a better knockout to show."

Pacquiao laughed. "Thank you, brother."

The conversation ended.

Manny laughed again and gleefully threw a straight left hand in slow motion into the air. "BOOM! Good-bye."

In his mind, the punch that sent Ricky Hatton into unconsciousness was the equivalent of a 500-foot home run into the bleachers, not an act of violence.

Meanwhile, Freddie Roach sat in a chair opposite the rubdown table, surveying the scene.

"Manny makes me look good," Roach said. "He's such a pleasure to work with. He was good when I got him and I knew there was room for improvement. But I wondered, 'How good can he really be? Will he listen?' Because a lot of guys get to the level Manny was at eight years ago and think they know everything. But Manny works hard. He listens. He keeps getting better and better. I know I have something to do with it. But really, the credit belongs to Manny."

Freddie smiled. "You know, you work on something in the gym again and again, and you hope you see some of it on fight night. And tonight. . . ."

Roach shook his head in wonder.

"Whenever Manny fights now, you see the things you worked on in the gym being executed perfectly, right in front of you."

In the far corner of the room, several members of Team Pacquiao had rewritten the lyrics to "London Bridge Is Falling Down" and were singing:

Ricky Hatton's falling down
Falling down
Falling down
Ricky Hatton's falling down
We love Manny

Pacquiao thrust his left hand into the air again and once again proclaimed, "BOOM! Good-bye." Then he began singing to the tune of "Winter Wonderland" (known in boxing circles as "Walking in a Hatton Wonderland"):

> There's no more Ricky Hatton
> No more
> Ricky Hatton

A reporter from a Filipino radio station reached toward him with a tape recorder in hand.

"No tape, please," Manny told him. "Ricky Hatton is a good fighter and my friend. I only want to show respect to him."

QUESTION FOR BOXING REFEREES: A fighter collapses when his knee gives way during the seventh round of a twelve-round fight. When he rises to his feet, he's in obvious pain and can't move properly or put weight on the leg. The fighter collapses several more times. His chief second advises the referee that he wants the fight to be stopped. The fighter wants to continue. The referee should: (a) ignore the chief second, tell the fighter to "suck it up," and allow the fight to continue; or (b) stop the fight.

The Appalling End to Foreman–Cotto
Yuri Foreman vs. Miguel Cotto—
June 5, 2010

On June 5, 2010, at Yankee Stadium, Yuri Foreman defended his 154-pound WBA championship against Miguel Cotto. Foreman was a Chabad rabbinical student and the first practicing Orthodox Jew to win a world title since Jackie "Kid" Berg in 1932. He was also the first Israeli citizen ever to win a world championship belt.

Foreman's ethnicity was central to the promotion of Foreman–Cotto. In that spirit, I'd planned to report on the fight in the form of a column explaining the action to my eighty-four-year-old Jewish mother.

"Foreman and trainer Joe Grier shmoozed in the corner between rounds. 'You want I should throw the jab?' Yuri asked."

If there was a controversial decision, I could write that the loser was "kvetching about the judges." If Yuri won, co-managers Murray Wilson and Alan Cohen would be "kvelling" with pride. The sanctioning body officials would be labeled "no-goodniks."

Then reality intervened in the form of what I believe was a gross error in officiating by referee Arthur Mercante that requires serious commentary.

Let's put the matter in context.

Foreman was born in Belarus. His family moved to Israel when he was eleven. "At first it was difficult," Yuri recalled. "I was missing my friends. And sometimes in Israel, there was discrimination between the Russians and the Jews. The Russians were also Jewish, but the Israelis would call us Russians and say we didn't deserve to be there, so there would be fights in school between the immigrants and the Israelis."

Foreman learned the rudiments of boxing in an outdoor lot. There was no ring, not even a heavy bag.

"They wouldn't give us a gym because we were just Russians," he said. "We went to City Hall and begged for a place to hang a bag and put up a ring. All they told us was, 'Go box with the Arabs.' So finally I went to the Arab gym. The first time I walked in, I saw the stares. In their eyes, there was a lot of hatred. But I needed to box. And boy, did they all want to box me. But after a while, the wall that was between us melted. We all wanted the same thing. I traveled with them as teammates. It helped that I won almost all the time. And finally, we became friends."

In Israel, Foreman was a three-time national amateur champion. In 2001, he came to New York to pursue a career in professional boxing. He turned pro in 2002, compiled a 28–0 record, and, on November 14, 2009, defeated Daniel Santos to claim the WBA junior-middleweight title.

The key to Yuri's style was to move constantly and use his legs to keep an opponent at long range. Footwork was crucial to everything he did. He was hard to hit and threw a lot of punches that kept opponents off balance. He boxed more than he fought. In 28 bouts, he had scored only 8 knockouts. His trainer was Joe Grier (a former police officer who fought professionally in the 1970s).

And there's another piece of information that's relevant. Yuri wore a brace on his right knee when he fought. "It's for an old injury," he said. "When I was fifteen, I fell off a bike."

Foreman was promoted by Top Rank, whose CEO (Bob Arum) has visions and implements them. As long as a fighter performs in the ring, Top Rank can get him to the dance. In this instance, the dance was Foreman vs. Miguel Cotto at Yankee Stadium. A win for Yuri would establish him as a star in the boxing firmament.

Outdoor fights in mammoth stadiums are part of American boxing lore. The original Yankee Stadium is at the heart of that tradition. Jack Dempsey, Gene Tunney, Rocky Marciano, and Sugar Ray Robinson are among the storied warriors who did battle within its walls.

Joe Louis fought in Yankee Stadium as a Black hope against Primo Carnera and Max Baer. By the time he entered the stadium ring to face

Max Schmeling on June 22, 1938, in what was arguably the most important prizefight of all time, Louis was America's hope. That night was the
first time that many people heard a Black man referred to simply as "the
American."

Times change. On June 5, 2010, when Foreman entered the ring
to face Cotto, an African American was president of the United States.
In 1938, the state of Israel didn't exist. Now an Israeli citizen would be
defending a world title in the main event.

The stadium venue was a key element in promoting the fight. The
other hook was Foreman's Israeli citizenship and status as a rabbinical
student. That distinction made him a magnet for publicity in the weeks
leading up to the bout. Yuri was the grand marshal in New York's annual
"Salute to Israel Parade" and a guest on *Jimmy Kimmel Live*. The *New
York Times* and *Wall Street Journal* ran feature articles about him. The *New
York Daily News* referred to Yuri and his wife, Leyla, as "the Brangelina
of boxing."

Foreman's ring walk, the media was told, would be preceded by the
sounding of the shofar (a horn, traditionally that of a ram, used in Jewish
religious rites).

"There will be two highlights for me on fight night other than the
fight," Arum proclaimed. "One will be when they play 'Hatikva' [the
Israeli national anthem] for the first time ever in the old or new Yankee
Stadium. The other will be when Yuri begins his ring walk to the sound
of the shofar. That's something that has never been seen or heard in
the whole long history of boxing. We are very fortunate to have Israel's
number one entertainer, Yoni Dror of Tel Aviv, attending the fight to
sound the shofar. Yoni is beyond compare when it comes to sounding
the shofar."

Yoni was also Arum's nephew.

On the day of the fight, Foreman observed the Sabbath (from sunset
on Friday until sunset on Saturday) in a Manhattan hotel room. He left
the hotel at 9:08 p.m. and drove with a police escort to Yankee Stadium.
In his dressing room, he taped an eight-foot-long Israeli flag over the
lockers at one end of the room. Then he took a Bible from his gym bag
and bowed his head while reading from the Book of Psalms. Five minutes
later, he kissed the book and put it back in his gym bag.

Top Rank's international television feed could be seen and heard on a TV set in the dressing room. Yuri stood silently as "Hatikva" was sung, shifting his weight from one foot to the other.

The referee for Foreman–Cotto was Arthur Mercante Jr. (son of Hall of Fame referee Arthur Mercante). Arthur Sr. was known throughout the boxing community as a man of integrity and competence. Over the years, his son had developed his own body of work.

The first part of Foreman–Cotto boiled down to boxing basics. Miguel was the aggressor. Yuri sought to stem the tide with lateral movement and enough punches of his own to keep Cotto from rolling over him. Foreman's punches stung. Miguel's were the harder blows. Cotto appeared to be more concerned with finding Yuri than he was with getting hit.

The third round saw the first of what would be several strange acts by Mercante. With 1:42 left in the stanza, Foreman's mouthpiece fell out of his mouth. Arthur saw it and immediately picked it up. There was a lengthy lull in the action, but he didn't call time. Instead, he waited more than a minute before leading Foreman to Cotto's corner. Emanuel Steward protested that he was the wrong guy to rinse the mouthpiece and put it back in, that Yuri wasn't his fighter.

"No! No! You clean it," Mercante ordered.

That was a clear departure from boxing protocol.

Round four was Foreman's best round of the fight. He landed several hard lead right hands after feinting with his jab and won the stanza on each judge's scorecard.

Round five belonged to Cotto. Round six was close.

Halfway through the scheduled twelve rounds, Miguel was ahead 59–55, 59–55, and 58–56 on the scorecards. Yuri had a bloody nose and a cut on his left eyelid. But he was still in the fight.

Then things got crazy.

Forty-five seconds into round seven, as Foreman was moving laterally to his right along the ring perimeter, his right knee gave way and he fell hard to the canvas. He rose in obvious pain, hobbling when he tried to walk.

"Walk it off, champ," Mercante told him. "Suck it up, kid. I'll give you five minutes." Then he asked, "Is it your ankle?"

Given the fact that Yuri was wearing a knee brace, an ankle injury wasn't the most likely possibility.

Foreman said no.

"Is it your knee?"

Yuri nodded.

"Suck it up, kid," Mercante repeated.

Less than a minute after Foreman went down, the action resumed. At that point, Yuri was a seriously compromised fighter. Forty-five seconds later, again with no punch being thrown, his knee buckled and he fell once more to the canvas.

"Oh, shit," Mercante muttered. His words sounded as though they were spoken more in anger than out of concern for the fighter. "Suck it up," he said. "Do you want more time? You're a game guy. Do you want to go?"

Foreman appeared to be in no condition to fight, but he was a champion with a champion's heart.

Mercante instructed that the action resume.

With one minute left in round seven, a Cotto left hook knocked out Yuri's mouthpiece. Mercante let the entire round finish without giving the mouthpiece to the corner to put back in.

Mercante's handling of round seven was bad. His conduct in round eight was worse.

Joe Grier readied Foreman for the eighth round in the hope that Yuri could regain his mobility. But it was quickly clear that, not only couldn't he move to avoid punches, he couldn't get power on his own blows. At the 1:30 mark, while trying to move laterally, he staggered and almost fell again.

"I knew then that it was a serious injury and that it wasn't something he could recover from," Grier said afterward. "Yuri had no mobility and he couldn't get leverage on his punches. He was just a target."

At that point, following proper procedure, Grier asked Ernie Morales (the New York State Athletic Commission inspector assigned to Foreman's corner) to tell Mercante that he wanted to stop the fight. Morales stood on the ring apron to get Mercante's attention. Arthur admitted after the fight that he saw and heard the inspector. And he knew that Morales was assigned to Foreman's corner because he'd seen him in

Yuri's dressing room when he gave the fighter his pre-fight instructions. But Mercante pointedly ignored the request.

"Yuri was starting to get banged up," Grier recounted later. "He couldn't properly defend himself because he only had one leg. The referee wasn't listening to the inspector. I had to get it stopped. I asked if I could throw the towel in, and the inspector said 'Go ahead.'"

With 1:15 left in round eight, Grier threw a white towel into the ring. Both trainers came through the ropes to embrace their respective fighters.

Then Mercante did a disservice to boxing. If he had doubts as to where the towel came from, he could have asked Grier if he'd thrown it in. Grier would have answered, "Yes, sir." The responsible thing for Mercante to say in response would have been, "Okay; the fight is over."

But that's not what happened.

Instead, Mercante shouted, "Everybody out of the ring. I don't want the towel. The corner is not throwing in the towel [apparently, he knew it came from the corner]." Then he turned to Foreman and asked, "You all right, champ?"

Obviously, Foreman wasn't all right.

"You're fighting hard. I don't want to see a move like that. Suck it up. Walk it off."

The action resumed. But as Grier said, Foreman was no longer able to properly defend himself. The fight was clearly unwinnable. In fact, it was no longer a professional prizefight. It was a beating.

Foreman's knee gave way and he staggered several more times before the end of the round.

After the eighth stanza, Mercante went to Foreman's corner. "Who threw in the towel?" he demanded.

"I did," Grier told him.

Mercante turned and walked away. He didn't even talk with Foreman. Grier, understanding that he'd been forbidden to stop the fight, reluctantly readied his charge for the ninth round.

Thirty seconds into round nine, Cotto landed a hook to the body. Yuri's knee gave out again and he fell to the canvas. Finally, Mercante stopped the bout.

In the dressing room after the fight, Foreman was disappointed but accepting of what had happened. "I felt a lot of pain," he said. "It was very sharp and my knee was weak. I didn't want to stop the fight, but I couldn't box like I had to. If the leg was fine, I would stay in my game plan. Without the leg, I couldn't move and I had no leverage on my punches."

Grier thanked Ernie Morales for doing what he could to stop the fight.

"The inspector did the right thing, and so did I," Joe said. "I'd throw the towel in again if I had it to do over. All that happened after that was, Yuri took unnecessary punishment. He was fighting with dignity, but he only had one leg. I wanted it to stop while he was still on his feet, not down on the canvas. I know you're not supposed to throw a towel in. I told the inspector I wanted them to stop the fight. The inspector told the referee. And the referee told them to keep fighting. What else was I supposed to do?"

Arthur Mercante came in the room to congratulate Foreman on his courage.

"You should have stopped it," Yuri's wife, Leyla, said.

"He wasn't going to get hurt," Mercante countered.

"You don't know that."

"Each time he collapsed, he got back up, throwing punches."

"It made no sense," Leyla pressed. "What did you expect was going to happen? Nothing was going to change. There was not going to be a miracle that he could start to move again."

Mercante left the dressing room, but not before pointing to several text messages he'd received on his cell phone telling him that the HBO commentators had praised his work during the fight.

Yuri lay down on a rubdown table, and a doctor put the first of seven stitches in his left eyelid. Six days later, he underwent knee surgery at NYU Medical Center to repair a torn meniscus muscle and rebuild his anterior cruciate ligament.

Subsequent to the fight, New York State Athletic Commission chairperson Melvina Lathan praised Mercante for his handling of the contest. "I think Arthur did a remarkable job," Lathan told writer Michael Woods. "He did what he was supposed to do. He knows the rules. He responded appropriately. All in all, it was a magical evening of boxing."

I have a different opinion. I think that Mercante's handling of the fight was appalling.

Let's start with some facts.

Early in round seven, as previously noted, Foreman's knee gave way
and he fell to the canvas. He rose, debilitated and in obvious pain.

New York State is a member of the Association of Boxing
Commissions. Section 33 of the *Referee Rules and Guidelines* adopted by
the ABC in 2008 states, "The referee must consult with the ringside physician in all accidental injury cases. The referee, in conjunction with the
ringside physician, will determine the length of time needed to evaluate
the affected boxer and his or her suitability to continue. If the injured
boxer is not adversely affected and their chance of winning has not been
seriously jeopardized because of the injury, the bout may be allowed to
continue."

Foreman's injury "seriously jeopardized" his chance of winning the
fight. Mercante is an intelligent man, so presumably he understood
that. Also, Mercante failed at that juncture to consult with Dr. Rick
Weinstein (an orthopedic surgeon, who was the ringside physician in
Yuri's corner) as required by Rule 33. Instead, he urged Foreman to
"walk it off" and "suck it up," and let the fight continue.

When Foreman's knee buckled and he collapsed again less than a
minute later, Mercante followed the same procedure.

The key to Foreman's success as a fighter has been his mobility. In
rounds one through six of the fight, Cotto had landed an average of
eleven punches per round. In round seven, with a disabled fighter in front
of him, he landed twenty-nine, including twenty-seven "power" punches.

Joe Grier understood Foreman's fighting heart and wanted to give
him every reasonable opportunity to win. But as round eight progressed,
it was clear to Grier that Yuri's injury was not something that the fighter
could "walk off" and that it would only get worse.

Corner inspectors are the eyes and ears of the commission. They
don't have the authority to stop a fight. But they do have the authority
to tell the referee that a fighter's corner wants the fight stopped. Midway
through round eight, when Yuri staggered and almost fell again, Grier
asked inspector Ernie Morales to tell the referee that he wanted to stop
the fight.

Morales relayed the request. Mercante refused to honor it.

At that point, with the inspector's permission, Grier threw a white
towel into the ring.

I'm hard pressed to think of another instance when a chief second asked that a fight be stopped (let alone, an instance when a fighter was hobbling around the ring on a severely injured leg) and the referee refused to stop it.

After the fight, when Mercante was interviewed by Max Kellerman on HBO, he was evasive, as evidenced by the following colloquy:

Kellerman: "Do you know who threw in the towel?"

Mercante: "At the moment, I didn't know."

Kellerman: "Do you know who it is now?"

Mercante: "I kind of know."

Kind of?

After round eight, Mercante had gone to the corner and demanded, "Who threw in the towel?"

"I did," Grier told him.

Arthur didn't ask, "Why?"

He didn't say, "Tell me what you're thinking."

He turned and walked away.

If that's standard protocol in New York, then New York needs to overhaul its standards.

After the fight, one of the things that Mercante said in support of his decision was, "There was no need to stop the fight. They were in the middle of a great fight. That's what the fans came to see."

But referees are taught from day one, "You don't worry about the crowd. You're there to ensure a fair fight and protect the fighters. You do what you have to do to fulfill these obligations whether or not it makes the crowd happy."

Shame on anyone who thought that seeing a one-legged fighter get beaten up was "entertainment."

Here, one might also note that Mercante was the referee on the night of June 26, 2001, when Beethavean Scottland fought George "Khalid" Jones in a bout that was nationally televised from the flight deck of the USS *Intrepid*.

Prior to Scottland–Jones, Mercante had been criticized for his performance in three high-profile bouts. On each of those occasions (Razor Ruddock vs. Michael Dokes, Pernell Whitaker vs. Diosbelys Hurtado, and Michael Bennett vs. Andrew Hutchinson), he'd allowed a fight to continue after one of the participants appeared to be unable to defend himself. Each time, an ugly knockout followed.

Ruddock–Dokes, Whitaker–Hurtado, and Bennett–Hutchinson involved split-second judgments. Scottland–Jones was a different matter. Scottland took a beating. On three occasions in three different rounds, there were cries from the crowd that the bout should be stopped. In round ten, Scottland was knocked unconscious. He died five days later.

Larry Hazzard is uniquely situated to comment on Foreman–Cotto, having been inducted into the International Boxing Hall of a Fame for his body of work as both a referee and chairman of the New Jersey State Athletic Control Board.

"Normally, I don't comment on situations involving a referee and a commission," Hazzard said after Foreman–Cotto. "And I don't like to criticize. But I'd be doing a disservice to the boxing community if I didn't speak out. The most important mission of the referee is to protect the health and safety of the fighter. Fighters are in danger every time they step into the ring. It's the referee's job to protect them when the danger becomes too great. The referee's mission is not to tell the fighter, 'Suck it up. Walk it off.'

"Walk it off? What does that mean?" Hazzard continued. "The referee should have called in the doctor when the fighter's knee gave out. Instead, the referee, on his own, made a medical decision that the fighter should continue. That's why we have a doctor in each corner. You call time and consult with the doctor. How can anyone argue with that? And how can you overrule the trainer when he wants to stop the fight? Nobody knows a fighter better than his trainer. When the inspector came up on the ring apron and told the referee that the trainer wanted the fight to be over, that should have been it. When Mercante threw the inspector out of the ring, he was throwing all the rules and a hundred years of boxing out of the ring. Right then, someone should have taken the fight out of his hands; because clearly, at that point, he wasn't acting properly. I hate to be this critical. But the way this fight was handled was horrible. In the whole history of boxing, to my knowledge, nothing like this has ever happened before. And it should never happen again."

Don Turner has been honored as "trainer of the year" by the Boxing Writers Association of America. "I didn't see the fight," Turner acknowledged. "But I heard about it. First, let me tell you about Joe Grier. He's a good trainer; he cares about his fighters; and he's a great guy. Second thing: the only problem I have with Joe Grier in this situation is that he was too nice a guy. If it had been me in there with my fighter and the referee told me I couldn't stop the fight, there would have been a bigger fight between me and the referee. All trainers want to win. The trainer does everything he can to keep his fighter in the fight. But the trainer knows better than anyone else when his fighter is in trouble and when a fight should be stopped. When the trainer reaches that conclusion, it's not about asking the fighter, 'How do you feel about me stopping the fight?' When the trainer says 'that's all,' the fight is over."

Finally, there was Emanuel Steward, respected throughout the boxing community as a trainer and HBO commentator. Steward had a unique view of Foreman–Cotto. He was in Miguel's corner as the drama unfolded.

"I usually defend referees," Steward said. "It's a hard job. And to be honest, I don't like to say things that upset officials because they might hold it against me down the road. But I'll talk about this because it was horrible. I don't think I've ever seen a referee do a job that bad. First, the referee was out of position all through the fight. No one is talking about that. Then there was the mouthpiece thing. That was crazy. And when the towel came in—that was awful. There are things we have in boxing to protect fighters from their own courage. There's the referee, the ring doctor, and the fighter's corner. The fighter's corner has always been able to stop a fight. The trainer knows his fighter better than the referee does. We're not stupid. If the trainer wants to stop the fight, you stop the fight. Yuri could have been killed. One punch can do it. And it was obvious to everyone except the referee that Yuri couldn't defend himself. Even if Joe Grier didn't want to stop the fight, the referee should have stopped it."

"If it was my fighter and I wanted to stop it," Steward concluded, "we would have had a real confrontation, in the ring right then and there. The referee could say anything he wanted. I'd have told him, 'I don't care what you say. The fight is over.' I have no idea what the man was thinking. The fighter's life was at risk. A bad call in another sport can cost you a point or maybe lose the game. Boxing is a whole different sport. If a referee doesn't understand that, he has a serious problem. The whole thing was weird and scary. This wasn't one bad spur-of-the-moment decision. Everything was wrong. There was bad refereeing and irrational behavior all night long. I've never seen anything like it before, and I hope I never see anything like it again."

There are those who say that it was appropriate to allow Foreman–Cotto to continue because Yuri had earned the right to "go out on his shield." That translates into, "Yuri had no chance to win. But the referee should have allowed him get to beaten up, rip open the cut on his left eyelid, shred whatever remained that was holding his right knee in place, and maybe get knocked unconscious. Then, since there were no shields at ringside, he could have been carried out on a stretcher."

Foreman didn't need that to establish his courage.

It's not a hard concept to grasp. If a fighter is hurt and his chief second wants to stop the fight, the referee should stop the fight. People can agree or disagree with me. But that's how I felt then. And more than a decade later, I still feel very strongly about it.

"A win would mean great things," John Duddy said three days prior to fighting Julio César Chávez Jr. "The winner has a good path in front of him."

John Duddy:
A Fighting Heart Isn't Enough
John Duddy vs. Julio César Chávez Jr.—
June 26, 2010

John Duddy sat in the "green room" at the Alamodome in San Antonio on the evening of June 26, 2010. The room was comfortably large, but it wasn't really a dressing room. There were no lockers or shower.

Decades of sacrifice, pain, passion, and dreams were about to crystalize into a fistfight. John would step onto a small square of illuminated canvas where he and Julio César Chávez Jr. would try to beat each other senseless.

There's an ebb and flow to a fighter's career. An unexpected loss can send his fortunes plummeting like a one-day 20 percent drop in the Dow Jones. On occasion, a fighter enters the ring, knowing in advance that he's about to engage in a crossroads fight. Win, and he takes a giant step forward. Lose, and he might never climb back to where he was before. This was a crossroads fight. It wasn't for a world title. But after this night, regardless of the outcome, Duddy's future as a fighter would be vastly different from what it had been before.

Duddy's pre-fight dressing room is always quiet. There's no music and little conversation. John sat silent for long periods, sipping occasionally from a bottle of Vitamin Water. At one point, he lay down on a black leather sofa, put his head on a pillow fashioned from towels, and closed his eyes, focusing on the task ahead.

Trainer Harry Keitt, cornerman Jihad Abdul-Aziz, cutman George Mitchell, and manager Craig Hamilton spoke in hushed tones when they spoke at all.

"I hate this part of it," Hamilton said. "Everything up until now, I could try to control. Now it's out of my hands."

Referee Jon Schorle came in and gave John his pre-fight instructions. One concern in the Duddy camp was that John cuts easily.

"I wish I didn't cut, but I do," Duddy had said. "If it bothered me, I wouldn't be a fighter."

In past fights against Yori Boy Campas and Walid Smichet, John had fought with horrific cuts above both eyes but emerged victorious each time. Team Duddy was afraid that Schorle might pull the trigger prematurely. It was an issue they'd planned to raise during the referee's pre-fight instructions.

Schorle brought the subject up himself. "I've seen you fight many times," he told John. "You cut easily. I'm not going to panic if I see blood. You've fought with bad cuts before and won."

The minutes passed. This wasn't *American Idol*. It wasn't about being voted off an island. John was about to fight for his career and to position himself to keep living his dream. Regardless of whether he won or lost, he would be punched again and again by a man trained in the art of hurting. It was inevitable that he would suffer physical damage. Much of it would be superficial. Some might be everlasting.

Duddy had turned pro in 2003 at age twenty-four after moving to New York from Ireland. His good looks, charisma, and action style of fighting made him a popular figure in the Irish American community. Women's hearts fluttered when he walked by. Men wanted to shake his hand. And he was winning: 23–0 with 18 knockouts.

How good was John?

Better than the guys he was fighting.

Then, on February 23, 2008, Duddy fought Walid Smichet (a free-swinging club fighter) at Madison Square Garden on the undercard of Wladimir Klitschko vs. Sultan Ibragimov. An impressive win would have put him next in line for a title shot against middleweight champion Kelly Pavlik.

It was a bad night for the Irish.

When an opponent throws punches in bunches, John tends to get hit. "Watching Duddy against Smichet was the first time I saw a guy get hit with every punch in a six-punch combination," George Kimball wrote afterward.

John won, barely. Both of his eyelids were ripped open. Thirty-two stitches were needed to close the wounds. "Boxing is hard enough when you're fighting smart," he acknowledged later. "There's no point in making things even harder by fighting stupid. Just because I can take a punch doesn't mean I have to. There's a time to stand and slug, but it's not as often as I've been doing it."

Then Duddy stumbled. After two more victories, he crossed the Hudson River to Newark, New Jersey, to fight journeyman Billy Lyell. Lyell had slightly faster hands than John and got off first for much of the night. In round three, an accidental head butt opened an ugly slice on Duddy's left eyelid. John finally got his jab untracked, backing Lyell up and splitting Billy's nose open in the process. The decision could have gone either way. Lyell won a split verdict.

After the loss to Lyell, Hamilton sat down with Top Rank (which had expressed interest in promoting John) to chart a course for the future. There was the usual back-and-forth with regard to money. During negotiations, Bob Arum was quick to point out Duddy's deficiencies as a fighter, which led Hamilton to complain, "Bob negotiates like a guy who's seducing a woman. He pursues her for a year. And when she finally agrees to go to bed with him, he tells her she's fat but he still wants to fuck her."

In the end, there was a meeting of the minds.

On October 10, 2009, Duddy pounded out a lopsided unanimous decision over Michi Munoz at Madison Square Garden on a Top Rank card headlined by Juan Manuel López and Yuriorkis Gamboa. Three months later, he returned to the scene and knocked out Juan Astorga in the first round.

The pieces of the puzzle that Arum and Hamilton were putting together were falling into place.

On March 13, 2010, John journeyed to Dallas for a showcase fight against Michael Medina on the undercard of Manny Pacquiao vs. Joshua Clottey at Cowboys Stadium. He controlled the action throughout the bout en route to a ten-round triumph.

Meanwhile, seven days after John Duddy made his professional debut at a small club-fight show in New York, Julio César Chávez Jr. entered the ring for the first time in Culiacán, Mexico.

Chávez had a hard act to follow. His father was one of Mexico's greatest fighters. Julio César Chávez Sr. won 107 times in a 115-bout career and captured championships at 130, 135, and 140 pounds.

Junior was brought along slowly by Top Rank against opposition that was suspect at best. Many of his opponents came from places like Indiana, Missouri, Oklahoma, Kansas, and Nebraska. The number of African Americans he'd faced in the ring could be counted on Arum's fingers with digits to spare. Yet, because of his name, he'd become a draw.

"Chávez," Bart Barry wrote, "built his following the old-fashioned way. He inherited it."

But in fairness to Julio, he'd turned pro with virtually no amateur experience, so it was logical for him to learn his trade against less-than-stellar competition. And by the start of 2010, his record stood at 40–0 with 1 draw. Anyone who's unbeaten in forty-one fights, no matter what the level of opposition, can fight a bit.

Chávez–Duddy was a fight that both camps had been pointing toward. Each fighter had a "name" and was marketable. Each fighter was confident that he could beat the other. It was the first time in John's career that he was the "B side" of a promotion. The fight would be for the World Boxing Council middleweight "silver belt." Significantly, that gave WBC president José Sulaimán control over the assignment of officials.

"Fighting Julio César Chávez Jr. for the WBC silver belt in Texas isn't a recipe for a fair fight," Hamilton acknowledged. "Texas has had problems in the past when guys come in to fight someone from Texas or a Mexican fighter. There's no question who José Sulaimán wants to win. And Julio is a cash cow for Top Rank. But there's really no choice. This is the right fight for John. It's a fight he can win, and winning will help him get to where he wants to be. Chávez isn't going to Ireland and we're not going to Mexico, so it makes economic sense to have the fight in Texas. All I can do is lobby for a fair fight and let people know that I won't go quietly if John gets robbed."

Duddy, for his part, said simply, "I'm coming to do my job, like I do for every fight. I don't appoint the referee and judges. I have to take care of my part of the bargain. After that, what happens happens.

"I think it will be a tough physical fight," Duddy continued. "The two of us are pretty aggressive fighters. I plan to keep the pressure on all night. I can box; I can punch; I can take a punch. And I can do it for twelve rounds. I've been in fights where I had to answer the question, 'Do I want to be a fighter or do I want to quit?' Chávez hasn't had to answer that question. I'll be going into waters where I've been before and Chávez hasn't."

And more important, Chávez had a reputation for coming into fights in less-than-stellar condition and fading late.

"Julio wasn't putting in the effort that is needed to be a world-class fighter," Bob Arum acknowledged. "You can have all the skills. But if you're not training properly and you struggle to make weight, you're not going to give a first-class performance. Finally, Julio listened. He understood that Duddy is better than all of the other guys he's fought and that he had to raise his game to beat John."

In the past, Julio had trained in Mexico with his uncles, Rodolfo Chávez and Miguel Molleda. For Chávez–Duddy, he trained in Los Angeles with Freddie Roach. And his conditioning regimen was overseen by Alex Ariza, who had a reputation for pushing the envelope where certain techniques were concerned.

For the first time in Duddy's career, he was an underdog. The odds were 7-to-2 in favor of Chávez. Once the bell rings, good looks and charm don't help. Moreover, as previously noted, there was a belief in some circles that the playing field would be tilted in Chávez's favor.

In the months leading up to the fight, Hamilton placed a series of telephone calls to Dickie Cole (administrator of combat sports for the Texas Department of Licensing and Regulation). Technically, the State of Texas would designate the referee and judges. But as a matter of course, Cole was expected to defer to José Sulaimán's recommendations.

Sulaimán was hardly an impartial observer. Twelve days before the fight, he declared, "This is now the time for Julio to prove if he's ready for a title challenge. If Julio wins, he'll fight for either the middleweight or super-welterweight championship, whichever is available. I believe he's going to be a world champion."

On June 7, the WBC advised Top Rank (which informed Hamilton) that the officials for Chávez–Duddy would be referee Jon Schorle (who has homes in Texas and California) and judges Glen Rick Crocker of Texas, Julie Lederman of New York, and Jurgen Langos of Germany. In Hamilton's mind, Langos's appointment cast a pall over the proceedings.

"We know that Sulaimán wants Chávez to win the fight," Craig noted. "If he's bringing a judge all the way from Germany to Texas for a fight between an Irishman and a Mexican, that judge is going to know it too. And the judge is going to understand that, if he scores the fight for Chávez, he's likely to get some very lucrative WBC judging assignments in the future. I know the crowd will be rooting for Chávez. I hope that doesn't include the referee and judges."

Duddy was philosophical when apprised of the situation.

"This is the biggest fight of my career so far," John said. "And I'm not going in it to lose. I know what I bring to the fight. If it's good enough, it's good enough. If it's not, it's not. It's not about Texas. It's not about Chávez's father. When the bell rings, it's just him and me. I expect that this will be the toughest fight of my career. And if I have my way, it's going to be the toughest fight of his career as well. One of two things will happen. If he quits, he quits. And if he fights, the better man will win."

In the end, it was a good, fast-paced action fight. Chávez was clearly the quicker of the two men and landed when he got off first. Julio didn't jab in the early going as much as Roach wanted him to. But he found a home for his left hook and lead right hand.

By round four, it was a slugfest. Duddy wanted to brawl. Chávez obliged him, landing the harder, more effective punches. Then in round six, John landed a hard counter right that buckled Julio's knees and left him looking momentarily like a man who was trying to walk in a canoe that was floating downriver.

After six rounds, two of the judges had the fight scored dead even. More importantly, it was a war of attrition, which was the fight that Duddy wanted. The second half of the bout was supposed to be his. But the first six rounds had taken more out of him than they'd taken out of Chávez. Julio had landed the harder punches. And he was better conditioned than he'd ever been before.

In round seven, Chávez started beating Duddy up. As the fight wore on, John absorbed hellacious punishment. His face turned an ugly shade of purple and began to swell. Time and time again, he was driven to the ropes. Julio landed blow after blow. John took the punishment and fired back.

"Go out and finish this guy," Roach told Chávez several times between rounds.

Chávez pounded Duddy mercilessly. John simply would not fall.

"Fuck," Freddie muttered more than once during the late rounds. "This guy won't quit."

"I thought about stopping it," Harry Keitt said afterward. "But each time John came back to the corner, he was alert and focused. He kept throwing back. He threw punches the whole twelve rounds."

Rounds eleven and twelve were a walk through fire for Duddy with no realistic hope of victory. Chávez was loading up on his punches, confident that John had lost the power to hurt him. But John kept fighting with everything that was in him. He wasn't just trying to survive. He was still trying to win.

Julie Lederman (117–111) and Glen Rick Crocker (116–112) turned in credible scorecards in favor of Chávez. Jurgen Langos watched the fight from La-La Land and gave every round to Chávez. Langos's responsibility was to turn in a scorecard that accurately reflected what happened in the ring. To score the fight a shutout for Chávez strained credibility. And it was particularly offensive given the courage that Duddy showed in the face of brutal adversity.

In the dressing room after the fight, Duddy looked like he'd been beaten up by three men in an alley. He was holding an icepack, shifting it from one eye to the other. His face was bruised, battered, and swollen.

"I'm sorry," John told Hamilton. "I let you down."

"Don't say you're sorry," Craig responded. "You did everything you could. You're my man."

A commission doctor asked for a post-fight urine sample. When the task was done, John signed a label that would be affixed to the tube and asked, "Do I have to walk in a straight line and touch my nose, or can I have my check now?"

Boxing is a humbling sport.

John left the room with a towel wrapped around his waist and went next door to shower.

"There's no way you can be around this guy and not fall in love with him," Hamilton said. "As a fighter, he gives you everything he has, in the gym and in every fight. As a person, you couldn't find a nicer guy. He's appreciative when you do something for him. He takes his responsibilities seriously, personally and professionally. I wish there were more people like him."

John returned, dried himself, and dressed.

"You don't have to go to the press conference," Craig told him.

"I don't mind," Duddy said. "If I can't deal with losing, I shouldn't be in boxing."

There was a quick call to his wife. "I'm all right," John assured her. "I tried my hardest. . . . I love you. . . . I'll see you tomorrow."

Then John went to the post-fight press conference and told the gathering, "Julio fought a good fight. There was a lot of pressure on him. He performed and answered all the questions I asked of him. I took him into deep water. And yes, he can swim."

One of the hardest things for an athlete to accept is that he loves his sport but might not have what it takes to get to the highest level.

Boxing is about more than a good support team, dedication, and heart. Duddy had fought with incredible courage and earned respect throughout his ring career. But he wasn't in boxing to win moral victories. He'd gone into the sport to make life-changing money and become middleweight champion of the world, not to be a contender. And he simply didn't have the physical gifts of an elite fighter.

As 2011 began, HBO offered John a six-figure purse to fight Andy Lee. A win would have put him in position to challenge for a world title. But it wasn't to be.

"I saw so many ex-champions who aren't doing well," Duddy said later. "Physically, mentally, they're having problems. I was getting into my thirties. I always got hit more than I should have as a fighter. And I realized that being a world champion wouldn't necessarily make me happy in the long run. Damage is a strong word. But in boxing, every time you fight, you lose a piece of yourself that you can never get back again. I didn't want to go on longer than I should."

Thus, on January 18, 2011, John issued the following statement:

After a great deal of soul-searching, I have decided to retire from boxing.

I started watching my father train in the gym when I was five years old. I began fighting competitively at age ten. For more than twenty years, I loved being a boxer. I still feel that it's an enormous honor to be a boxer. But I don't love it anymore.

I no longer have the enthusiasm and willingness to make the sacrifices that are necessary to honor the craft of prizefighting. I used to love going to the gym. Now it's a chore. I wish I still had the hunger, but I don't. The fire has burned out. And I know myself well enough to know that it won't return.

It would be unfair to my fans, my trainer and manager, and everyone else involved in the promotion of my fights for me to continue boxing when I know that my heart isn't in it. I've always given one hundred percent in the gym and in my fights. I have too much respect for boxing and the people around me to continue fighting when I know that I can't do that anymore.

I haven't accomplished everything that I wanted to achieve in boxing. But I've had a rewarding career. I've enjoyed the satisfaction of winning twenty-nine professional fights and learned lessons from my two losses. I've experienced the thrill of fighting in Madison Square Garden, Cowboys Stadium, and, also, my beloved Ireland with crowds cheering for me. I look forward to finding future challenges that bring as much passion and joy into my life as boxing has over the past twenty years.

Barry McGuigan was one of my childhood heroes. His photograph was one of the first things that visitors saw when entering our home in Derry. He had great influence on me when I was a boy. Barry McGuigan once said, "Fighters are the first people to know when they should retire and the last to admit it." I know that it's time for me to retire from boxing, and I'm admitting it.

I'm fortunate to have had the support of many good people throughout my career. To my fans, to the people in the boxing business who have been part of my team over the years, and most of all, to my wife Grainne and the rest of my family; thank you for your love and support.

I give you my word; I will not come back.

And he didn't.

Manny Pacquiao at his best seemed as unbeatable as a video-game action hero.
Would challenging the much larger Antonio Margarito be a bridge too far?

Manny Pacquiao in Texas
Manny Pacquiao vs. Antonio Margarito—
November 13, 2010

On November 13, 2010, Manny Pacquiao added another page to his boxing legacy when he fought Antonio Margarito at Cowboys Stadium in Arlington, Texas, for the vacant World Boxing Council 154-pound title.

Outside the ring, fully clothed, Pacquiao looks almost delicate and vulnerable. The first reaction many people have on meeting him is surprise that he's so small. But in the ring, he's a destroyer.

Pacquiao won his first world title in 1998 at 112 pounds and had compiled a 51–3–2 record with 38 knockouts by the time he fought Margarito. At age thirty-one, he'd earned belts against credible competition in seven weight divisions. More significantly, three times during the preceding twenty-three months, Pacquiao had moved up in weight and destroyed bigger men.

"It's not just about beating opponents," former featherweight champion Barry McGuigan observed. "It's the way that you beat them. Pacquiao went through Oscar De La Hoya like a sparring partner. The way he knocked out Ricky Hatton was staggering. He just pole-axed him. Then he systematically took apart Miguel Cotto in a way no one could have predicted."

Pacquiao's journey from abject poverty to wealth and fame almost beyond imagination had made him an icon in his native Philippines. And his celebrity status exploded after his stoppage of De La Hoya.

"The broad outlines of his legend," *Time* magazine declared, "have made him a projection of the migrant dreams of the many Filipinos who leave home and country for work. Some spend decades abroad for the sake of the ones they love. Everyone in the Philippines knows a person who has made the sacrifice or is making it. Pacquiao gives that multitude a champion's face of selflessness, the winner who takes all and gives to all."

In May 2010, the people of Sarangani Province elected Pacquiao to Congress. Unlike many politicians, he meant it when he told voters that he saw the struggle of every Filipino in his own torturous journey.

"I feel what they are feeling because I have been there," Pacquiao said. "I slept in the streets. I ate once a day. Sometimes I just drank water, no food. That was my life before. So hard. I understand the needs of people who need help. My heart hurts when I see people in the street, sleeping. I remember my past when I was young."

"Manny Pacquiao," HBO Boxing commentator Jim Lampley observed, "is having a lovefest with the world while beating the crap out of people."

The lovefest continued when Pacquiao squared off against Margarito.

Pacquiao–Margarito was seen by many as a morality play of the highest order. Margarito had fashioned a 38–6 (27 KOs) ring record and previously held the World Boxing Organization and World Boxing Association welterweight titles. The latter prize was attained by virtue of a 2008 knockout of Miguel Cotto in a brutal encounter. Then, in his next outing, Antonio fought Shane Mosley. In his dressing room prior to that fight, illegal inserts were found in Margarito's handwraps. They were removed and Mosley knocked him out in the ninth round.

Margarito's trainer at the time, Javier Capetillo, took responsibility for the incident, saying that he'd grabbed the wrong knucklepads "by mistake" and that Antonio was unaware of the problem. Thereafter, Capetillo was banned from practicing his trade in the United States and Margarito's license to box was revoked by the California State Athletic Commission. The boxing community was split on whether Margarito should have been given the opportunity to fight Pacquiao. Some thought that the decision by the Texas Department of Licensing and Regulation to license him was a thumb in the eye for the sport. Be that as it may, Pacquiao–Margarito was contracted for at a catchweight of 150 pounds. That enabled the WBC to put its 154-pound belt on the line and allowed the promotion to talk about the possibility of an unprecedented eighth world title for Pacquiao.

In late October, Team Pacquiao journeyed from the Philippines to Los Angeles for two weeks of final preparation. Then it descended on Dallas.

There's no entourage like a boxing entourage, and Pacquiao's was substantial. Manny had chartered an American Airlines 757 that brought 180 people from the Philippines to the United States. "Air Pacquiao" cost him $120,000 plus food, lodging, and fight tickets for many of the travelers. Peter Nelson, then a freelance writer and later the head of HBO Sports, heralded their arrival.

"When Pacquiao fights in Cowboys Stadium," Nelson wrote, "his countrymen will colonize Arlington, Texas, forming a populace replete with advisors, cooks, priests, security, political chiefs-of-staff, a five-piece band, mentors, apprentices, past exiles for crimes now forgiven, future ones for crimes yet committed, and, of course, his mother. Where he goes, his people follow. They have nowhere else to be but living on his largesse. Manny Pacquiao has become the 7,108th island of the Philippines."

On Wednesday of fight week, Pacquiao worked out in Longhorn Exhibit Hall E (a huge room in the Gaylord Texan Hotel that had been converted into a makeshift gym). Then a hundred invited guests gathered at the far end of the room. Pacquiao donned a straw hat and walked over to a group of musicians that included three guitarists, a keyboard player, and drummer (known collectively as "The Manny Pacquiao Band"). Two backup vocalists joined them. For the next seventy-five minutes, Manny sang.

"I bless the day that I was born for you. . . . Two hearts that beat as one. . . . I can't resist your touch. . . ."

"At this point, it's all about keeping Manny happy," Rob Peters (the point man in Pacquiao's security detail) explained. "He loves doing this. It relaxes him. Right now, he's having fun, singing love songs. And Margarito is on a treadmill somewhere, killing himself to make weight."

Weight and size were Margarito's perceived edge in the fight (if he had any edge at all). Pacquiao was a 4-to-1 betting favorite. But Manny had begun his career at 106 pounds. Two days hence, he would weigh in at 144½ pounds, while Margarito (five inches taller) would tip the scales at 150. On fight night, there would be a 17-pound weight differential between them.

"Size doesn't win fights," Freddie Roach (who trained Pacquiao) said. "Skill does. And Manny is the most skilled fighter in the world."

But size in boxing translates into power and the ability to take a punch. That's why the sport has weight divisions. At some point, big becomes too big to handle. Margarito's battle plan would be to apply pressure, pressure, and more pressure. Wear Pacquiao down. Suffocate him with punches.

"He's a great fighter," Margarito said of Pacquiao. "We all know that he's fast and lands punches from all angles. But I think it's impossible that he'll have the power of a super-welterweight. He might hit me with five to one at first, but I'm too strong for him. I will gradually break him down and knock him out."

★★★

On fight night, Freddie Roach arrived at dressing room F300 at Cowboys Stadium at 5:45 p.m. Peter Nelson and training assistant Billy Keane were with him. A commission inspector was already there.

Pacquiao was Roach's signature fighter. They'd begun working together in 2001. At the time, Manny had awesome physical gifts but was largely a one-dimensional boxer. Jab, jab, straight left hand. Roach improved his charge's footwork, balance, and defensive skills; added a right hook to his arsenal; and brought consistency to his technique.

How good a trainer was Roach?

Paulie Malignaggi said that, when he watched a tape of the HBO telecast of his own fight against Amir Khan, he listened to Roach's corner instructions.

"After the third or fourth round," Malignaggi recounted, "Freddie told Amir, 'I need you to feint. If you feint, he's going to drop down and then you do this.' I'm saying to myself, 'Wow. That is my reaction to a feint. I never focused on it before, but that is how I respond.' Freddie knew me better than I knew myself."

When a fighter's hands are wrapped before a fight, the man doing the wrapping runs long strips of tape between each finger other than the thumb on each hand. Most trainers apply the tape flat, six strips in all. Roach likes to roll each strip vertically so they resemble sticks of incense. He calls the strips "ligaments."

Sitting in Pacquiao's dressing room, Roach began rolling the strips while conversing with Nelson and Keane.

"Manny loves to watch himself on television," Freddie said. "Between rounds in Vegas, he watches himself on those big video screens. The first time it happened, I tapped him on the cheek to get his attention and he told me, 'I'm listening.' In Cowboys Stadium, he can't see the screen because it's above the ring so I won't have to compete for his attention."

Cutman Miguel Diaz entered the dressing room. He was wearing black pants. Pacquiao won't wear black for a fight and he doesn't like anyone in his corner to wear black either.

"Don't worry about it," Roach told Diaz. "You're wearing a red jacket. Manny won't notice."

At 7:20 p.m., by prearrangement, an observer from Margarito's camp entered. Because of the Margarito handwrap scandal, it had been agreed that each side would have a representative in the opposing fighter's dressing room for the entire pre-fight proceedings and each trainer would fashion his fighter's knucklepads in front of the observer and a commission inspector.

Billy Keane left for Margarito's dressing room.

Roach began folding gauze into knucklepads.

At 8:05, Buboy Fernandez (Pacquiao's assistant trainer and longtime friend) arrived—a sure sign that Manny was in the building.

Buboy arranged Pacquiao's trunks, robe, and shoes (a color-coordinated white with gold trim) on a rubdown table.

Diaz's red corner jacket was adorned with advertising logos from a previous fight.

"Buboy," Miguel queried. "Is the advertising on this jacket okay, or will it be a problem?"

"No problem for me," Buboy answered. "They're not paying me for the advertising. They're paying Manny."

At 8:10, Pacquiao entered with thirty-six people in tow.

In due course, the dressing room was cleared of nonessential personnel.

Pacquiao put on his trunks and did some stretching exercises.

"I'm going over to watch Margarito wrap," Roach told him. "If you need anything, ask Miguel. Is that okay?"

Pacquiao nodded.

With Diaz assisting him, Manny started to wrap his own hands. Margarito's representative objected to virtually everything, including the tape provided by the commission and the knucklepads approved by the commission. The inspector overruled the objections.

Margarito's co-manager, Sergio Diaz, entered and lodged more objections. They too were overruled.

Roach returned.

Diaz finished wrapping.

At 9:30, there was a problem. Billy Keane telephoned Pacquiao's strength and conditioning coach Alex Ariza (who was now in the dressing room with Manny) to report that Margarito was about to take ephedrine (an appetite suppressant and stimulant) nasally.

"When you stack ephedrine with caffeine and aspirin," Ariza noted, "you get speed."

Keane said that three cups of coffee had just been delivered to Margarito's dressing room.

"It won't show up in his urine unless we test him before the fight," Ariza told Roach. "An ECA stack burns out quickly. A post-fight test will be too late."

William Kuntz (executive director of the Texas Department of Licensing and Regulation) and Dickie Cole (administrator of combat sports) were summoned to Pacquiao's dressing room.

"I want a drug test right now," Roach demanded.

"You focus on what you have to do," Ariza told Pacquiao. "Let the rest of them handle this bullshit."

Pacquiao did some more stretching exercises and began shadow-boxing.

Robert Garcia (Margarito's trainer) entered and complained that no one from the Margarito camp had been present when Roach rolled the ligaments earlier in the evening. He wanted Pacquiao to rewrap.

"It's pieces of tape," Roach countered. "Your guy looked at them and didn't have a problem."

Tempers flared. People from both camps started shouting. Pacquiao looked at Nelson and winked.

Kuntz and Cole announced that they wouldn't administer a pre-fight urine test even though ephedrine is a controlled drug and its use would be against commission regulations.

Garcia's complaint was overruled.

Keane reported that Margarito had agreed to not use the ephedrine.

Pacquiao finished warming up.

Once a fighter steps into the ring and the bell for round one sounds, nothing that he has accomplished before matters.

Prior to the fight, Roach had declared, "I'm not worried about Margarito. He's made to order for us. Margarito is tough. He'll come to win. But I've watched tons of film on him. He's always the same, completely predictable. He winds up on all of his punches so you can see them coming. He likes to exchange and he's hittable. He has poor footwork. He doesn't cut the ring off. And he's too slow to beat Manny. You can watch Manny on TV and say, 'Oh he's fast.' But you don't know how fast until you get in the ring with him. Manny will beat him up badly. This will not be a difficult fight for us. I don't see any issues."

That said, it was a hard-fought battle. The first two rounds were cautiously contested. Margarito was a bit less aggressive than expected. In round three, he began stalking in more determined fashion. Pacquiao circled, darting in and out, alternating between getting off first and landing sharp counter blows.

In round four, the landscape tilted lopsidedly in Manny's favor. One minute into the stanza, after raking Margarito with lightning-fast punches. he landed a hard left uppercut. Seconds later, Antonio's face was grotesquely swollen and discolored beneath his right eye and blood was dripping from a cut that would require six stitches to close.

The cut wasn't a major problem. What was happening beneath the cut was. The area swelled up so quickly and so dramatically that one could assume there was a fracture (which there was). That led to further splintering of the bone as the fight progressed and problems with the muscles and nerves around the eye.

Now Margarito was on his back foot, giving ground. Round five was more of the same. But at the start of round six, Manny looked a bit tired. Take away the swelling beneath Antonio's right eye and Margarito might have seemed the fresher of the two men. With thirty seconds left in the round, he backed Pacquiao into the ropes and dug a vicious left hook to the liver. Manny doubled over in pain and spent the next twenty seconds in retreat.

"I was a little worried in the sixth round," Roach admitted afterward.

"He hurt me," Pacquiao later acknowledged.

At that point, Margarito was behind in the fight but very much in it. He'd entered the battle in top physical condition, and the energy level between the combatants seemed to be shifting.

Margarito began round seven by going to the body. Pacquiao, as he'd done before, circled and darted in and out. The combatants resembled a grizzly bear swatting with his paw at a swarm of killer bees. Over the next few rounds, Manny landed the more numerous blows. Then the bout began to take on the look of a man smashing a large boulder to pebbles with a sledgehammer.

By round ten, Margarito's right eye was useless and his left eye was closing, which meant that he was fighting with half an eye. The right side of his face was disfigured to the point of mutilation. Referee Laurence Cole stopped the action, raised his left hand to cover Margarito's right eye, and asked the fighter how many fingers he was holding up. Margarito answered. The action resumed. But Antonio was now defenseless against Pacquiao's onslaught.

With twenty seconds left in round ten, as Margarito was plodding hopelessly forward, Pacquiao landed a sharp right hook to the jaw. Antonio's legs buckled and Manny followed with a barrage of punches that left his opponent lurching back to his corner at the bell. Margarito had been blasted with sixty-four punches during the round; fifty-seven of them, power punches.

The ring doctor examined Margarito briefly from outside the ropes. He couldn't look into Antonio's right eye with a penlight because the eye was swollen shut.

Round eleven was target practice. On three occasions, Pacquiao stopped his assault and looked toward Cole—in effect, asking him to stop the fight. "Boxing is not for killing," Manny said afterward. But Cole ignored the gesture and the carnage continued, although Pacquiao fought the rest of the bout with what seemed to be a blend of caution and compassion. The judges scored the contest 120–108, 119–109, and 118–110 in Manny's favor.

After the fight, Pacquiao went to Margarito's dressing room, where Antonio's cuts were being stitched up. The two men embraced and exchanged words of mutual respect. Then Manny hugged Antonio's wife and left.

Meanwhile, Roach was critical of Robert Garcia for allowing the fight to continue.

"There's no doubt at all in my mind that he should have stopped it after the eighth round," Freddie said. "Margarito had no chance to win by then and his face was a mess. After round ten, I thought, 'They have to stop it now. If the corner doesn't stop it, someone else will.' But they didn't. Margarito might never fight again after this. For sure, he won't be the same fighter."

Bernard Hopkins once said, "If you don't know how to control your emotions, that's a signed death warrant in boxing." Chad Dawson controlled his emotions when it mattered most—in the ring during his rematch against Hopkins.

Chad Dawson's Revenge

Chad Dawson vs. Bernard Hopkins— April 28, 2012

On April 28, 2012, Chad Dawson fought a rematch against Bernard Hopkins at Boardwalk Hall in Atlantic City. Hopkins's World Boxing Council light-heavyweight title was on the line. But the stakes were higher than that for Dawson.

Dawson got into boxing at a young age. His father, Rick Dawson, fought professionally from 1982 through 1984 and compiled a 1–6–1 record. The one fighter he did beat finished his career with 3 wins against 48 losses and 30 KOs by.

Prior to facing Hopkins, Dawson had beaten some good fighters, most notably Eric Harding, Tomasz Adamek, Glen Johnson (twice), and Antonio Tarver (twice). His one loss was a technical-decision defeat at the hands of Jean Pascal in a fight cut short by an ugly gash caused by a head butt above Chad's left eye. At various time, he had held the WBC and IBF 175-pound titles.

"My father took me to the gym when I was eight and put me in the ring with my older brother, Ricky," Chad would reminisce at the peak of his own career. "Ricky gave me a bloody nose, but it was no big thing. He did that at home all the time.

"This is just my opinion," Dawson added, choosing his words with care. "But my father didn't have a good career and the truth is, I don't think he expected me to make it. He looks at me now, and I think he's saying, 'I was there; I could have done it.' All the things he wanted to do in boxing, I'm doing them now. And he says to himself, 'That should have been me.' He doesn't get as much joy out of what I've done in boxing as I'd like him to."

Four years after Rick Dawson retired, Bernard Hopkins turned pro following a fifty-six-month period of incarceration in Graterford State Penitentiary.

"I didn't plan what happened to me in boxing," Hopkins said later. "I planned to not get in trouble again. I never wanted to go back to prison. So I did things right and made myself the best that I could be, and great things happened."

In the ring, Hopkins projected an aura of strength, physically and mentally. He talked like a street fighter but fought like a scientific one.

"I love the fundamentals of boxing," Bernard said. "I love the art of boxing. I love the hit and not get hit. I love that you can be aggressive but you can be aggressive smartly. It keeps my fire always burning. Yes, you're seeing talent. Yes, you're seeing genetics and a little bit of good fortune. But what you're really seeing are the benefits of planting my crops; taking care of my life, my body, and my mind. I've invested in eating the best foods, staying away from drinking and smoking and partying. There's people who hate me but they respect me. I didn't kiss ass. I didn't sell out. I didn't buck dance. Nobody gave me anything. I fought my way to the top. I took it. I'm cut from a different cloth than other fighters."

Hopkins and Dawson had met in the ring once before—on October 15, 2011, with Bernard's WBC title on the line. In round two, Dawson had picked up the pace with Hopkins trying to blunt the action. With twenty-two seconds left in the stanza, Bernard missed with a right hand, leveraged himself onto Dawson's upper back, and appeared to deliberately push his right forearm down on the back of Chad's neck. At the same time, he wrapped his left arm around Dawson's torso to steady himself and apply additional pressure to Chad's neck.

"Bernard was on his back and was more physical than he should have been," HBO commentator Emanuel Steward noted later.

Consider for a moment what it feels like to have Bernard Hopkins climb onto your back and jam his forearm into your neck. The intelligent response is to throw him off as fast as possible, which is what Dawson did to keep Hopkins (who was fouling) from damaging the back of his neck.

Chad rose up and, using his shoulder, shoved Bernard up and off. Hopkins fell backward to the canvas, landed hard on his left elbow and shoulder, and lay there in apparent pain. In response to questioning from a ring physician and referee Pat Russell, he said that he couldn't continue unless it was "with one hand." Russell then ruled that Bernard's trip to the canvas was not caused by a foul and declared Dawson the winner by knockout at 2 minutes, 48 seconds of the second round.

"He ran from me for three years," Dawson said in a post-fight interview. "I knew he didn't want the fight. He keeps talking about Philly and about being a gangster. He's no gangster. Gangsters don't quit. He's weak physically and mentally. He has no power. I was going to get on him, and he knew it."

Then, after a hearing, the California State Athletic Commission reached the dubious conclusion that the result of the fight should be changed to "no contest." That ruling allowed Hopkins to retain his *Ring Magazine* and WBC belts and led Dawson to declare, "I really don't believe Hopkins was hurt. We didn't see any doctor's notes or anything like that. I'm going to keep saying this—Bernard did not want to be in the ring with me that night. Maybe he undertrained and he didn't expect to see what he saw. Maybe he needed more time to get in better shape. I don't know, but I know I looked into Bernard's eyes, and Bernard did not want to be in the ring that night.

"Courage isn't crying and complaining and pretending you got hit low or your shoulder is hurt when things aren't going your way," Dawson continued. "A real champion gets up off the canvas and tries to fight. Bernard Hopkins is the opposite of courage. What he did to me in that fight—that was going to be my night, and he took it away from me by play-acting and crying. I lost all respect for him that fight. I don't like him, and I think he's a phony."

In due course, the fighters signed for a rematch. But Dawson was forced to accept the short end of a 70–30 purse split as a consequence of Hopkins's "injury" in their first encounter. That left Chad uncharacteristically angry.

Dawson is a soft-spoken man with a gentle demeanor, on the shy side with strangers but talkative when he feels comfortable with someone.

"My father had seven children by the time he was twenty-one," Chad told this writer in the days leading up to Hopkins–Dawson II. "I have four brothers and two sisters. None of us has ever been in jail. We might not be the smartest people you'll ever meet, but none of us has a criminal record. Our parents taught us to be good."

Chad and his wife, Crystal, had four sons.

"I enjoy being a father," Dawson said. "I'm most happy when I'm in my house with my kids. When I was little, my father never took me to school. I take the three oldest to school every morning; pick them up after school too. Having kids made me grow up a lot. I'm a lot more responsible now than I was before. My brothers and sisters and I grew up poor. I don't want my kids not to have the things they need to live right, but there's a line you have to draw. I'm still learning how to say 'no' to them.

"It's hard to get me mad," Dawson continued. "I'm not an angry person. But some of the stuff that goes on in the world. . . . I watch the news a lot and I hate it when I see people hurting other people, especially kids. I don't understand how a father and mother can hurt their own kids, but they do."

The knock against Dawson was that he lacked the fire inside that makes a fighter great; that he fought like he'd rather be doing something else.

"I hear the criticism," Chad said, "But most of it comes from guys who never put on a pair of gloves in their life, so I brush it off."

Still, Dawson was prone to adding to the conventional perception of his approach to boxing with thoughts like, "When I'm waiting in the dressing room before a fight, I want it to be over. . . . Training camp is hard for me. Most of the time, I'd rather not be there. One of the kids starts talking and I'm not with him to hear it or there's something else I miss that's going on with my family. . . . Right now, boxing is more of a job for me than anything else. . . . I don't like stupid stuff, ugliness, greed, disrespect. And I've been in boxing a long time, so I've run into a lot of stupid. If I didn't have a wife and kids, I'd probably have given it up by now. But if I wasn't in boxing, I don't know what I'd do. Probably nine-to-five somewhere, go home at the end of the day, and not worry about getting hit. You don't want to get hit. It's a bad feeling."

Meanwhile, Dawson's disdain for Hopkins was on display when the fighters met at Planet Hollywood in New York for a press conference to promote their rematch.

"I want to make one thing clear," Chad told the assembled media. "I came to fight, and he pulled a stunt. Legends don't act the way this guy acts. Legends don't do the things this guy does. Legends don't punk out."

Then Dawson stepped away from the podium, stared directly at Hopkins, and challenged, "Don't be a punk this time."

★★★

Chad Dawson arrived in his dressing room at Boardwalk Hall on fight night at 8:20 p.m. The core of Team Dawson was with him. Trainer John Scully, lawyer-advisor Walter Kane, cutman Rafael Garcia, strength and conditioning coach Axel Murrillo, Steve Geffrard (one of three sparring partners Chad had worked with in training camp), Chad's father, his brother Jermaine, camp aide Charles Robinson, and "G" (a close friend).

Dawson sat on a cushioned folding metal chair and put his feet up on another chair in front of him. He spent next the thirty-five minutes in that posture, listening to music through a pair of headphones with his eyes closed, nodding his head in rhythm to the sounds that were echoing through his mind.

At 8:55, referee Eddie Cotton came in to give Chad his pre-fight instructions.

"The referee will be important," Scully had said earlier in the day. "We need a referee who's smart enough to see what Bernard is doing and also has the mindset to stop it when Bernard goes over the line, which he'll do as long as he gets away with it."

Dawson removed his headphones. Cotton went through the standard litany of instructions ending with, "Do you have any questions?"

Scully held out his hands, palms up. "You know," he began.

"I know," Cotton interrupted. "I saw the last fight."

Scully proceeded to list a series of tactics that Hopkins had employed throughout his ring career.

Cotton, as referees always do, promised to keep a close eye on things.

After Cotton left, Dawson put his headphones back on and resumed listening to music. At 9:15, with the headphones still on, he put on his ring shoes, stood up to see how they felt, and sat down again.

Rick Dawson went down the hall to watch Hopkins's hands being taped. Naazim Richardson (Bernard's trainer) arrived moments later to watch Garcia tape Dawson's hands.

Garcia worked quickly. In twenty minutes, the job was done.

All the while, Chad's headphones were on.

At 9:55 p.m., Dawson took off his navy-blue track suit and put on his protective cup followed by steel-gray trunks with green trim. Then he began shadow-boxing in the center of the room, his first exercise of the evening.

Garcia gloved him up.

At 10:25, Chad and Scully went to work, hitting the pads in earnest. Earlier in the day, the trainer had told his charge, "There will be times tonight when you wonder what Hopkins is doing." At that point, Scully had postured, wiggled his body, and moved his shoulders in exaggerated fashion. "He's resting, is what he's doing. Don't let him do it."

More importantly, the trainer had told Chad, "You can't go into this fight walking on pins and needles because of what happened last time. If he pulls down on your neck again, you have to throw him off again. You cannot let him manhandle you."

Now the instructions were oriented toward technique.

"Jab. . . . Jab. . . . There you go. You got it. . . . One jab. . . . One jab. . . . Double jab. . . . When his hands go up, go to the body. . . . Don't let him get comfortable. . . . Push him back. . . . One-two. . . . Hook up top. . . . There you go; perfect. . . . If he gives you rounds, take them big. . . . Nasty jab. . . . Nasty jab. . . . That's it. Stick him. . . . If he comes inside, dig to the body. . . . Jab. . . . Long left. . . . You got the legs; he doesn't. . . . One-two. . . . That's it. . . . Don't try to be perfect. Let your hands go and you'll hit what's there. Anything you can hit, hit it. . . . Stay mentally strong. . . . Close the show."

Fifteen minutes later, Dawson was sweating profusely. Garcia helped him into his robe and Scully offered some final words of motivation.

"You got too much for him, but you got to bring it. You know what you can do. Go out and do it. Be what you're supposed to be. Take what's yours."

Despite being the challenger, Dawson was a 7-to-2 betting favorite. The general view was that he was too fast and too strong for the forty-seven-year-old Hopkins to handle. But there was an alternative view. Too often, Dawson was a reactive fighter rather than a proactive one. His work rate could be slowed by an opponent's inactivity. And Hopkins had a master's degree in delay, frustration, and opportunistic counterpunching.

The ethos of the fight was set early with Dawson seeking to engage and Hopkins fighting as though he wanted a twelve-round staredown. Bernard avoided exchanges to the greatest extent possible by means of lateral movement and retreat. When that didn't work, he clutched, grabbed, led with his head, mauled, went low, hit on the break, and did everything else he could to blunt Chad's assault.

After round four, HBO commentator Jim Lampley advised a national audience, "Somewhere, there are some great light-heavyweights rolling over in their graves at the dreadful action so far."

Lampley's comment came shortly after a key moment in the fight. Thirty seconds into the fourth stanza, a Hopkins head butt opened an ugly gash on the outside of Dawson's left eye.

"Keep your composure," Scully told his fighter between rounds. "Keep fighting. Let the cutman do his job."

Garcia controlled the flow of blood from that point on.

Near the end of round five, Dawson spun Hopkins around and Bernard made a beeline for the ropes, looking very much like a man who wanted to dive through them to end the fight. The crowd reacted accordingly.

"It looked to me like he was starting to jump out of the ring," Chad said in his dressing room after the fight. "And then he figured the fans wouldn't buy it."

As the bout progressed, Hopkins showed that he had one of the best chins in boxing. And he pulled the trigger on his right hand lead pretty fast for an old man. When Dawson landed solid shots to the head, which he did on occasion, Bernard fired back. That said, by the late rounds, Chad was landing two-for-one in exchanges and scoring well to the body.

In round eleven, Hopkins was clearly tired and looking for a breather. Toward that end, he sank to the canvas in a clinch and, moments later, tackled Dawson in a move that sent both men to the canvas. Cotton had warned Bernard for infractions on several occasions earlier in the fight but had never taken a point away for cumulative fouling. That would have been an ideal time to do it.

Then came the decision of the judges. Luis Rivera's score was announced first: 114–114, a draw. When the fighters entered the ring, Hopkins had been cheered and Dawson booed by the crowd. But the fans in attendance were fair minded enough to react derisively to Rivera's scorecard. Steve Weisfeld and Richard Flaherty restored sanity to the proceedings with 117–111 ledgers in Dawson's favor.

"He's a slick-ass fighter," Chad said in his dressing room after the fight. "Low blows, hitting on the break; you name it, he did it. He head-butted me seven, maybe eight times. It was obvious that the head-butt that caused the cut was on purpose. There were a couple of times when I almost lost my composure because of all the dirty things he was doing. But Scully kept telling me to stay disciplined, keep the heat on, keep my composure. Don't throw it all away on something dumb."

Chad shook his head and smiled.

"It's funny the way things work. Now that I beat him, there's a different feeling inside me about him than I had before. I don't feel sorry for him. But a lot of the bad feeling I had is gone."

High Drama in Las Vegas

Sergio Martínez vs. Julio César Chávez Jr.—
September 15, 2012

An athlete's life is characterized by peaks and valleys.

When Sergio Martínez was seventeen years old, he played forward in the #7 slot for a team called Defensoris in a junior amateur football (soccer) league in the province of Buenos Aires.

"We were playing against a team called Sportman," Sergio said, sitting in his suite at the Wynn Las Vegas Resort and Casino two days before his middleweight championship fight against Julio César Chávez Jr. "It was a tournament that was important for me to play well in. There were a lot of professional scouts in the stands. If I did well, it could take me places.

"I was very inspired that day," Sergio reminisced. "We won 4-to-0, and I scored three goals. On the first goal, there was a free throw from one of my teammates and I lifted it in an arc with my right foot over the goalie. That put us ahead in the score. The next goal was my best of the game. I stopped the ball with my chest, dribbled it past four defenders, and scored on a finesse kick with my right foot. The third goal was at the end of the game. Their goalie was at midfield. I got the ball, dribbled all the way in, and scored on an empty net. After each goal, everyone was celebrating and hugging. It was an incredible feeling.

"I wasn't born with the instincts that a great football player has," Sergio continued. "My technique wasn't good, but I was fast and strong. My emotions were my Achilles heel. I was very emotional when I played football. The next game was for the championship. There was a tie and the game went to penalty kicks. If I make my kick, we play on. If I miss it, we lose.

"I placed the ball down in front of the goal," Sergio recalled. "Then I got nervous. The goalie got bigger and bigger in my mind and the goal got smaller and smaller. I kicked the ball and it went slowly to the goalie, right to his hands. He didn't even have to move to field it. I was humiliated and embarrassed. It was one of the worst moments of my life. Because of my failure, we lost the championship game. I was so devastated that I quit the team."

Martínez has come a long way in the world of sports since then. On September 15, 2012, he and Julio César Chávez Jr. did battle at the Thomas & Mack Center in Las Vegas for the middleweight championship of the world in the most-anticipated fight of the year.

Martínez was born into poverty. Sports were his way out of the Argentinian ghetto. At age twenty, he walked into a boxing gym for the first time. That's late in life to begin learning the sweet science. "But I started at the right time for me," Martínez said later. "Too many fighters are pushed into boxing. When I began, I could make the decision to box as an adult."

Martínez turned pro in 1997 and fought twenty-four of his first twenty-five fights in Buenos Aires. In 2002, he moved to Spain and met trainer Gabriel Sarmiento. Sampson Lewkowicz became his co-manager in 2007 and brought him to the United States where Sergio lived in California and was promoted by Lou DiBella.

Martínez won the World Boxing Council middleweight crown in 2010 with a twelve-round decision over Kelly Pavlik. He successfully defended his title with knockout victories over Paul Williams, Sergeiy Dzinziruk, Darren Barker, and Matthew Macklin. At age thirty-seven, he had a record of 50 wins, 2 losses, and 2 draws. Regardless of the games that boxing's sanctioning bodies play, he was widely recognized as THE middleweight champion of the world.

Julio César Chávez Jr. traveled a road that was very different from the road Martínez traveled. Chávez was born in Culiacán, Mexico, on February 16, 1986. His father was widely regarded as Mexico's greatest fighter. Julio Jr. grew up as a child of privilege, the "son of the legend." But if life was a bed of roses for Julio Jr., there were a lot of thorns with the flowers. His parents divorced when he was young, which is difficult for any child. And his father, in addition to being a Mexican icon, was an alcoholic and a drug addict.

Julio Jr. turned pro in 2003 with no amateur fights on his résumé. His ring career was nurtured on weak opponents who were only marginally trained in the art of hurting. Eventually, Top Rank (his lead promoter) brought Freddie Roach in as Julio Jr.'s trainer and his maturation as a fighter began. By mid-2011, he had 42 victories and 1 draw in 43 fights.

Then the powers that be engaged in an ugly sleight of hand.

Martínez was the WBC middleweight champion by virtue of his victory over Kelly Pavlik. But Chávez Jr. was the godson of WBC president Jose Sulaimán. Martínez was stripped of his title and a WBC "world championship" bout was arranged between Chávez and Sebastian Zbik with the understanding that the winner would fight Martínez.

Except after Chávez beat Zbik, he refused to fight Martínez. Instead, he defended his belt in succession against Peter Manfredo Jr., Marco Antonio Rubio, and Andy Lee.

Finally, Julio César Chávez Jr. vs. Sergio Martínez was signed. But Martínez was deeply resentful of the fact that his championship had been unfairly taken from him and handed to Chávez. Worse, when the fight was made, Sergio was on the short end of a 60–40 purse split and Chávez got top billing in the promotion.

Despite his hard journey through life, Martínez has a warmth and elegance about him accentuated by charismatic good looks. One can imagine him formally attired, dancing the Argentinian tango. After winning the title, he became an advocate for women who were subjected to domestic violence and children who were targeted by bullies in school. He'd never been a trash-talker and steadfastly avoided demeaning opponents. But the build-up to Chávez–Martínez brought a new range of emotions to him.

"I've known Sergio for a long time," Sampson Lewkowicz said. "I've never seen him this angry. He has always treated his opponents with respect. But he feels that something was stolen from him and given to Chávez and that Chávez let it happen."

The trash-talking began on the kickoff media tour and continued up until the fight. Among other things, Martínez said, "Chávez has been hiding in the hen house. Now it's time for the chicken to come out. . . . I do not respect Chávez as a champion. The only reason he is called a champion is because of his last name and who his father is. . . . A victory for me would be justice because Chávez is a lie. . . . I'm not insulting him. I'm just telling the truth."

There was a buzz in the media center at the Wynn Resort and Casino during fight week. Chávez–Martínez was a fight that boxing people wanted to see. Stylistically, the matchup all but guaranteed excitement. By Tuesday of fight week, the Thomas & Mack Center was sold out.

Martínez was a 7-to-4 betting favorite (the first time in Chávez's career that he would enter the ring as an underdog). The assumption was that Julio had never been hit as hard as Sergio would hit him, that Sergio's southpaw stance would give Julio trouble, and that Chávez would be unable to adjust as the fight wore on.

Chávez's training regimen was also a factor for those who thought that Martínez would win. It's axiomatic that, if a fighter doesn't give 100 percent in training, he won't be at 100 percent during a fight. And it was common knowledge that Julio had slacked off in training for Martínez.

That said, Chávez appeared to be in good condition at the weigh-in. After struggling to make weight for recent fights, he tipped the scales for his confrontation with Martínez at 158 pounds; two pounds under the middleweight limit and one pound less than Sergio.

Moreover, Martínez was thirty-seven years old with a lot of wear and tear on his body. Throw out his perfect one-punch knockout of Paul Williams two years earlier and, in recent years, he'd looked like a gifted but vulnerable fighter.

★★★

Martínez arrived at his dressing room at the Thomas & Mack Center on fight night at 5:30 p.m. Red-cushioned folding metal chairs ringed the room. The walls were cream-colored cinderblock. The three men and one woman who would be in Sergio's corner during the fight were with him—trainer Pablo Sarmiento, assistant trainer Naazim Richardson, Dr. Roger Anderson (Sergio's cutman), and Raquel Bordons.

Bordons taught and practiced physical therapy in Spain. She had been in Sergio's camp for the final few days prior to his two most recent outings. This time, she'd been summoned ten days before the fight to deal with a slight muscle tear on the upper left side of Sergio's ribcage. The injury was painful and had interfered with his breathing.

Sebastian Martínez (Sergio's brother), Miguel Depablos (a friend), and Nathan Lewkowicz (Sampson's son) rounded out the group.

Normally, Martínez listened to music in his dressing room in the hours before a fight. But the speakers he'd brought with him weren't working. He took a smartphone from his pocket and began to text.

Nathan Lewkowicz went next door to wish Matthew Macklin well in an undercard bout that he'd be fighting against Joachim Alcine. Six months earlier, Martínez had knocked Macklin out in eleven rounds at Madison Square Garden.

Lewkowicz returned with a prize. Macklin had offered his speakers to Team Martínez. Soon, Latin rap sounded throughout the room.

During the next few hours, Sergio talked with members of his team, texted well-wishers, and tended to the rituals of boxing. For much of that time, Bordons massaged his upper body.

Macklin vs. Alcine appeared on a large flat-screen television mounted on the wall at one end of the room. Their encounter was brief. Macklin stopped Alcine in the first round.

"I am happy for him," Sergio said. "I like Matthew. Tonight he is my friend."

Referee Tony Weeks came into the room and gave Sergio his pre-fight instructions.

Macklin followed, fresh from his ring triumph.

Sergio's face lit up. "Matthew!" he exclaimed.

The two men embraced.

Macklin offered a quick "Good luck" and left.

Martínez began moving slowly around the room in rhythm with the music. Then he lay down on the industrial gray carpet. Bordons stretched his legs and massaged his upper body. When she was done, Sergio rose and moved around the room again; this time, jabbing and shadow-boxing.

At eight o'clock, Sarmiento gloved Martínez up.

Sergio hit the pads with Pablo for the equivalent of three rounds with a minute between each segment.

Roger Anderson greased Martínez down.

Bordons massaged Sergio's upper body one last time.

Sarmiento helped the fighter into his ring jacket.

One consideration to be factored into determining whether a fighter will win or lose is whether he really wants to be in the ring that night.

Sergio had the fight he wanted for the largest payday of his career. There was no place on earth that he would rather be.

★★★

The atmosphere inside the arena was electric. It was a pro-Chávez crowd, but Martínez had his followers.

Prior to the bout, Roach had cautioned, "I've told Julio again and again, 'You can't just follow Martínez around the ring. If you do, you'll walk into a left hand. You have to cut the ring off.' Julio doesn't miss a beat in the gym. In the gym, he has the strategy down perfectly based on the way Martínez moves. But the gym and the fight are two different places."

"And another thing," Roach continued, "We've watched the tape of Sergio's fight against Pavlik a lot. He took some of the middle rounds off. Julio can't let him rest. When Sergio tries to rest, Julio has to make him fight."

Chávez had echoed that theme, saying, "I have to stay on top of him all night long; don't give him room to move or time to think."

But once the fight began, those plans didn't come to fruition.

Chávez fought cautiously in the early going, allowing Martínez to circle, dart in and out, and control the distance between them. Also, Sergio threw punches—a lot of punches, mostly jabs and straight left hands—that landed consistently. His jab, in particular, discouraged Julio from coming forward aggressively. When Chávez did manage to work his way inside, rather than tie him up, Martínez drove him off with punches or pushed him back with the superior strength of his legs and upper body.

In round three, a left uppercut opened a cut inside Chávez's mouth. By round five, the skin around his left eye was discolored and swollen. In round six, he began bleeding from the nose.

Round after round, Martínez potshotted his opponent and rested when he wanted to. The only difference between one round and the next was that Chávez got beaten up more badly in some rounds than others. The fight had the look of a matador versus an overmatched bull.

There were times when Sergio chose to trade punches. Almost always on those occasions, he got the better of the action. Chávez showed a good chin but not much more. He might have made a greater effort to take the play away from Martínez. But that's easier said than done when an adversary is getting off first and throwing seventy-five punches a round. Julio simply couldn't solve the puzzle in front of him.

In the late going, Martínez was standing in the center of the ring at the start of each round, while Chavez was slow to get off his stool. After round nine, Roach threatened to stop the fight if his charge didn't show him something in the next three minutes that indicated he could win. But the boxing lesson continued with Sergio circling, jabbing, and getting off first.

A clash of heads in round ten opened a gash on Martínez's scalp to go with a cut above his left eye. But Julio looked far worse for wear than Sergio.

In round eleven, Chávez managed to corner his foe on several occasions. But each time, Martínez's punches drove him off.

Going into the final round, Martínez had outlanded Chávez by a 314–141 margin. The fight was a shutout on two of the judges' scorecards with Julio winning a solitary round on the third. Chávez could have won the last stanza 10–0 and it wouldn't have mattered.

Then the matador got gored.

Chávez started slowly in round twelve, moving forward with his hands held high. His left eye was swollen shut. His right eye was ringed by abrasions and his lips were puffy.

Martínez kept circling, jabbing. Twenty-eight seconds elapsed before Julio threw his first punch of the round, a tentative stay-away-from-me right hand. Ten seconds later, he offered a meaningless jab. Both punches missed.

One minute into round twelve, Chávez had thrown three punches and landed none. Then he stepped up the pace and forced Martínez against the ropes. With 1:28 left, Julio scored with a sharp left hook up top. Sergio was hurt.

Two more hooks landed flush.

Suddenly, with 1:23 left in the fight, Martínez was on the canvas and in trouble.

There was pandemonium in the arena. For Martínez, that "pandemonium"—translated in classic Greek—was "the region of all demons."

Getting up off the floor comes from pride and a fighter not wanting to go back to that place in his life where he came from.

Sergio crawled to the ropes and lifted himself up at the count of six.

Referee Tony Weeks beckoned Chávez in. Julio had seventy seconds to finish the job. Those seventy seconds showed why many people feel that boxing at its best is the greatest sport of all.

Chávez now loomed very large in front of Martínez, and the ring seemed very small.

Julio went for broke. Sergio, too dazed and weak to tie Chávez up and with his legs too unsteady to move out of danger, hurled punches back at his foe.

With one minute left in the fight, Martínez tried to clinch and Julio dismissively threw him to the canvas. Sergio staggered to his feet. Weeks, appropriately, chose not to give him extra time to recover and ordered that the action resume immediately without wiping Sergio's gloves.

Fifty-two seconds remained. But now, Chávez too was exhausted.

At the final bell, both fighters knew that Martínez had won.

In the dressing room after the fight, Sergio had bruises beneath each eye. Five stitches would be needed to close the cut above his left eye and two staples to close the gash on his scalp. He'd also suffered a hairline fracture of his left hand (most likely in round four) and torn ligaments in his right knee (when knocked down in the final round).

Martínez and Bordons embraced. During the fight, Raquel had worked on Sergio in the corner after round four and again after round seven.

"Without you, this wouldn't have been possible," Martínez told her.

Then Sergio and Raquel broke down in tears.

Seanie Monaghan took it for granted that, each time he fought, there would be damage to his face. "I was at a bar that James Moore [a retired boxer] owns the other night," Seanie told me. "There was James, John Duddy, Matthew Macklin, Michael Conlan, Seamus McDonough, and myself. I was looking at the faces, thinking, 'We all have scars.' It's the price we pay. You just don't want to pay a price where something like your eye is functioning differently for the rest of your life. But if you're thinking about things like that too much, you shouldn't be a fighter."

Seanie Monaghan Loved to Fight

Seanie Monaghan vs. Rex Stanley— April 13, 2013

Fighting in the new millennium, Seanie Monaghan was a "throwback fighter." In the 1940s, he would have been a neighborhood fight club headliner and local hero.

Seanie is the oldest of four children. His parents immigrated to the United States from Ireland and settled in Long Beach, a town of thirty-three thousand located on a barrier island east of New York City. Long Beach faces the Atlantic Ocean. There was a time when it styled itself as "the Riviera of the East" and vied with Atlantic City as a tourist destination for New Yorkers during the hot summer months. That time is long gone. In recent decades, the town has gone through cycles of urban decay and renewal.

Seanie grew up in Long Beach and still lives there. His father ran an upholstering business. His mother was a physical therapist. His paternal grandmother was one of seventeen children, so he has a large family, many of whom still live in Ireland. His wife earned a master's degree in special education from Hofstra University. They have a young son and daughter.

But there's a painful backstory.

"I was a lost teenager," Seanie told this writer. "I had no ambition or direction. Everything was short-term. I didn't care where I was going. I smoked weed every day. I wrestled a bit in high school and played some sports like football and lacrosse. But the other guys were better than me. And if I wasn't good at something right away, instead of working to get better, I gave up on it."

Seanie graduated from Long Beach High School in 1999. "Barely," he acknowledged. But trouble was brewing.

"There was an unhealthy culture in Long Beach and I got caught up in it," Seanie recalled. "I wasn't a bad kid. My mother and father are good hard-working people. I came from a decent home. I wasn't a street guy. I never stole anything or sold drugs. But a lot of people in my family have had drinking problems. I was drunk a lot and I tried just about every drug there was except heroin.

"Around the time I was fifteen," Seanie said, "I started getting into bar fights. I was working as a barback [a bartender's assistant] and was surrounded by grown men who were drinking and I'd try to keep up with them. A fight would start, sometimes with me. Or if it started with someone else, I'd jump in. People would crowd around and cheer. I'd always wanted to be really really good at something. And there it was. Knocking guys out. It felt so good. There were a lot of fights, fifty or sixty over the years. My nose got broken. I was constantly hurting my hands. I'd come home with a black eye or cuts and try to hide it from my mother. I look back on it all now and say, 'Forget about everything else. Look at the stress I put my mother through.' I wasn't a bad kid. I got along with people, all kinds of people, when I wasn't fighting. But it was like, if there was a problem, I was the Long Beach representative. One time in a bar fight, I got stabbed in the throat and needed thirty or forty stitches. I was arrested a few times. The last time was for assaulting a police officer who was trying to break up one of the fights. I didn't know he was a police officer. He grabbed me from behind and I threw him off. The judge gave me a break. He put me on probation and told me, 'If I see you in my courtroom again, you're doing five years hard time.' That straightened me out. I stopped drinking and doing drugs. I don't drink or smoke at all now. I haven't had a drink in more than ten years. Casual drinking is okay if you can do it, but I couldn't."

As part of Seanie's probation, he was required to attend meetings at Alcoholics Anonymous and Narcotics Anonymous and also attend an anger management course.

"The anger management course really pissed me off," Seanie said "I didn't think I needed to be there. But over time, I realized that little things were making me furious and I was getting mad for no reason. Even though I might not have been starting the fights, I was looking for them. It took me a while, but finally I understood that I had to change. I learned to take a step back when there was a problem and how to control my emotions. I had relatives in Ireland who were telling me, 'You're on probation. Come back here before they throw you in jail.' But the problem wasn't that I was in Long Beach. The problem was me.

"Then I looked at my life as a whole. I hadn't built anything. All I was doing was drifting from day to day. I was in danger of losing any chance I had for a good future. My whole personality is different now. I've learned discipline and how to dedicate myself to things that are important to me. I'm a much better husband and father than I could possibly have been back then. I'm much happier than I used to be."

After Seanie stopped drinking, a friend named Bobby Calabrese suggested that he try his hand at boxing. That sounded like a good idea, so he went to the PAL gym in Freeport, which had a boxing club run by a firefighter named Joe Higgins.

"Two guys were in the ring, sparring," Seanie remembered. "I liked what I saw. There was a trainer there. I told him, 'I'm Seanie Monaghan from Long Beach. I want to be a boxer.'"

"He was a real character," Higgins recalled. "A kid off the street with a chip on his shoulder. He told me he wanted to spar that day, and I started laughing. He said, 'I knock guys out on the street.' And I said, 'Yeah; but this ain't the street.'"

The next six weeks were about footwork, balance, head movement, and how to throw a jab.

"Finally, Joe said I could spar," Seanie said with a smile. "And the first punch I got hit with, I went down on my butt."

Seanie had fifteen amateur fights starting at age twenty-six and turned pro in 2010. By age thirty-one, he'd had eighteen pro fights in less than three years. Joe Higgins was still his trainer. His manager was P. J. Kavanagh.

"I'm usually the aggressor," Seanie said of his fighting style. "I come at you, go to the body a lot, and don't stop coming. Getting hit doesn't bother me that much. I kind of zone out when I'm in a fight. The biggest problem I have is that I cut too easily. My biggest fear is that I'll be in a fight I know I can win and it's stopped on cuts. And I have to get past my natural instinct to try to just smash everybody."

"Seanie works so freakin' hard," Higgins declared. "He takes a week or two off from the gym after a fight; but even then, he runs. And outside of those breaks, he hasn't missed a day in the gym since I started with him. He does everything I ask him to do. He's in monster shape every time he fights. I tell the other guys in the gym, 'Study this guy. Be like him.'"

But Monaghan had started boxing late in life and was relatively slow in a sport where speed kills. Top Rank matchmaker Brad Goodman, who took a special interest in Seanie, observed, "The first time I saw him, he had no technical skills. But he had some natural ability and I'm impressed with how much he has improved since then. It's our job as matchmakers to see that he isn't in with an opponent who's too advanced for him at this stage of his career because Seanie has a warrior mentality. He'll fight anyone you put in front of him."

TV commentator Steve Farhood noted, "Seanie is a good example of a fighter who started out with limited skills and has made something of himself through determination and hard work. He's always in better shape than his opponent. There was, and still is, a lot of room for improvement. But he's now a competent fighter. He's also one of those guys who's easy to root for. He's very likeable and unpretentious. You hope he succeeds."

And promoter Lou DiBella added, "Seanie will never be on a pound-for-pound list. He'll probably never be a world champion. But he's a blood-and-guts warrior. His arsenal consists of heart and balls. He's a good guy. And I'd sure as hell rather watch Seanie in a good club fight than a lot of so-called world-class fighters."

There was a buzz in the room whenever Seanie fought. And more important, there were asses in seats. Seanie started out as a Long Beach attraction. And his fan base grew after that. This appeal enabled him to remain a promotional free agent. Because he was a ticket-seller, promoters were willing to use him on a fight-by-fight basis without requiring him to sign a long-term promotional contract.

That led to Seanie vs. Rex Stanley on the undercard of an April 13, 2013, title bout between Nonito Donaire and Guillermo Rigondeaux promoted by Top Rank at Radio City Music Hall.

Stanley was thirty-six years old. Prior to the fight, his record stood at 11–4 with 7 knockouts. But he'd won only once in the preceding thirty-five months (a four-round decision twenty-three months earlier over an opponent whose record was 0–1 at the time). Stanley hadn't fought since then.

Radio City Music Hall bills itself as "the biggest stage in New York." It's a long way from fighting on the street outside a Long Beach bar.

Seanie spent fight day at a Manhattan hotel and arrived at his dressing room at Radio City at 8:00 p.m. Higgins and cutman George Mitchell were already there. Joe had put in a full day at the gym in Freeport before driving to Manhattan for the fight.

Team Monaghan was sharing the dressing room with seven other undercard fighters. This was the "red corner" dressing room. All eight of the fighters in it were expected to win. The "blue corner" dressing room was within shouting distance down the corridor.

Donaire and Rigondeaux each had his own dressing room where they could dictate the mood—whether or not there was music, who said what. Undercard fighters can't control their surroundings. They coexist with other fighters and their teams.

Some of the fighters near Seanie were sitting quietly. Others were laughing and talking loudly.

The room was hot and stuffy with a claustrophobic feel; long and narrow with a low ceiling and thirteen vanity mirrors. Fifty people, many of them physically active men, were crammed into a space designed for thirteen chorus girls.

Seanie was wearing faded blue jeans, a black T-shirt, and blue sweatshirt. His fight was scheduled for ten o'clock. For a while, he talked quietly with Higgins, sipping occasionally from a bottle of water.

At 8:20 p.m., Juan Perez of Top Rank came into the room and told Seanie, "Your opponent's not here yet. I hope he comes."

"Me too," Seanie said.

The undercard bouts were visible on a television monitor at the far end of the room. In the third fight of the evening, Tyler Canning (who'd been flown in from Wyoming on the assumption that he'd lose to prospect Dario Socci) scored an upset decision triumph. Cheers erupted in the "blue" dressing room down the corridor.

Seanie lay down on the carpet in a corner of the room and closed his eyes.

Socci returned, angry. "Un-fucking-believable," he said to no one in particular. "What the fuck were the judges looking at?" Then he picked up his cellphone and started texting.

Other fighters fought and returned, some with their faces bruised and swollen. In boxing, even winning takes a toll.

At nine o'clock, Seanie got up from the floor and sat on a chair. Higgins began taping his hands. P. J. Kavanagh came in to wish his fighter well. When the taping was done, Seanie put on his shoes and trunks. At 9:45 p.m., trainer and fighter went into the corridor and began working the pads.

"Start with the jab," Higgins instructed. "That's it. . . . Work with the jab from the opening bell. Then go after his body. . . . Turn the hook over. . . . Good. That's what I'm looking for. Show me that again. . . ."

Down the corridor in full view, Rex Stanley and his trainer were engaged in a similar exercise.

"One-two," Higgins continued. "Again. . . . One more. . . . Jab. . . . Hook. . . . Keep everything nice and short. No gorilla punches. . . . Beautiful. . . . Nice deep breath."

When they were done, Seanie sat on a stool in the corridor and closed his eyes.

"I was thinking about my son," he said later. "Sammy is going to see this fight someday, and I wanted it to look good for him. And I was thinking, I can do all the work in the world in the gym, but it doesn't mean anything if I don't perform when it counts."

Moments before leaving for the ring, Seanie put on his last piece of clothing; a faded Kelly green sweatshirt that he'd worn for his first pro fight. There had been a problem on that night in 2010. Once Seanie had gloved up, the sweatshirt wouldn't fit over his gloves. Higgins had to cut a slit in each cuff to get it on.

"People tell me all the time that I should get a fancy robe," Seanie noted. "But why change what works."

This was the second fight card in the history of Radio City Music Hall. Roy Jones vs. David Telesco on January 15, 2000, had headlined the first. Like its predecessor, this card sold out. Seanie's purse was $20,000. Team Monaghan would also receive 20 percent of the revenue from the tickets it sold. Seanie had sold five hundred tickets and come back for more, but none were available.

Radio City Music Hall was built for large stage spectacles, not boxing. The sight lines are good, but most of the seats are far away from the action. For most of the night, the capacity crowd of 6,145 relied on four large video screens to see what the two small figures in the ring were doing.

There were cheers from the crowd as Seanie made his way to the ring. "This place is so big that the fans were a little far away this time," he said afterward. "It means a lot to me that they're there. But to be honest— and this is no disrespect to my people; I love them—I used to think about my fans during a fight. Then I realized that my mind can't be in two places, so I kind of block them out once I get to the ring."

Seanie vs. Rex Stanley was scheduled for eight rounds. It was much shorter than that. Stanley had some skills but he didn't have a chin, which is a prerequisite for a professional fighter. Seanie fought like a professional and did what he had to do, taking his time and moving forward behind a stiff jab. Midway through the first round, he backed his opponent into a corner and landed an overhand right flush. Stanley dropped to the canvas and rose on wobbly legs. He might have twisted an ankle, but the rest of him didn't look so good either. Referee Harvey Dock appropriately halted the bout before another punch was thrown. The time was 1:51 of round one.

After beating Stanley, Seanie won ten more fights in a row against relatively low-level competition.

"Seanie believes in himself, and that's important for a fighter," Brad Goodman observed. "He's moving up in the rankings now. Maybe a champion will be looking for a soft touch and figure Seanie for an easy mark. It would be a nice payday for Seanie. And let me tell you something: Seanie is not soft. Seanie would be in shape. He'd fight his heart out. And this is boxing. On a given night, anything can happen."

But success at the highest levels of boxing wasn't to be. On July 15, 2017, Seanie fought undefeated Marcus Browne and was stopped in the second round. Then, after a comeback victory against Evert Bravo, he lost by decision to Sullivan Barrera and was knocked out by Callum Johnson. After losing to Johnson, he retired from boxing with a 29–3 (7 KOs) ring record.

Gennady Golovkin's Kingdom
Gennady Golovkin vs. Curtis Stevens—
November 2, 2013

Times Square in New York City is often referred to as "the crossroads of the world." On November 2, 2013, the crossroads moved nine blocks south to Madison Square Garden, where Brooklyn and Kazakhstan converged for the middleweight title fight between Curtis Stevens and Gennady Golovkin.

Golovkin was born in Kazakhstan in 1982. He turned pro after winning a silver medal as a middleweight at the 2004 Athens Olympics and had a reported amateur record of 345 wins against 5 losses. Prior to facing Stevens, he was undefeated in 28 professional bouts with 25 knockouts and had never been knocked down as an amateur or pro. Sergio Martínez might have been the "lineal" middleweight champion at the time. But Gennady (the WBA champion) had come to be regarded as the best 160-pound fighter in the world.

Golovkin introduced himself to the American public with a fifth-round knockout of Grzegorz Proksa on HBO in 2012. Explosive triumphs over Gabriel Rosado and Matthew Macklin followed. In the ring, he was like a threshing machine cutting through a wheat field. Or a tank firing live ammunition. Choose your metaphor. He was a technically sound predator who had mastered the art of controlling the distance between himself and his opponent and methodically destroyed adversaries with hard precision punching and a pressure assault. Abel Sanchez (then Gennady's trainer) likened his pupil's relentless attack to that of Julio César Chávez in his prime.

Cornerman Al Gavin once said, "If you're making a list of all the attributes a fighter needs, start with a chin. If you don't have a chin, forget about being a fighter."

Golovkin's chin seemed to have been carved out of granite. One could argue that he didn't move his head enough and got hit more than he should have. But Freddie Roach, who knew greatness as Manny Pacquiao's trainer, opined, "Golovkin is a great fighter. He's strong. He has good fundamentals. He cuts the ring off well. I've watched his ring generalship. It's fucking great. Ring generalship is a lost art, but Golovkin has it. Ninety-five percent of the time, he's in the right position. If you do that, you win fights. He's heavy-handed. He's a nice kid. I'm a big fan."

Some fighters keep the "0" on their record by avoiding other top fighters. Golovkin hadn't turned down a single opponent. The converse wasn't true. More than a few top fighters were avoiding Gennady. HBO had a November 2 date for Golovkin and needed an opponent. Twenty-eight-year-old Curtis Stevens stepped into the void.

Stevens was born and raised in the Brownsville section of Brooklyn where he lived with his mother (a counselor at the New York City Department of Juvenile Justice) and younger sister. Often when he was young and did roadwork in the morning, his mother had ridden on her bike behind him. Over time, words and images chronicling the streets where Curtis ran were inked into his skin as tattoos:

On his back—"Brownsville"
On his neck—"Don of Dons"
On his right biceps—"Showtime" ("That's my street name," Stevens explained.)
On his left forearm—The image of a heart and crucifix with the words "Pain Is Love" and "Tanya" (his mother's name)
On his right hand—"Brother," "Hood," and "D.B.D" ("'Death before dishonor.' That's the code I live by.")
On his left hand—"R.I.P Lo Bloccs" ("'Lo Bloccs' is what we called Anthony Reid. He was a friend of mine. He died on New Year's Day 2003. A cop shot him. Wrong place, wrong time.")

"I know the streets," Stevens acknowledged. "But I know the boundaries of life too. Don't be out there selling drugs because, sooner or later, you're gonna get locked up. Don't get in a fight that will land you in trouble. With every option there's a repercussion, so think before you make a move. My mother raised me to respect people."

Stevens's fistic education began at age five when an uncle took him to the Starrett City Gym in Brooklyn. He had his first amateur fight at age eight. The high point of his amateur career were twin 178-pound championships in 2002 at the United States Amateur Championships and National Golden Gloves. He turned pro in 2004 and came into the Golovkin fight with a 25–3 record. Most his bouts had been at light-heavyweight. He was undefeated with three first-round knockouts in four fights after going down to 160 pounds.

Standing only five feet, seven inches tall, Stevens was a puncher with an aggressive attacking style. "I put on a show," he said. "I knock people out. I demolish them. I'm fast. I have power. My hook is like a meteorite. You know how, if a giant meteorite hits the earth, we'd all be gone. Well, if I hit you with my hook, you're gone. I can hit you one time, and the fight's over. And I can finish. Once I hurt you, I'm gonna take you out."

"Outside the ring, I'm a nice person," Stevens continued. "In the ring, I'm a different man. In the ring, I'm someone you don't want to mess with. I get angry; I get violent and crazy. In the ring, I'm the most dangerous person in the world."

Golovkin had made his Madison Square Garden debut ten months earlier with a seventh-round knockout of Gabriel Rosado. Golovkin–Stevens would be his second appearance at The Mecca of Boxing.

Outside the ring, Gennady has a gentle demeanor that masks how brutally he practices his trade. He's laid back and smiles a lot. On the street, he could pass for a computer geek. His first language is Russian, but he speaks fluent Kazakh and some German. In interviews with the American media, he often waits for a question to be translated into Russian before answering in English.

There was a modest amount of trash-talking in the week leading up to Golovkin–Stevens, most of it coming from Curtis, who called Gennady "an overrated hype job" and promised to "knock him the fuck out."

That earned a rejoinder from Golovkin, who observed, "Dangerous atmosphere, different style. I am sportsman. He has big mouth."

"Gennady doesn't get angry," Abel Sanchez noted. "He gets focused." Then Sanchez said of Stevens, "He's going to get destroyed. He doesn't belong in the ring with Triple-G. You've seen what Gennady has done so far. He can do that to anybody."

That led Curtis to respond, "Abel is saying I'm gonna get knocked out in three rounds. Abel is saying I'm gonna get knocked out in six. Abel is stupid."

Meanwhile, in a calmer moment, Stevens acknowledged, "This is something that I dreamed about since I was eight years old and stepped in the ring for the first time. And to be here and to have it in my grasp, it's amazing. I think about it every night. Some nights, there's anxiety from thinking about it too much and I don't get good. So in my mind, I'm saying, 'You've just got to grab it. You're either gonna give it up or go in there and take it right out of his hands.' Come November second, I'm gonna be great."

"Golovkin is a fighter," Curtis added. "He might not look like one outside the ring, but I know he's good. People are saying he's the best middleweight in the world. After I beat him, what does that make me?"

★★★

Gennady Golovkin arrived at his dressing room on the second floor of The Theater at Madison Square Garden on fight night at 8:05 p.m. Max Golovkin (his brother) and two other team members were with him.

The room was small, roughly twelve feet square, with cream-colored cinderblock walls and a speckled-gray tile floor. A large blue-and-gold Kazakhstani flag hung from the wall above a rectangular plastic table. Television cables taped to the floor and seven folding metal chairs with black cushions made the space seem smaller than it was.

Gennady began doing stretching exercises. At 8:20 p.m., Abel Sanchez came in. The trainer had three fighters on the undercard including heavy-weight Mike Perez, who would be in HBO's first televised fight of the evening. Sanchez would move back and forth between dressing rooms for much of the night.

Other members of Team Golovkin came and went. Gennady checked his cell phone for text messages. Music at a low decibel level sounded in the background; an eclectic mix ranging from a woman's soft voice over a gentle rock beat to gangsta rap.

There was little conversation. Most of the time, Gennady was on his feet, pacing, stretching. At one point, he sat down and massaged his own fingers, hands, and wrists. At nine o'clock, he took a milk chocolate Hershey bar out of his gym bag and peeled off the wrapper.

"Is that for energy?" a state athletic commission inspector assigned to the dressing room asked.

"No. I'm hungry and it tastes good."

All fighters are aware of the stakes involved when they fight—financially and in terms of their physical well-being. But they process it in different ways. At a time when many fighters' nerves are gyrating on the edge, Golovkin seemed calm and emotionally self-sufficient, almost serene.

Referee Harvey Dock came in and gave Gennady his pre-fight instructions.

"The three-knockdown rule is waived. . . . The Unified Rules of Boxing are in effect. . . . If your mouthpiece comes out, keep fighting until I call a lull in the action. You have two mouthpieces, correct?"

"Three," Sanchez answered.

Abel wrapped Gennady's hands.

There was more moving about. The stretching became more vigorous. Golovkin lay down on a towel and contorted his body into positions that most people would find troubling. Then he rose, took a jar of Vaseline, and greased down his own face.

Sanchez gloved Gennady up. Max massaged his brother's legs, back, and shoulders.

Golovkin's eyes hardened. A transformation had begun. The gentle smile was gone. Now he was stomping around the room, growling, flexing his muscles. Most athletes, not just fighters, need meanness in them to be great. The meanness was there.

Round one of Mike Perez vs. Magomed Abdusalamov came into view on a small television monitor. Sanchez had opted to remain with Golovkin. Ben Lira was the head man in Perez's corner.

Gennady hit the pads with Abel for thirty seconds. Each punch was thrown with technical precision and thudding power. Then he paced and stretched some more before hitting the pads for another thirty seconds. Finally, he slapped himself on the temple with closed gloves. Left, right, left, right. More than a tap.

Sanchez applied more Vaseline to Gennady's face.

Perez vs. Abdusalamov dragged on.

"What round is it?" Abel asked.

"Six."

Twenty minutes lay ahead before Golovkin would leave for the ring. He paced, shadow-boxed, and paced some more before sitting on a chair in a corner of the room where he bowed his head in concentration.

"It was for focus," he later explained. "This is a serious business. I understand my situation. It was for concentration in the fight. To concentrate on speed, power, and distance. To concentrate on what I must do to win for myself and my family."

Perez–Abdusalamov ended with Perez winning a unanimous decision. No one knew it at the time, but hours later, Abdusalamov would be in critical condition, in a coma after emergency surgery to relieve bleeding and swelling in his brain. He would survive but never be whole again.

★★★

A casual observer who saw Golovkin and Stevens at the opening bell and knew nothing about either man might have thought that Gennady was a sacrificial lamb. Curtis was shorter but more visibly muscled with a particularly menacing aura about him. He could beat a lot of middleweights, but Golovkin wasn't one of them.

Stevens had the proper mindset but he was competing against a different class of fighter. Or as former WBO heavyweight champion Lamon Brewster observed after disposing of hopelessly overmatched 309-pound Joe Lenhart, "It's like when you look at a lion and he's about to eat you. It's not about what you're thinking. It's what the lion is thinking."

Golovkin began by working off of, and controlling the fight with, his jab. Stevens cranked up left hooks from time to time but couldn't connect solidly. With thirty seconds left in round two, Gennady fired a short compact textbook left hook that landed flush on Curtis's jaw and deposited him on the canvas.

Stevens struggled to his feet, dazed, and survived till the bell. Thereafter, he tried valiantly to work his way back into the fight. There was no quit in him. Late in round four, he flurried off the ropes and landed some good shots. Midway through round five, he scored with a solid hook and right hand up top followed by a hook to the body. But Golovkin took the punches well and was soon stalking his man again.

It was the kind of fight that keeps fans on the edge of their seats. Both fighters were throwing bombs and both fighters were dangerous. It seemed as though—BOOM—at any moment, something might happen. But most of the "booms" were coming from Golovkin.

Gennady showed once again that was a complete fighter. His foot-work was such that there were times when he seemed to be gliding around the ring. He was always looking to attack and do damage. He was relentless but not reckless and cut off the ring well. His jab, straight right, hook to the head and body, and uppercut were all in working order.

Stevens started round six aggressively. Then Gennady unloaded on him. Boxing demands courage of fighters, and Curtis showed it. But from that point on, Golovkin–Stevens was a one-sided display of brutal artistry.

A minute and 15 seconds into round eight, Golovkin landed two thudding hooks to the body that hurt Stevens. Curtis backed into the ropes, and Gennady battered him around the ring with sledgehammer blows to the head and body. Stevens refused to submit, but his cause was helpless.

At the end of the round, referee Harvey Dock followed Curtis to his corner and told trainer Andre Rozier, "That's it."

"Okay," Rozier responded.

An hour later, Golovkin was in his dressing room. He was pleased with the outcome of the fight and satisfied with his performance. He had showered and dressed and was packing his gym bag when the door opened and a short stocky man wearing a navy-blue hoodie and dark glasses to obscure the bruises around his eyes walked in.

Curtis Stevens extended his hand and spoke his next words with sincerity and respect: "Champ; you're a great fighter. Congratulations."

Behind the Scenes with Tim Bradley

Manny Pacquiao vs. Timothy Bradley—
April 12, 2014

Shortly after one o'clock on the afternoon of April 10, 2014, Manny Pacquiao concluded a series of satellite interviews that were conducted in section 118 of the MGM Grand Garden Arena in Las Vegas. The interviews were designed to promote his April 12 rematch against Tim Bradley, and everything had gone according to plan. After the interviews ended, Pacquiao was leaving the makeshift set when a voice from across the arena shouted out loud and clear: "Manny, we love you. Manny, we love you. Manny! Manny!"

Pacquiao turned to acknowledge the fan, one of many who follow him wherever he goes. Then his face broke into a broad smile. The man shouting was Tim Bradley.

Manny waved. Tim waved back. In two days, they would try to beat each other senseless in a boxing ring. But for the moment, there was fondness between them.

Pacquiao's saga is well known. In an era of phony championship belts and unremitting hype, he has been a great fighter and a true people's champion.

Unlike Pacquiao, Bradley hasn't had to make his way through a mob of adoring fans each time he steps onto the street. But the more time that people spend with Tim, they more they like him.

Bradley is a man you'd let babysit for your children. He's devoted to his wife, Monica, and has a smile that lights up a room when he enters. There are no allegations of domestic violence, no conspicuous spending. The thought of Tim blowing twenty thousand dollars in a strip club is ludicrous. When he takes his children to school in the morning, it's not a designed photo op for television cameras.

"I try to be the best person I can be," Tim has said. "I love friends and family. I stay out of trouble. I always try to do the right thing. I don't like a lot of drama in my personal life. I'm outgoing, stubborn, ambitious. I work hard and do whatever it takes to get what I want. I don't want anything given to me. I want to earn it. Whatever life brings me, I deal with it."

Bradley came as close to getting 100 percent out of his potential as any fighter in boxing. His success in the ring was based in large part on physical strength and a will of iron. Roy Jones called him "a 147-pound Evander Holyfield without the punch."

"I'm not the most talented fighter in the division," Tim acknowledged. "There are guys with better skills and better physical gifts than I have. Where I separate myself from other fighters is my determination. I wear the other guy down. That's what it is; hard work and determination. I work my butt off. I come ready every time."

Bradley turned pro in 2004 and, over time, crafted a 28-and-0 ring record en route to annexing the World Boxing Council and World Boxing Organization junior-welterweight crowns. That led to June 9, 2012, when he traveled to Las Vegas to challenge Manny Pacquiao who, at the time, held the WBO welterweight title.

"First round of the Pacquiao fight," Tim later recalled, "I was like, 'Wow—this is it?' This is the best fighter in the world? I can deal with him.' Second round, I stepped on the referee's foot and felt something pop. I'm like, 'Damn! I think I broke my foot. I can't believe this is happening.' I'd spent years trying to get to that place. It was the biggest fight of my life. So I told myself, 'Forget about the pain. Do what you gotta do.' So I bit down hard on my mouthpiece and kept fighting. I fought every minute of every round. Then, trying to protect my left foot, I sprained my right ankle. So now I had pain wherever I put my weight. And I had a lion in front of me. All I could do was take it round by round. And it wasn't enough to survive each round. I had to win them. It was a close fight. I thought I'd done enough to win, and the judges agreed with me. I was on top of the world. And then the roof caved in."

An overwhelming majority of onsite media had scored the fight for Pacquiao. Jerry Roth agreed that Pacquiao had won, although his 115–113 scorecard was closer than some observers thought appropriate. Duane Ford and C. J. Ross ignited a firestorm of protest, scoring the bout 115–113 in favor of Bradley. Brian Kenny (who handled the blow-by-blow commentary for promoter Top Rank's international feed) also scored the bout for Bradley. But his voice was drowned out in the tumult that followed.

Suffering from severely strained ligaments, Bradley was rolled into the media center in a wheelchair for the post-fight press conference. There, Bob Arum (who promoted both fighters but whose financial fortunes were linked to Pacquiao) declared, "I have never been as ashamed to be associated with the sport of boxing as I am tonight. To hear scores like we heard tonight; it's unfathomable. This is an absurdity."

Much of the debate in the days that followed focused on round seven, which HBO labeled "the smoking gun." The CompuBox "punch-stats" had Pacquiao outlanding Bradley in round seven by a 27–11 margin. Yet all three judges scored the round for Bradley.

A smoking gun?

This writer went to HBO headquarters a week after the fight and watched a video of round seven in its entirety from multiple camera angles . . . several times . . . in slow motion. . . . In reality, Bradley out-landed Pacquiao 16–12 in round seven. It was a close fight, and Bradley deserved better treatment than he got from fans and the boxing estab-lishment afterward.

"It should have been the happiest time of my life," Bradley said of the weeks that followed. "And I wound up in the darkest place I've ever been in. You prepare your entire life to get to a certain point. You get there. And then it all gets taken away. I was attacked in the media. People were stopping me on the street, saying things like, 'You didn't win that fight; you should give the belt back; you should be ashamed of yourself; you're not a real champion.' I got death threats. I got hate mail like you wouldn't believe. I turned off my phone. The ridicule got so bad that there were times when I didn't know if I wanted to fight anymore. All I did was do my job the best way I could, and it was like I stole something from the world.

"I watched the tape of the fight again and again," Bradley contin-ued. "I can be obsessive. I watched the tape maybe fifty times. I think I won. Part of the problem, I believe, was that the HBO announcers had Pacquiao on a pedestal. It was like they were calling *The Manny Pacquiao Show*. Don't get me wrong. I like HBO. But their call was way off that night. A lot of the punches the announcers said were landing didn't land. And everything they said was going into viewers' minds. I was shattered. It was a dark time for me. I was walking around angry, bitter. Finally, my wife asked me, 'Aren't you tired of this?' I said, 'You're right. Enough is enough. This isn't me. I'm not going to let these people change who I am. The fight is over. It's in the past.'"

In Pacquiao's next fight, he suffered a one-punch knockout loss at the hands of Juan Manuel Márquez. Eleven months later, he rebounded to decision Brandon Rios. Meanwhile, Bradley edged Ruslan Provodnikov in a thriller and outboxed Márquez en route to another split-decision triumph. That brought Tim's record to 31–0 and set the stage for his rematch with Pacquiao.

Bradley was the reigning champion, but Pacquiao was the engine driving the economics of Pacquiao–Bradley II. Each fighter felt that there was unfinished business between them.

Pacquiao was a 9-to-5 betting favorite, down from 4-to-1 in their first encounter.

Bradley was confident. "The first time we fought," he said, "I didn't know how much intensity Manny brought to the ring. He throws so many feints and closes the distance so fast and punches from all angles. He always keeps you guessing when he's going to come in and out. Now I know what to expect. I was able to make adjustments in the first fight, and Manny had problems with me when I was moving. With two good feet, I'll be able to move quicker this time and set down harder on my punches. With two good feet, I can adjust my footwork to deal with whatever Pacquiao brings to the table. Pain-free is another dimension, and I'll be pain-free this time. I'm a more mature fighter now than I was two years ago. I'm better at getting in and out on guys and controlling the distance between us, which I showed in the Márquez fight. I'm a better fighter now than I was the first time Pacquiao and I fought. And Manny can't say that."

Indeed, the main concern in Bradley's camp was that the judges might overcompensate for the perceived injustice of the scoring in Pacquiao–Bradley I and, fearing ridicule, have a default setting on close rounds that favored Pacquiao.

On fight night, Tim Bradley arrived in dressing room #1 at the MGM

Grand Garden Arena at 6:00 p.m. His father (known as "Big Ray"), Joel Diaz (who had trained Bradley from his first pro fight), assistant trainer Samuel Jackson, conditioning coach James Rougely, and attorney Gaby Penagaricano were with him. Big Ray had helped train his son from the early days of Tim's career.

Bradley sat on a cushioned metal chair and rested his feet on another chair in front of him. HBO production coordinator Tami Cotel entered the room and asked if Tim would weigh in on HBO's fight-night scale. Bradley complied. One day earlier, he'd tipped the official scale at 145½ pounds. Now he weighed 152. Minutes earlier, Pacquiao (who'd weighed in officially at 145) had registered 151 pounds.

After his weight was checked, Tim sat back on the chair and closed his eyes, envisioning the battle ahead. His family's financial future, his physical well-being, and his legacy as a fighter were all on the line. He was as well prepared as he could be. But in all likelihood, so was Pacquiao.

At 6:25 p.m., Freddie Roach (Pacquiao's trainer) came into the room to watch Bradley's hands being wrapped. Tim took off his wedding ring and handed it to his father for safekeeping. Joel Diaz began taping. Roach's own hands were shaking visibly, a symptom of his Parkinson's condition. Big Ray offered him a chair. Roach gestured "no, thank you."

No one spoke. At 6:40, the taping was done. Tim took off his jacket and shadow-boxed for ten minutes, stopping twice to sip water from a bottle that his father was holding. Then he sat down again.

Bradley gets his game face on earlier than most fighters. "On the day of a fight," he has said, "it's like there's this huge rock on my back and I want to get it off." The next few hours would be about fighting, not charm school. The look on his face said, "Don't fuck with me."

Joel Diaz went next door to watch Roach wrap Pacquiao's hands.

Tim stayed on his chair—sometimes with his eyes closed, sometimes open; sometimes with his head up, sometimes down—playing different fight sequences through in his mind.

If I do this, Pacquiao will do that. If Pacquiao does that, what do I do next?

The mood in the dressing room was intense. There were no attempts at levity, no smiles, no upbeat conversation. Few words were spoken.

At 7:10 p.m., Big Ray spread two towels side by side on the floor. Tim lay down and began a series of stretching exercises; first on his own, then with his father's assistance. The exercises grew progressively more rigorous. At 7:40, Big Ray picked up the towels and Tim shadow-boxed again.

Referee Kenny Bayless entered and gave the fighter his pre-fight instructions.

Bayless left and Tim resumed shadow-boxing. Big Ray stepped in front of his son with a folded-up towel in each hand, assumed a southpaw stance to emulate Pacquiao, and aimed punches at his son.

"Don't let him get lower than you," Big Ray cautioned.

At eight o'clock, Tim sat again and stared silently ahead.

Big Ray, Joel Diaz, and Samuel Jackson took on the role of a Greek chorus, voicing thoughts one at a time.

"Fast, like lightning."

"Stay loose."

"Control the pace. Make him do things he doesn't want to do, and he'll get tired."

"Don't be a gentleman. Rip his ass up on the inside."

The voices were complementing, not competing with, each other.

"It ain't about strength. It's about knowledge."

"That right hand will get him every time."

"Fight like a cat."

"Fight smart."

Big Ray slammed the palm of his hand down hard on the table beside him.

"Do not be on the ropes," he warned. "Do not be on the ropes. You're in deep shit if you're on the ropes."

Diaz gloved Tim up.

There was more shadow-boxing.

Again, the Greek chorus.

"That's the way. Snap those punches."

"On the inside, keep both hands up by your head."

"Watch for his right hook on the inside."

"It's your night, baby. It's your night."

Tim sat.

"I'm excited," he said. Then he fell silent, his face registering a range of emotions.

The Greek chorus continued.

"Right hand to the body. Hook to the body. Tear that body up."

"If he gets under you, come up with the uppercut."

"The conditioning is there. He won't be able to deal with the pace."

"Control him. Don't let him control you."

"Patience is a virtue. Take your time. If it goes twelve, amen."

"We're happy, man; we're happy. Have fun"

"Fight smart."

"You're the real deal, babe."

Bradley rose and began hitting the pads with Joel Diaz.

"Right over the top," Diaz instructed. "Beautiful. You got twelve rounds, twelve fuckin' rounds to time that punch. You're the champion. You're the boss. You're the big dog. You're the man."

The padwork ended. Pacquiao could be seen on a television monitor at the far end of the room, leaving his dressing room and walking to the ring.

"It's fun time, baby," Bradley said.

Then the members of Team Bradley joined hands in a circle and Tim led them in prayer. He asked for the strength to prevail in the battle ahead. He asked that both he and Pacquiao emerge in good health. And he closed with a final thought for the Creator: "Love you, man."

The fight itself was heartbreak for Bradley. After a tactical first round, the combatants exchanged in the second stanza with Pacquiao getting the better of the action. In round three, Manny scored big early and maintained his edge with speed and angles. Then Bradley found a home for his right hand, buzzed Pacquiao with a hard right up top, and took rounds four and five.

At that point, Bradley seemed to be where he wanted to be in the fight. Two of the judges (Michael Pernick and Craig Metcalfe) had him leading three rounds to two while Glenn Trowbridge's card was the reverse. Tim's strategy from day one had been premised on the idea that the second half of the fight would belong to him.

But the unthinkable was happening. After round three, Bradley had returned to his corner and told Joel Diaz, "I pulled a muscle in my calf."

Now Tim's gastrocnemius muscle was tearing apart.

"You're losing your rhythm," Diaz told his charge after round six. "What the fuck is wrong?"

"I'm hurting," Tim answered.

The rest of the fight belonged to Pacquiao. Except for a right hand to the body that hurt Manny visibly in round seven, Bradley couldn't do much more than survive. The grinding aggression typical of his style was missing. He was an impaired fighter. And round by round, the injury was getting worse. Tim backed into corners, beckoned Manny in, and swung for the fences with wild right hands up top. It was an inexplicable strategy unless one knew that he was fighting on one leg.

The final scoring of the judges was anticlimactic: 118–110, 116–112, 116–112 for Pacquiao.

Monica Bradley was waiting for her husband when Tim returned to the dressing room after the fight. Their fourteen-year-old son, Robert, and Tim's mother were with her.

A large lump was visible on the back of Bradley's right calf. He was limping badly.

"What's up, baby?" Tim asked as he hugged Monica.

Then father and son embraced. "Some you lose; some you win," Tim said. "A champion has to accept defeat when it comes. I tried my best."

A kiss for Kathy Bradley was next. "I love you," Tim told his mother.

Joel Diaz took out his cellphone and began snapping photos of the lump on Bradley's calf.

A commission doctor came in to examine the injury.

"I don't want to go to the emergency room," Tim told the doctor. "And no wheelchair. I'm walking out on my own tonight."

Reflecting on his journey through the sweet science, Sergio Martínez said, "Life sometimes takes you through a path where the lighter thing is boxing." That says all one needs to know about the circumstances of Sergio's life when he was young.

Two Good Men, One Would Lose
Sergio Martínez vs. Miguel Cotto— June 7, 2014

A fighter's dressing room is a sheltered world in the hours before a big fight. At 9:15 on the night of June 7, 2014, Sergio Martínez entered dressing room #5 at Madison Square Garden with trainer Pablo Sarmiento, cutman Roger Anderson, and physical therapist Raquel Bordons. Cornerman Russ Anber and Nathan Lewkowicz (the son of promoter Sampson Lewkowicz) followed. The room was small and angularly shaped with brown industrial carpet and cream-colored cinderblock walls. Two doors down the corridor, Miguel Cotto was ensconced in dressing room #3.

In two and a half hours, Martínez and Cotto would battle for the middleweight championship of the world. Sergio was the defending champion, but his dressing room was one-third the size of Miguel's. Other slights had cut deeper.

The fight and all promotional material for it had been styled "Cotto–Martínez" rather than the other way around. "It bothers me," Sergio admitted, "because it's disrespectful to the history and traditions of boxing. But Cotto said there would be no fight if his name wasn't first on the posters. I can imagine that, on June 7, he will ask for rose petals to be thrown at his feet or he won't walk to the ring."

More significantly, the finances of the fight were weighted in the challenger's favor. Cotto and Top Rank (Miguel's promoter) had retained Puerto Rican television rights off the top. The first $15 million in net revenue after that would be split 55 percent to Cotto and Top Rank, 45 percent to Martínez and his promoters (DiBella Entertainment and Sampson Promotions). Thereafter, the split would increase to 60–40.

To Cotto, that was fair and logical. "Two times in my career—when I fought Pacquiao and when I fought Mayweather—I was the champion but I was the B-side," Miguel noted. "I understood my position. Sergio Martínez is a great fighter, but boxing is a business. For this fight, I am the one who sells the tickets."

Taken severally, Martínez's features aren't classically handsome. But they fit together well and his smile further binds them. Fashion designers love to hang clothes on him. He has a strong physical presence and carries himself with grace. Every now and then, a hard look creeps into his eyes, as though he's remembering the hardships of his youth or the demands of the boxing trade.

Like most fighters, Martínez came from a hard world. Growing up in the slums of Buenos Aires, he didn't know what "dinner" was. The family didn't sit down together at an appointed hour. When food came into the home, they ate it.

"When you are very small, a child, you don't know that you're poor," Sergio said, reflecting back on that time. "Even though you're hungry and cold, if you have the love of your parents, you're happy with what you have because you're used to that life and it's all you know. Then you become an adolescent. You start to realize what you don't have and begin to think about how to get what you want. You can work hard or you can take the shorter path and turn to crime. If you have good parents, it makes a big difference in deciding which path you take. When you are an adult, you realize fully what you missed as a child. And again, you have a choice. You can feel sorry for yourself or you can feel pride at where you came from and where you've gotten to in life. I give thanks to the fact that I grew up poor because it helps me appreciate what I have now."

Boxing was Martínez's route to a better life. "I was a good student," he said. "But my family didn't have the money to continue my education. Without my physical gifts, I don't think I would have found my way out of poverty. But I believe that everyone has a path if they choose to follow it. Everyone has a talent that's special.

"The very poor identify with boxing," Sergio continued. "They look at boxers and relate to the economic conditions that we came from and to our struggle. They admire the courage we have to fight to get to the next level. The very wealthy look at boxers as two animals trying to kill each other for their entertainment. They don't identify on a human level with the fighters. Many of them—I truly believe this—want to see me fail in the end, lose all my money, and go back to nothing. It's like a game for them. And sadly, most boxers who go from very poor to very rich go back quickly to being poor again."

Martínez turned pro in 1997 and fought in obscurity for much of his career. Now, fourteen years later, he had lost only twice in fifty-five fights. The first defeat came in 2000 at the hands of Antonio Margarito. "I was trained but I was not prepared," Martínez said of that fight. "I started well, but it was impossible for me to win that night. He was a professional boxer, a great champion. And at that moment, I was a boxer who, three or four years before, was working on roofs. I was playing soccer with my friends when Margarito had already been a professional boxer for six or seven years. What had to happen happened. In terms of spirit, I never was down after that defeat."

The second loss was a controversial majority-decision defeat in a 2009 bout against Paul Williams. Martínez rebounded from that setback by dethroning middleweight champion Kelly Pavlik on April 17, 2010, and knocking Williams unconscious with a single punch in the second round of a November 20, 2010, rematch. Those victories earned him recognition from the Boxing Writers Association of America as the 2010 "Fighter of the Year."

A tattoo of a dragon was imprinted on the outside of Martínez's left arm from his shoulder to his elbow. In January 2013, he'd added the word "resistencia" (resistance) on the inside of his right forearm and "victoria" (victory) on the inside of his left forearm.

"The life I have chosen revolves around those two words," Sergio said, explaining the latter two tattoos. "When I was preparing to fight Chávez [in September 2012], they were constantly in my head. Then I signed to fight Martin Murray. I wasn't motivated, and I thought the tattoos would help motivate me. There will be no more tattoos. I don't like tattoos. I never wanted tattoos. I hate tattoos. It is a contradiction, I know. I cannot explain it except to say, in two brief moments in time, I thought it was important to have these tattoos on my body."

Cotto–Martínez harkened back to a time when New York was the capital of the sports world. Earlier in the day, California Chrome's pursuit of racing's Triple Crown had drawn a crowd of 102,000 to the Belmont Stakes. Now Cotto was bidding to become the first Puerto Rican to win titles in four weight divisions. This would be his ninth fight in the big arena at Madison Square Garden and the first for Martínez. Three thousand fans had attended the Friday weigh-in. It would have been more, but the doors to The Theater at the Garden were closed an hour before the fighters stepped on the scales.

Martínez was a 2-to-1 betting favorite, but the outcome of the fight was very much in doubt.

The case for a Martínez victory began with the belief that Cotto wasn't "Cotto" anymore. Miguel had lost two fights in a row (to Floyd Mayweather and Austin Trout) before blowing out journeyman Delvin Rodríguez the previous October. Prior to those fights, he'd been brutalized by Antonio Margarito and Manny Pacquiao and looked ordinary in victories over Yuri Foreman and Ricardo Mayorga as well as in a rematch against Margarito.

Trout was thought to have given Martínez a roadmap for beating Cotto. Like Sergio, Austin was taller than Miguel and a southpaw. Twelve months earlier, he'd outpointed Cotto 119–109, 117–111, 117–111. Asked at a sit-down with reporters about the parallels between Trout and Martínez, Miguel responded, "I fought Trout in 2012. Now it is 2014. I never saw that fight after that night, and I have no plans to see it again."

That seemed like a bad case of denial. Moreover, for the first time in a long time, Martínez would be entering the ring with a height (three inches) and weight (four pounds) advantage over his opponent.

"I like to watch my opponents," Martínez has said. "I like studying them a lot. More than what they do, it's how they think. I want to know what my opponent is thinking. Once I've seen them, I can figure them out; the ideas they have, their plan, their strategy."

Watching Cotto, Sergio had seen Pacquiao and Mayweather beat Miguel with speed and Margarito beat him with power.

"Cotto does not have the same power at this weight that he had at 147," Martínez declared. "I am the power-puncher of the two of us. When I start to find my rhythm, my timing, and the right distance, the fight will be over."

Team Cotto, of course, held to a contrary view.

Cotto would be the most intelligent and technically skilled opponent that Martínez had faced. Freddie Roach (Miguel's trainer) was confident that edge would enable his fighter to exploit the flaws in Sergio's style.

"Martínez is a great athlete," Roach said. "I wouldn't call him a great boxer. If you keep yourself in a good position, most of the time you'll control the fight. Sergio's footwork is reckless. He's all over the place. Miguel can take advantage of that. And I think Miguel can beat Martínez down the middle. Sergio's defense is not all that good—if you exchange with him, let your hands go, he's very hittable. Chávez didn't do that until the last round, and you saw what happened when he did. I think Cotto's boxing ability will be too much for Martínez to handle."

On the issue of size and power, Cotto declared, "It's not about gaining the weight. It's about not having to lose the weight. For the first time in my career, I'm not concerned about making weight. I can eat to be strong."

"We moved up the weight a little bit and put on more muscle," Roach added. "I think Miguel will be stronger on the inside and much more physical on the inside than Martínez is. We're going to push him around with no problem. On the inside we're the bigger, stronger fighter."

But the biggest issue surrounding Cotto–Martínez was Sergio's physical condition. Virtually everyone believed that Martínez was fragile. Forty-three months had passed since Sergio's demolition of Paul Williams. Subsequent to that, he had looked vulnerable. More than most fighters, Martínez fought with his legs. But in recent fights, his legs had betrayed him.

After decisioning Martin Murray in 2013, Martínez underwent major knee surgery. "The recuperation was very painful," Sergio acknowledged. "I was on crutches for nine months, and it is very hard to come back from that. But this is the road that I chose, and I enjoy the achievement of coming back from something like this. Right now, I am just the same as when there were no knee problems. I have overcome all obstacles."

That thought was echoed by physical therapist Raquel Bordons, who said in the dressing room an hour before the fight, "Sergio's condition is more than I could have hoped for. He is very very good now."

But was Martínez fully repaired after the surgery, or was he a thirty-nine-year-old athlete with substandard body parts? Tom Gerbasi framed the issue when he wrote, "It's almost as if Martínez making it to the ring is the equivalent of New York Knicks captain Willis Reed limping out of the tunnel for Game Seven of the NBA Finals against the Los Angeles Lakers on May 8, 1970, to inspire his team and get them off to the start they needed to win the game and the title. It's got that feel, that buzz, that for one more night, a great champion can be great. Saturday night is Sergio Martínez's Game Seven. But this is no basketball game. Martínez can't hit two baskets, go back to the bench, and leave his teammates to finish the work like Reed did. This is a fight, twelve rounds with the best fighter Martínez has ever been in with. Thirty-six minutes of wear and tear, physical and mental warfare."

"Who do you like in the fight?" boxing maven Pete Susens was asked.

"Whichever guy has one last big fight left in him," Susens answered.

The hour of reckoning for Martínez and Cotto was drawing closer.

Referee Mike Griffin came into Martínez's dressing room and gave Sergio his pre-fight instructions. Russ Anber wrapped Martínez's hands. Sergio put on his shoes and trunks and shadow-boxed briefly. Then he pulled a protective latex sleeve up over each knee. "A precaution," he explained. "Not a necessity."

Pablo Sarmiento gloved Martínez up. Earlier in the evening, New York State Athletic Commission inspector Ernie Morales had initialed Sergio's handwraps. Now Sue Etkin (the other inspector assigned to Martínez) wrote "Sue" on the tape covering the lace on each glove.

Sergio hit the pads with Sarmiento.

Music played—"Out of Control," sung by You Aren't Going to Like This. The same song, again and again.

There was anticipation in Martínez's eyes. Some fighters are intimidated by a big-fight atmosphere. Sergio thrived on it. He loved the spotlight.

For Muhammad Ali, boxing was a sport. Joe Frazier treated it as combat. In Martínez's mind, he was preparing for a sporting competition. Two doors down the corridor, Miguel Cotto was preparing for combat. A short walk from each fighter's sanctuary, a screaming bloodlust crowd of 21,090 waited.

During the buildup to Cotto–Martínez, Sergio had told the media, "It has been my dream for a long time to fight in the big room at Madison Square Garden."

On fight night, that dream turned into a nightmare.

The heavily pro-Cotto crowd was chanting "Cotto, Cotto" even before the bell to start round one rang. It didn't have to wait long for satisfaction. One minute into the first stanza, Cotto staggered Martínez with a left hook up top. A barrage of punches put Sergio face down on the canvas. He rose on unsteady legs and, a minute later, was decked again by a right hand. Once more, he struggled to his feet. Almost immediately, a body shot put him down for the third time.

That left Martínez with a gaping hole to climb out of on the judges' scorecards. And worse, he was now a debilitated fighter.

"The first punch that hurt me, after that, I never recovered," Sergio said in his dressing room after the fight. "I wasn't the same after that. I couldn't do anything. My mind was disconnected from my body. My mind told me to do something, and my body wouldn't do it."

A brutal beatdown followed. Cotto punished Martínez almost at will to the head and body. Everything that Miguel landed seemed to hurt. Sergio's only hope was that Cotto would fade in the late rounds, as had happened in several recent outings. But with each passing round, it became more unlikely that Martínez would have anything left if and when that eventuality occurred. As the fight wore on, the question was not who would win but how much punishment Martínez could take. Sergio wasn't just being outpointed. He was getting beaten up. All that he had left was his heart.

After nine rounds, Pablo Sarmiento stopped the carnage.

In the dressing room after the fight, the trainer recounted, "I told him, 'Sergio, champion, you mean more to me than I mean to myself. I am stopping it now.' Sergio pleaded with me, 'One more round.' I told him no, and he accepted that."

If Cotto–Martínez was Miguel's finest hour, it was also Sarmiento's.

As Pablo spoke, Martínez sat on a cushioned folding chair. His face was bruised and swollen. There was a cut on his right eyelid and an ugly gash on top of his head. The right side of his body, where Cotto's left hook had landed again and again, ached. Fortunately, a post-fight trip to Bellevue Hospital for a precautionary MRI revealed nothing more serious than a broken nose.

Prior to fighting Cotto, Sergio Martínez told this writer, "I want to be remembered first as a good person and a man of integrity. After that, if people remember me as a good fighter, that would be nice."

History will record that he was both.

"The fans don't fully understand what it means to be a fighter," Miguel Cotto once said. "They see the fight, and most don't understand even that. But even fewer understand the sacrifices that a fighter must make, the pain he suffers, just to get to the fight. For myself, I'm not a real big fan of boxing. I just enjoy boxing when I'm boxing."

In Celebration of Miguel Cotto
Miguel Cotto vs. Daniel Geale—
June 6, 2015

Miguel Cotto entered his dressing room at Barclays Center on June 6, 2015, at 8:25 p.m. He was casually dressed, wearing faded blue jeans, a well-worn gray T-shirt, a blue leather jacket, and loafers with no socks.

There was a time when winning a world championship was boxing's equivalent of a mobster becoming a made man. No more. In an era characterized by multiple sanctioning bodies and more than a hundred world "champions" at any point in time, only a handful of fighters matter to the public.

Miguel Cotto matters. His journey through boxing began in 1992. "I was a chubby child," he later recalled. "I weighed 162 pounds at age eleven. My sport was to sit in front of the TV and eat. I started boxing to lose weight and fell in love with it."

Cotto turned pro in 2001. At his peak, he'd been a destructive force, devastating good fighters like Zab Judah, Carlos Quintana, and Paulie Malignaggi and outpointing great ones like Shane Mosley. Then something bad happened.

On the morning of July 26, 2008, Cotto was undefeated in thirty-two fights and ranked in the top five on most pound-for-pound lists. That night, he fought Antonio Margarito at the MGM Grand in Las Vegas and was brutally beaten into submission. Most knowledgeable observers of the boxing scene now believe that there were illegal inserts in Margarito's handwraps that night.

Following the loss to Margarito, Miguel was a different fighter. On November 14, 2009, he was on the receiving end of another brutal

beating—this one administered by Manny Pacquiao. He fought sporadically after that, besting Yuri Foreman, Ricardo Mayorga, and Margarito
(in a rematch), but was outpointed by Floyd Mayweather and Austin
Trout in back-to-back outings.

After the loss to Trout, Cotto's days as a star attraction seemed to be
over. On October 5, 2013, he scored a third-round knockout over Delvin
Rodriguez. But Rodriguez had won only four of eleven fights dating
back to 2008, so that didn't count for much in the eyes of the boxing
establishment.

Then, on June 7, 2014, Cotto challenged Sergio Martínez for the
middleweight championship of the world and, defying the 2-to-1 odds
against him, forced Martínez's corner to call a halt to the action after
nine one-sided rounds. But it was an open issue as to whether Miguel
had looked good or Sergio (who'd undergone extensive knee surgery
prior to the fight and would require more surgery afterward) looked bad.

The victory over Martínez brought Cotto's record to 39 wins against
4 losses with 32 knockouts and gave him renewed bargaining power. In
January 2015, he signed a lucrative three-fight contract with Roc Nation
that included a substantial signing bonus, a contribution to a charity created by Miguel in Puerto Rico, and an agreement that Roc Nation and
Cotto Promotions would co-promote a series of boxing cards and rock
concerts on the island.

In the aftermath of the signing, there were harsh words from Todd
DuBoef of Top Rank (Cotto's former promoter). At a February 5,
2015, luncheon to formally announce the deal, a reporter asked Gaby
Penagaricano (Miguel's attorney) about DuBoef's negative comments.

"I am going to be the only one to talk about it," Cotto interrupted.
"We had a fight-by-fight deal with Top Rank. I expect respect, and a lot
of people I knew from the beginning of my career didn't show that."

Later, when asked if there was any lingering bitterness between him
and Top Rank, Miguel answered, "If they want to say hi to me, they have
my number."

Cotto's opponent at Barclays Center on June 6 was Daniel Geale.
Geale had been competitive in past outings against fighters like Darren
Barker, Anthony Mundine, and Felix Sturm. But when last seen in New
York, he'd been knocked out by Gennady Golovkin in three rounds in a

fight that evoked images of a bug flying into the windshield of a sixteen-wheel truck on an interstate highway.

"I didn't come here for a holiday," Geale said of his impending confrontation with Cotto. "I came here to fight."

But Daniel was a 5-to-1 underdog and had been brought in on the assumption that he would lose. He was a respectable but "safe" opponent. Not too fast, not too skilled, not a big puncher. He wouldn't bring anything to the table that Miguel couldn't deal with.

Furthering Cotto's advantage, the fight was to be contested at a catchweight of 157 pounds even though Miguel's 160-pound title was at stake.

Barclays Center is the home of the NBA Brooklyn Nets. Cotto was treated like visiting royalty. Geale had been given an ordinary dressing room. Team Cotto was ensconced in the Nets suite.

The dressing area was a spacious enclosure, thirty-six feet long and thirty feet wide with a twelve-foot-high ceiling and recessed lighting above. A white Brooklyn Nets logo was woven into plush black carpet. There were twelve separate dressing stations, each with its own vertical closet, sliding drawer, and swivel chair. The name and uniform number of a Nets player was on a placard affixed to the wall by each dressing station. The rest of the suite consisted of a lounge, lavatory, shower room, whirlpool room, and medical area.

For the first two hours after Cotto's arrival, well-wishers came and went. Family members and friends, sanctioning body officials, representatives of Roc Nation. Through it all, the core group remained the same. Trainer Freddie Roach, assistant trainer Marvin Somodio, cutman David Martinez, strength and conditioning coach Gavin MacMillan, and Bryan Perez (Miguel's closest and most trusted friend).

Former New York Yankee great Bernie Williams (who'd been asked by Miguel to walk him to the ring) sat quietly to the side.

The mood was relaxed, almost festive. Cotto smiles more in the dressing room on fight night than he does at press conferences and other media events. As time passed, he chatted casually with Perez, Somodio, and others as though he were circulating at a cocktail party. Other times, he sat alone with his thoughts or paced wordlessly with his arms folded, sipping from a bottle of water.

Referee Harvey Dock gave Cotto his pre-fight instructions.

Miguel applied underarm deodorant before putting on his boxing gear and checked his smartphone for messages.

Times have changed. It's hard to imagine Rocky Marciano applying underarm deodorant and checking a smartphone for messages in the dressing room before a fight.

At 9:00 p.m., the salsa music of Ismael Miranda wafted through the air, adding to the festive aura.

Roach stood off to the side. Cotto–Geale was the third fight that he and Miguel had prepared for together.

In an earlier incarnation, Roach had compiled a 39–13 ring record as a combatant. He's still every bit as much a fighter as the men he trains. But now he's fighting a different kind of battle, against the ravages of Parkinson's syndrome.

Miguel had called Freddie "the best thing that ever happened to my career" and said, "Freddie brought confidence back to me. He comes every day to the gym and gives his best. The only way you can pay a person like that back is to give your best."

Now Roach was reflecting on the time he'd spent with Cotto.

"Miguel has a great work ethic," Freddie said. "Once he's in the gym, it's all work. He's one of the most disciplined fighters I've seen in my life. He's very quiet. Every now and then, he tells a joke. He's a pleasure to work with."

"The biggest thing when I started with Miguel," Roach continued, "was, I said to him, 'When you were an amateur, you were a boxer. Why are you throwing every punch now like you want to kill the other guy? It's not enough to have skills. It's not enough to have heart. You have to fight smart.' And Miguel listened. He tries to do what I tell him to do. You'll see that tonight. I don't know if Geale will come at us and try to impose his size or run all night. Either way, he'll keep his hands high. That's what he always does, so we'll attack the body."

Roach went down the hall to watch Geale's hands being wrapped.

Cotto began stretching his upper body and leg muscles.

At 9:30 p.m., Marvin Somodio started wrapping Miguel's hands, right hand first.

Miguel whistled in tune with the music as Somodio worked.

"Miguel loves fight night," Bryan Perez said. "He's enjoying the moment."

Roach returned.

"Geale got a terrible handwrap," Freddie announced. "I don't think his guy knows how to wrap hands. The way he did it, there's not much protection or strength."

That led Roach to reminisce about an oddity that had occurred years earlier when he was training Virgil Hill.

"I went in to watch the opponent getting his hands wrapped, and the guy who was wrapping had no idea what he was doing. Finally, the fighter said, 'Freddie, will you wrap my hands?' I said, 'I can't. You're fighting my guy.' He said, 'Please!' So I did it."

At 9:50, Cotto lay down on a towel on the floor and Somodio began stretching him out.

Miguel shadow-boxed briefly.

Somodio gloved him up.

At 10:27, Miguel began hitting the pads with Roach. It was his first real physical exertion of the night. Four minutes later, they stopped.

At 10:40, a voice sounded: "Okay, guys."

It was time to fight.

This was Cotto's first fight at Barclays Center. Geale had a decided size advantage. One day earlier, Miguel had weighed in at 153.6 pounds while Daniel tipped the scales at 157. During the ensuing thirty hours, Geale had gained approximately twenty pounds. He weighed 182 in street clothes on fight night. But size was his only edge.

Cotto–Geale was a craftsman versus an ordinary fighter. It was clear from the start that Miguel was faster and the better boxer.

For the first three rounds, Cotto piled up points with his jab and did damage with hard hooks to the body. Thirty-two seconds into round four, a picture-perfect left hook up top smashed Geale to the canvas and left him on his back with his upper torso stretched beneath the bottom ring rope.

Daniel rose on unsteady legs at the count of nine and managed to stay upright for another thirty seconds before a barrage of punches punctuated by a short right hand deposited him on the floor for the second time.

Once again, he beat the count.

"Are you okay?" referee Harvey Dock asked.

Geale shook his head.

"No," he said.

Dock stopped the fight.

There was joy in Cotto's dressing room after the fight. It wasn't that he'd beaten Geale as much as the way he beat him that impressed.

"Miguel boxed very well tonight," Roach said. "The angles were good. He got off first and went to the body a lot." Freddie smiled. "It's a lot easier when the fight happens the way you planned it."

While Roach was holding court, Cotto showered and put on the same faded blue jeans, gray T-shirt, blue leather jacket, and loafers without socks that he'd worn earlier in the evening. He looked like a factory worker getting ready to go home after an honest night's work. How many more fights he had left in him would depend on how much punishment he took in those fights and how much each training camp took out of him. He was much closer to the end of his ring career than the beginning.

Asked about his place in Puerto Rican boxing history, Miguel Cotto declared, "I am going to be wherever the fans put me. I am never going to claim something that the people won't give me. Wherever they are going to put Miguel Cotto, I am going to be happy. All I want is to be Miguel Cotto."

Miguel Cotto's Last Fight
Miguel Cotto vs. Sadam Ali—
December 2, 2017

On Saturday, December 2, 2017, at 7:15 p.m., Miguel Cotto walked into a dressing room at Madison Square Garden preparatory to fighting for the last time.

In recent decades, there has been a premium in boxing on trash-talking and glitz. That was never Cotto's way. He's soft-spoken and polite with an aura of dignity about him. His low, monotone voice doesn't travel far and can be reassuring, grave, even gentle, depending on the moment. Often, one has to lean close to hear him speak. As his ring career progressed, he conducted interviews with the English-speaking media without an interpreter but was more expressive when speaking in Spanish.

The gravity of what Cotto once did for a living is etched on his face. There's an aura of solemnity about him. He doesn't smile often in public and gives the impression of being on guard at all times. One might describe him as "stoic" (a person who endures hardship and pain without complaint and rarely shows his true feelings). But he has expressive eyes that can be soft, hard, thoughtful, happy, lonely. His smile is genuine and warm.

"No matter what my face might say, I am a happy guy," Miguel once said. "But I am a shy guy. Most people don't realize that. I don't prefer the spotlight."

Hard work has been a constant in Cotto's life. So have the themes of dignity and respect. His creed was always, "Work hard, don't cut corners, and do the best you can." A soldier going to war would want Miguel fighting beside him.

Cotto followed Félix Trinidad as the standard bearer for Puerto Rican boxing and is on the short list of greatest Puerto Rican fighters of all time. Touted as boxing royalty from early in his pro career, he was near the top of most pound-for-pound lists for years. At his best, he could choose between outboxing opponents and mauling them in the trenches.

Cotto turned pro in 2001 and moved quickly through the 140-pound ranks before capturing the WBO crown with a 2004 knockout of Kelson Pinto. A run of successful title defenses and a natural evolution to welterweight followed. He was at his best fighting at 140 or 147 pounds, weights at which he was able to impose his size and physical strength on opponents. Opponents said that his hook to the body felt like an iron wrecking ball.

On the morning of July 26, 2008, Cotto was 32–0 as a pro with 26 knockouts. That night, he stepped into the ring at the MGM Grand in Las Vegas to face Antonio Margarito and suffered a horrific beating. The weight of the evidence strongly suggests that Margarito's gloves were "loaded" that night.

Miguel wasn't the same fighter after that. On November 14, 2009, he absorbed another beating at the hands of Manny Pacquiao. Thereafter, he fought sporadically, earning victories over Yuri Foreman, Ricardo Mayorga, and Margarito (in a rematch) before being outpointed in back-to-back losses to Floyd Mayweather and Austin Trout.

At that point, Cotto's days as a star attraction seemed to be over. Then, on June 7, 2014, he challenged Sergio Martínez for the middleweight championship of the world. Cotto knocked Martínez down three times in the first stanza. The fight was stopped after nine lopsided rounds. That was followed by an impressive fourth-round knockout of Daniel Geale. A loss by decision to a younger, stronger Canelo Álvarez and a decision victory over Yoshihiro Kamegai for a vacant 154-pound WBO belt brought Miguel to Madison Square Garden on the night of December 2, 2017.

Cotto was now thirty-seven years old. His record stood at 41 wins against 5 losses with 33 knockouts. He had come a long way since 2004, when he journeyed to Las Vegas to fight Randall Bailey. On that occasion, a security guard at Mandalay Bay had seen him walking around the casino, evaluated him as an undesirable, and asked him to leave the casino floor.

The storyline on December 2 was simple. Cotto had pledged that, win or lose, this would be his last fight. The opponent was Sadam Ali, a twenty-nine-year-old former US Olympian who had been unable to rise to the top as a pro. One year earlier, Ali had stepped up in class to fight Jessie Vargas for the vacant WBO welterweight title and been stopped in the ninth round. Cotto–Ali would be Sadam's first fight at a contract weight of 154 pounds.

Ali had been chosen as Cotto's opponent on the assumption that he lacked the essentials to pose a serious threat. It would be better to see Miguel leave boxing on a victory over a lesser fighter than to exit in the manner of so many great champions who lost in the final bout of their ring career.

Sadam himself acknowledged during a pre-fight media conference call that it was "a little scary" to be fighting "a legend who I grew up watching."

Cotto had more than boxing on his mind when he entered his dressing room at Madison Square Garden on the night of his last fight. Nine weeks earlier, his Puerto Rican homeland had been devastated by a historic hurricane that shattered the island's infrastructure and killed almost three thousand people. But those thoughts would have to be put on hold in the hours ahead.

The dressing room was a large oval enclosure that housed the New York Rangers hockey team on game nights. Locker stalls with a plaque bearing the name and uniform number of each Ranger player ringed the room. Rolls of tape lay scattered about, a reminder of the team's 5–1 victory over the Carolina Hurricanes the previous evening.

Cotto was wearing black pants, a burgundy jacket over a white T-shirt, and blue track shoes. His mother, wife, two sons, one of his two daughters, trainer Freddie Roach, assistant trainer Marvin Somodio, cutman David Martinez, strength and conditioning coach Gavin MacMillan, and Bryan Perez (his closest friend) were with him.

Miguel checked his email, put on some music, and sat down on one of two brown leather sofas that had been placed on opposite sides of the room. Over the next forty-five minutes, he texted, talked intermittently with Perez, and ate half of a large container of fruit salad. That left Roach with time to reflect on his six-fight tenure with Cotto.

"I'm glad Miguel is retiring on his terms," Freddie said. "That it's not some commission saying, 'You're all washed up, you're done.' I wish more fighters made decisions like that. I know I couldn't do it. I fought five times after I should have quit and lost four of them. The last fight I had was in Lowell, Massachusetts, which was my favorite place to fight. I embarrassed myself. I didn't even try to win. After that, I knew it was time."

In 2009, Roach had trained Manny Pacquiao for his brutal demolition of Cotto. Did he feel badly about that, given his fondness for Miguel?

"No," Freddie answered. "That was my job then. But I'm on Miguel's side now."

Roach paused.

"You know, Miguel and Manny are the two most talented fighters I've had. A trainer is lucky if one fighter like that comes his way in a lifetime. I've had two of them. But this is a must-win fight for Miguel. After everything he's accomplished, he doesn't want to go out on a loss."

At eight o'clock, Cotto left the dressing room and accompanied his family to their seats inside the main arena. After returning, he chatted with Robert Diaz (the matchmaker for Golden Boy Promotions, which was promoting the fight) and Cotto Promotions vice president Hector Soto. Then he left the room again, this time with a New York State Athletic Commission inspector for his pre-fight physical examination. He returned at 8:40, took off his pants, put on his boxing shoes, and handed his watch and necklace to Bryan Perez for safekeeping. Then he opened a sealed bottle of Fiji water he'd brought with him and began eating the rest of his fruit salad.

New York State Athletic Commission inspector Ernie Morales informed him that this was a problem. If Miguel ate anything more now, he'd have to provide another urine sample. And under NYSAC rules, he could only drink water provided by the promotion, which, in this case, consisted of twenty-four bottles of Dasani on a table at the far end of the room.

"But I like Fiji," Miguel protested. "Water is water."

Morales held firm.

Robert Diaz dispatched someone from Golden Boy to buy ten bottles of Fiji water for Cotto and ten more for Sadam Ali so each camp would be treated equally.

Roach went down the hall to watch Ali's hands being wrapped.

Miguel turned his attention to a large television monitor and stretched while watching an early preliminary fight.

The ten bottles of Fiji water arrived.

Andre Rozier (Ali's trainer) came into the room and watched as Somodio taped Miguel's hands. When the wrapping was done, Cotto lay down on the blue-carpeted floor and Marvin stretched him out. Then Miguel put on his protective cup and trunks, shadow-boxed for a while, and circled the room offering a kind word and physical gesture to everyone there.

Oscar De La Hoya, Golden Boy president Eric Gómez, and director of publicity Ramiro González came in to wish Miguel well. They were followed by referee Charlie Fitch, who gave Cotto his pre-fight instructions.

There was more shadow-boxing.

Shortly after 10:00 p.m., Miguel went into an adjacent room with Perez and Soto for a brief prayer.

Somodio gloved him up.

There was more shadow-boxing.

Cotto hit the pads with Roach for five minutes, took a minute off, and did it for five minutes more.

Another break. . . . More padwork.

Rey Vargas vs. Oscar Negrete (the co-featured fight of the evening) ended.

Miguel put on his robe, left the room, and walked to a boxing ring as an active professional fighter for the forty-seventh and final time in his storied ring career.

Cotto–Ali was Miguel's tenth fight at Madison Square Garden. Ticket sales had been hurt by an attractive slate of televised college football conference championship games that evening. More significantly, the core of Miguel's fan base in New York was the city's Puerto Rican community, and many would-be ticket buyers were sending whatever discretionary income they had to relatives on the island who'd been hard hit by the hurricane.

Cotto had weighed in for the bout at 151.6 pounds, his lowest weight since fighting Floyd Mayweather in 2012. Ali had weighed in at 153, his highest weight ever.

Miguel was the heartfelt favorite of almost everyone in the arena. But there's no room for sentiment in a boxing ring.

In the early going, Ali's handspeed and elusive footwork gave Cotto more than a bit of trouble. Sadam had come to win and was getting off first, while Miguel moved methodically forward but was unable to land effectively. Cotto was also having difficulty getting out of the way of punches, which happens to fighters when they get old. A sharp right to the ear followed by a right to the temple wobbled Miguel in round two.

Then Cotto began using his jab effectively and landing hooks to the body. By round six, Ali was tiring. There was swelling around his right eye. And Miguel's bodywork was taking a toll.

One moment can change everything in boxing.

Early in the second half of the fight, most likely in round seven or eight, Cotto tore a tendon in his left biceps.

As Bart Barry wrote long ago, "There's the pain of torn flesh or cramped muscles or wheezing breathlessness. And then there's injury. Injury is a non-negotiable signal sent to the central nervous system. One doesn't make his living in athletics without knowing the difference."

The torn tendon was an injury. It caused acute pain and rendered Cotto unable to effectively jab or hook. After eight rounds, Miguel was leading on two of the judges' scorecards and was even on the third. But now he was a one-armed fighter.

Ali continued to fight a disciplined fight, following the formula of getting off first and not waiting for a receipt. As Sadam's confidence grew, he fought more aggressively and won the last four rounds on each of the judges' scorecards. The judges got the final tally right: 116–112, 115–113, 115–113 in Ali's favor.

It wasn't supposed to end this way. But boxing is rarely about happy endings. Sadam Ali was thought to have been a "safe" opponent. But Father Time isn't.

Cotto was in obvious pain in his dressing room after the fight. New York State Athletic Commission chief medical officer Dr. Nitin Sethi and Dr. Kevin Wright (an orthopedic surgeon) examined his left arm and confirmed that he'd suffered a torn tendon in his left biceps. Worse, the tendon had been torn away from the bone. It was impossible to separate the injury from the outcome of the fight.

IN THE INNER SANCTUM

"Sadam caught Miguel with a good right hand in the second round," Roach acknowledged. "He was more explosive than I thought he'd be. But Miguel's jab was working well and he was doing good body work with the hook until he tore his biceps. He came back to the corner with a look on his face like he was in pain. I asked what was wrong, and he told me his arm was killing him. I've see that injury before. It takes your power away. And it hurts like hell."

Meanwhile, Cotto was philosophical about the night's events.

"This was the last chapter of my book on boxing," he said. "Now I have another book to write that will be more about my family."

One can argue that there's nothing noble about one man trying to render another man unconscious by inflicting concussive blows to the brain. But Miguel Cotto ennobled boxing. His legacy is that of a warrior who carried himself with dignity and grace in and out of the ring. His motto was simple: "I do my best every time I fight." He would have been respected as a fighter in any era.

Katie Taylor Can Fight
Katie Taylor vs. Victoria Noelia Bustos—
April 28, 2018

Jimmy Wilde reigned as the world's first flyweight champion and is regarded by some as the greatest British fighter of all time. Wilde once declared, "The idea of women in the boxing ring is repulsive and will receive no support from real lovers of the art. Girl boxers will ruin their matrimonial chances. No man could fancy a professional bruiser for a bride."

That was long ago. In recent years, women's boxing has begun the march toward acceptance by mainstream sports fans. But the talent pool is thin and many women boxers have limited skills.

Katie Taylor has contributed mightily to changing the perception of women's boxing. Christy Martin was a blip on the radar screen by virtue of her appearance on Mike Tyson undercards. Laila Ali garnered attention because she was Muhammad Ali's daughter. Lucia Rijker, the best female boxer of her era, was largely unknown. Taylor can fight and has earned recognition for it.

"When people watch me box," Katie told this writer, "I hope they see a boxer, not a female boxer. I would love to bring the sport to another level and take women's boxing to a place where people really respect it."

Both of Taylor's parents were involved with boxing. Her father, an Englishman, married an Irish woman and moved to Bray, County Wicklow, where Katie was born on July 2, 1986. He boxed as an amateur and was Katie's first coach when she took up the sport at age ten. Her mother was one of Ireland's first female boxing judges. Katie has three older siblings, one of whom is a professor of mathematics at Trinity College.

Taylor grew up physically gifted, competitive, and loving sports. She was an elite athlete at a young age in both boxing and soccer. The downside to being a fighter is that fighters get hit. But in the end, she gravitated to boxing.

Later, she would explain, "There comes a point in the life of all junior boxers, when you hit fourteen or fifteen years old, when the punches start to hurt and you have to decide whether you're going to take it seriously or not at all. There's no middle ground."

At age fifteen, boxing as an amateur, Taylor participated in the first officially sanctioned woman's match in the history of Ireland. Thereafter, she won six gold medals at the European Championships and five at the Women's World Championships. She was the flag bearer for Ireland at the 2012 London Olympics and became a national hero after winning a gold medal at those games.

"Listening to the anthem [at the awards ceremony]," Katie later reminisced, "was the proudest moment of my life."

Then came what Taylor calls "the lowest moment of my career." At the 2016 Rio de Janeiro Olympics, she lost in the first round to Mira Potkonen of Finland.

"I just didn't perform well," Katie said of that outing. "It's a simple as that."

Taylor turned pro in late 2016 and won the World Boxing Association title by decision over Anahi Ester Sánchez one year later. After successfully defending her tiara against Jessica McCaskill, she journeyed to America for a title unification bout against IBF beltholder Victoria Noelia Bustos at Barclays Center in Brooklyn.

Taylor vs. Bustos was on the undercard of an April 28, 2018, doubleheader on HBO featuring Danny Jacobs vs. Maciej Sulecki and Jarrell Miller vs. Johann Duhaupas. Bustos had 18 victories and 4 losses on her ring ledger but had never fought outside of Argentina. More significantly, in twenty-two professional fights, she had never scored a knockout. The odds favoring Taylor ran as high as 20-to-1 despite the fact that Bustos had been the IBF lightweight champion for over a year.

There was a problem during the medical examinations one day before the fight when a New York State Athletic Commission doctor noticed a cold sore on Bustos's lip. One doesn't normally think of a cold sore as preventing a fight. But Victoria was told that she needed a clearance letter from a dermatologist. The dermatologist then sent a letter to the commission saying that the sore was "likely" to be contained. That wasn't good enough for the NYSAC, which consulted next with an infectious disease specialist. It wasn't until 1:15 p.m. on fight day that Team Taylor was advised the fight was on.

Taylor's status as a star and also her gender dictated that she not share a dressing room with other fighters on fight night. Carrying her own gym bag, she arrived at room 1B11.09 at Barclays Center at 6:45 p.m. She was wearing black pants, a black T-shirt, gray sneakers, and a black jacket with "Katie Taylor" emblazoned in gold on the back. Her long dark hair was pulled back in a single braid. Trainer Ross Enamait and manager Brian Peters were with her.

The dressing room was fifteen feet long and ten feet wide with black industrial carpet, pale yellow walls, and recessed lighting above. A gray table built into one of the walls ran the length of the room with a wall-to-wall mirror above it. Seven black cushioned folding metal chairs were set against the table. A black leather sofa stood against the opposite wall.

Tomas Rohan (who works with Peters) and filmmaker Ross Whitaker joined the trio. It was a small group. No expanding circle of family, friends, and hangers-on.

Enamait unpacked his gym bag and put the tools of his trade on the table.

Veteran cutman Danny Milano (who would be working Katie's corner for the first time) brought in a half-dozen white terrycloth towels.

"I've been following the women for a while now," Milano had said earlier in the day. "They tend to lose their composure more quickly than the men when things aren't going their way. But not this one."

Katie sat on the sofa, propped her feet up on a chair, and sipped from a bottle of water.

At 7:10, Enamait asked a New York State Athletic Commission deputy commissioner if Bustos had arrived at the arena.

She hadn't.

"I'll feel better when I know she's here," the trainer said.

At 7:20, Brian Peters left the room to see if Bustos was on site yet. Five minutes later, he returned.

"She's here."

It was a quiet dressing room. For much of the time that Katie was there, she sat alone on the sofa, watching undercard fights on a TV monitor. Other times, Enamait or Peters sat beside her, engaging in quiet conversation.

Male or female, the rituals for battle are the same. A pre-fight physical examination and the taking of a urine sample were followed by the referee's dressing room instructions.

Occasionally, Katie stood and stretched. She has a well-muscled frame with shoulders that are broader and thighs that are more powerful than might appear at first glance.

At 7:40, Taylor put on a pair of black-and-gold boxing trunks, a matching top, and a fuchsia T-shirt with words from Psalm 18 in white letters on the front ("It is God who arms me with strength") and back ("He trains my hands for battle").

Enamait began taping Katie's hands, right hand first. At 8:15, the job was done.

Katie stretched on her own and shadow-boxed briefly.

Enamait greased her hair with petroleum jelly to hold it in place.

The assumption was that Katie would win. But boxing is boxing. She was about to venture into the unknown. In less than an hour, a woman trained in the art of hurting would try to hurt her.

"I get nervous before every fight," Taylor has said. "I'd be worried if I wasn't nervous. But I feel like I'm most alive when I'm in the ring. You don't know what will happen. That's what makes it so exciting."

There was more shadow-boxing. Katie's face looked harder now. She was transforming into a warrior.

Enamait gloved her up.

Trainer and fighter worked the pads together.

"Don't give her any free shots," Enamait cautioned.

Brian Peters helped Katie into a black robe with gold trim.

At nine o'clock, a voice instructed, "It's time to walk."

The fight went largely as expected.

Taylor has good footwork and good handspeed coupled with a nasty jab, a sharp straight right, an effective left hook, and a serviceable uppercut. She's not a big puncher but she mixes her punches well.

Fighting at a distance in the first half of the bout, Katie was in total control. In rounds eight and ten, she chose to trade on the inside (which was the only place Bustos could reach her), stayed in the pocket too long, and took some unnecessary punches. The judges were on the mark with their 99–91, 99–91, 98–92 verdict.

After the fight, Katie returned to her dressing room and sat on the sofa. There were ugly welts on her back and shoulders, a bruise on the left side of her forehead, and a smaller bruise beneath her right eye.

"I'm tired," she said.

Pressed for more, she elaborated on her performance.

"I can always do better, but I did okay tonight. She [Bustos] was durable, and it was a different style from what I'm used to fighting. I'm still learning my trade. There's a big difference between the amateurs and the pros. The pros are more physical. But I'm happy with the win, and I'm happy to be a unified champion."

In her next eight fights, Taylor beat Kimberly Connor, Cindy Serrano, Eva Wahlström, Rose Volante (adding the IBF title to her collection), Christina Linardatou, Miriam Gutiérrez, and Delfine Persoon (twice). In the process, she consolidated all four major sanctioning body 135-pound belts.

Her two fights against Persoon were the most telling. The first was contested at Madison Square Garden on June 1, 2019, on the undercard of the initial bout between Anthony Joshua and Andy Ruiz. Persoon brought the WBC strap to the table. Taylor was defending her WBA, WBO, and IBF titles.

It was a good fight. Taylor was the better boxer and landed the sharper, cleaner punches. Persoon was stronger and kept forcing the action. As the rounds passed, Persoon kept fighting, and Taylor kept boxing. What was clear, though, was that Katie was tiring and not hitting hard enough to keep Delfine off.

The fight devolved into a bloody slugfest. Each fighter's face became more bruised and swollen. Persoon kept moving inexorably forward, throwing inartful clubbing right hands. An exhausted Taylor kept firing back. Katie's power was gone. Her strength was gone. All she had left were the remnants of her conditioning and her will to survive.

The consensus at ringside was that Persoon had forced the action effectively enough to deserve the nod. But the decision went to Taylor by a 96–94, 96–94, 95–95 margin. Afterward, Carl Frampton told BBC

Radio 5, "The judges have got it wrong, and it is heartbreaking to see Delfine Persoon in tears. I thought she won that fight by miles. That was a disgraceful decision."

Eddie Hearn (Taylor's promoter) said that he'd scored the fight a draw and conceded, "Quite a few people had Persoon winning." He also quoted Katie as saying, "We've got to fight her again, straight away."

Unlike many fighters who duck tough opponents after a narrow escape on the judges' scorecards, Taylor was true to her word. On August 22, 2020, the two women met in the ring again. As in their first encounter, Persoon was the physically stronger fighter. She moved forward for the entire ten rounds, mauling and brawling as best she could. This time, though, Katie boxed more and stood her ground less, rendering Delfine's pressure tactics less effective.

Taylor tired a bit as the fight wore on. Her punches lost some of their sting and she got hit with some good shots. She was never able to discourage Persoon but she did outbox her. There was no controversy as to the winner. Katie emerged with 96–94, 96–94, 98–93 triumph.

"She deserves this time to win," Persoon acknowledged.

In recent years, championships have been sadly devalued in boxing. And that's particularly true on the women's side of the ledger where "championships" are dispensed like trinkets from a gumball machine.

The world sanctioning bodies, motivated by an insatiable lust for sanctioning fees, have created 110 different women's titles. This means that, assuming each title is available in 17 weight divisions, the sanctioning bodies have belts for 1,870 women's champions. Meanwhile, according to John Sheppard of BoxRec.com, as of this writing there are 1,493 active women boxers.

Do the math. This means there are 1.25 titles available for each woman boxer fighting today.

In this nonsensical world, Taylor stands out as a "real" champion. No one should be fooled by her gentle outside-the-ring demeanor. She's a tough, skilled professional fighter.

Katie is confident but not arrogant with regard to her ring skills. She laughs easily and is poised, gracious, articulate, and unfailingly polite. She likes attention but is wary of it. In recent years, she has spent most of her time in Connecticut, an ocean away from many of her loved ones.

"I love the fact that I'm anonymous in America," Katie has said. "I can go for walks and be left alone when I want to be alone. I can just be myself over here."

There's a private, somewhat shy, person behind the public facade.

As Taylor ages, her years in the sweet science are numbered. But as women's boxing advances to the point where there can be a serious pound-for-pound conversation, many knowledgeable observers believe that Katie belongs in the #1 slot on today's list.

Men's boxing has a storied tradition. Today's male fighters can look back in time and say, "I would have loved to have fought Sugar Ray Robinson. Or Muhammad Ali. Or Joe Louis." Maybe someday, young women fighters will look back on this era and say, "I would have loved to have fought Katie Taylor."

The Validation of Canelo Álvarez
Canelo Álvarez vs. Gennady Golovkin—
September 15, 2018

Boxing is a mess. Speculation regarding which big fights might be scheduled is an unsatisfying substitute for the fights themselves. But on occasion, the best do fight the best. When that happens, a great fighter can emerge. Such was the case when Canelo Álvarez fought Gennady Golovkin.

Canelo and Golovkin fought twice. Their first encounter, on September 16, 2017, resulted in a controversial draw. Their second meeting, one day shy of a year later, validated Canelo's standing as an elite fighter and justified his status as boxing's biggest box-office star and pay-per-view attraction.

Álvarez has been in the spotlight since he was an adolescent. The weight of great expectations in his Mexican homeland has been on his shoulders for more than a decade. He turned pro at age fifteen and, prior to meeting Golovkin for the first time, had fashioned a 49–1–1 (34 KOs) ring record. He was willing to go in tough and had defeated some of boxing's biggest names including Shane Mosley and Miguel Cotto. There were also victories over Erislandy Lara, Austin Trout, and Amir Khan. But with each win, there was a caveat attached. This opponent was too old. That one was too small. And there was a 2013 loss to Floyd Mayweather when a too-young Canelo was outslicked over twelve long rounds.

Gennady Golovkin was born in Kazakhstan. After compiling a reported 345–5 amateur record and winning a silver medal at the 2004 Olympics, he turned pro and won his first 37 professional bouts, scoring 33 knockouts and claiming the WBC, WBA, and IBF 160-pound titles. At his best, he relentlessly ground opponents down. The one important element missing from his résumé was a victory over an elite boxer in his prime.

The first meeting between Canelo and Golovkin was the most-anticipated fight of the year. It generated a live gate of $27,059,850 at

T-Mobile Arena, the third largest in boxing history. The 22,358 fans in attendance comprised the largest indoor crowd ever for a fight in Las Vegas.

It was a spirited contest with most observers believing that Golovkin deserved the nod. Dave Moretti scored the bout 115–113 for Gennady. Don Trella had it even. Adelaide Byrd turned in what might have been the worst scorecard ever in a major fight: 118–110 for Canelo.

Clearly, a rematch was in order. A contract for a May 5, 2018, encore was signed. Then there was a problem. A big one. On March 5, it was revealed that two urine samples taken from Canelo by the Voluntary Anti-Doping Association (VADA) had tested positive for clenbuterol.

The Álvarez camp maintained that the positive tests were the result of Canelo having inadvertently eaten contaminated beef. To this day, Canelo maintains his innocence. Regardless, on April 3, 2018, he announced that he was withdrawing from the May 5 rematch. Then, on April 18, the Nevada State Athletic Commission unanimously approved a settlement agreed to by Álvarez that called for the fighter to be suspended for six months retroactive to the date of his first positive test for clenbuterol. There was no admission of wrongdoing on Canelo's part. But there was an acknowledgment that clenbuterol had been present in his system.

With Álvarez temporarily out of the picture, Golovkin fought Vanes Martirosyan. Then negotiations for Canelo–Golovkin II resumed. On June 13, the two camps agreed to a September 15, 2018, rematch at T-Mobile Arena.

It would be a legacy fight for both men. But for Canelo, it was something more. Canelo–Golovkin I had been for history and glory. This one, because of the fallout from the positive drug test, was for Canelo's honor.

Canelo–Golovkin I had been conducted in an atmosphere of mutual respect. It was a feel-good promotion and a celebration of boxing. Two elite fighters had fought one another in the spirit of goodwill.

Canelo–Golovkin II was a different matter. Leading up to the rematch, the antipathy between the fighters was such that they declined to participate in traditional marketing ventures and, prior to the fight, appeared together only for the final pre-fight press conference and weigh-in. There was no kickoff promotional media tour. In its place, the two teams participated in a split-screen media conference from their respective training camps in Guadalajara and Big Bear.

"It doesn't matter if he likes me, loves me, doesn't like me," Golovkin said. "I wouldn't say I hate him. It's just that my opinion of him has changed completely."

Golovkin's grievances began with his belief that Canelo had used illegal performance-enhancing drugs while preparing for their first fight. Canelo, in turn, was resentful that he was being called a "cheater." No fighter had been tested by VADA more often and without a problem over the years than he had. And while the standard for the presence of clen-buterol in an athlete's system is qualitative, not quantitative, the amount found in his urine had been small enough to be consistent with the inadvertent ingestion of tainted beef.

Golovkin was also upset by the decision in Canelo–Golovkin I.

"Canelo lost that fight," Gennady said. "That's it. He lost the fight according to all standards. I thought I didn't understand something, but then I reviewed the fight. These people [the judges] are like terrorists. They're killing sport. People like that should be in prison."

Then Golovkin and his trainer, Abel Sanchez, began saying that Canelo wasn't a true "Mexican" fighter.

In the past, Team Golovkin had gone to great lengths to market Gennady as a "Mexican-style" fighter.

"There is no such thing as a Mexican style," Canelo had noted. "There have been many fighters from Mexico with different styles. My style is mine. I'm Mexican, and that's what is important."

But Sanchez roiled the waters. After calling Canelo "a man without character," he questioned his credentials as a representative of the Mexican people. Then he added, "I hope Canelo was able to see a transmission specialist for the rematch because in the first fight he was stuck in reverse. He was a runner."

"I outboxed him," Canelo responded. "I went on the ropes. I made him miss. I controlled the center of the ring. I'm not a jackass who just comes forward throwing punches and gets hit. He believes he is a great coach. He does not know what boxing is. He does not know what it is to have technique, what it is to box, what it is to make a move, knowing how to adapt to the circumstances of the fight, not just going forward throwing punches. I hope he goes home tonight and really thinks about what he says. Because he's saying stupid idiotic things."

Then Golovkin added fuel to the fire, saying, "This wasn't boxing by Canelo. It was running. He always has a way of running in the ring. However, in our last fight, he was really avoiding fighting close to me. I felt a couple of slaps. Slap! Slap! I didn't feel real power, punch power. He's fast; he's quick. He is good fighter but he is not at my level."

Canelo stated the obvious when he observed, "The cordiality we had is over. The respect that I had, that we had, it has been lost. They disrespected me for everything they have been saying, everything they have been doing, all their actions. Now it's different. This fight is personal because of all that has been said, and it will be difficult to regain the respect we once had."

Who would win?

Golovkin was a 13-to-10 betting favorite. Both men were big punchers. Each had a granite chin. Golovkin liked to force his opponent to the ropes. Canelo liked to counter off them. Each fighter knew that, on fight night, more than a few liver shots would be aimed in his direction.

★★★

Canelo Álvarez arrived at dressing room #1 at the T-Mobile Arena on fight night at 5:10 p.m. A five-by-ten-foot Mexican flag hung on the wall opposite a large flat-screen television monitor.

Two hours earlier, a seven-man film crew working for Canelo had set up in the room. The crew was gathering material for a documentary about his life. It also fed content to Canelo's 3.6 million Instagram followers, his 1.3 million Twitter followers, and the 2.9 million people in his Facebook community. The cameras recorded his arrival in the dressing room with Chepo Reynoso (his manager) and Eddy Reynoso (Chepo's son and Canelo's trainer).

Canelo sat on a black imitation-leather armchair to the left of the flag. No one knew it at the time, but this would be HBO's last pay-per-view fight. Three months later, the network would leave the boxing business.

HBO production coordinator Tami Cotel came in and positioned Canelo for a pre-fight interview with Max Kellerman. When the interview was done, Canelo returned to the armchair and, arms crossed across his chest, began watching the first pay-per-bout of the evening on the TV monitor. Román González knocked Moisés Fuentes unconscious in round five. Canelo nodded in acknowledgment.

David Lemieux vs. Gary "Spike" O'Sullivan—the second televised bout of the evening—began. Canelo turned his body slightly to the right in his chair, crossed his right leg over his left thigh, and studied the action with his right hand pressed against his chin. The fight didn't last long. Lemieux KO'd O'Sullivan 2 minutes, 44 seconds into round one.

Two fights. Two reminders of how suddenly and brutally a fight can end.

Soft Latin music began playing in the dressing room.

The TV monitor showed Gennady Golovkin arriving at T-Mobile Arena.

Several sponsor representatives entered. Canelo rose to greet them and posed for photos before returning to his chair. Video footage from his first fight against Golovkin began to play on the monitor. Canelo watched impassively.

At 6:05, clad in a tuxedo, Julio César Chávez came in to conduct an interview for Mexican television. That was followed by a visit from Nevada State Athletic Commission executive director Bob Bennett, who arrived with several commission dignitaries and referee Benjy Esteves, who gave Canelo his pre-fight instructions.

Golden Boy publicist Gabriel Rivas and matchmaker Robert Diaz appeared from time to time to attend to various matters.

The video of Canelo–Golovkin I ended.

More well-wishers, family members, and friends came and went. Canelo rose from his chair to greet each one with a welcoming smile and embrace.

At 6:20, Canelo's girlfriend came into the room with his daughter, an adorable toddler named Maria Fernanda Álvarez. Canelo took his daughter in his arms and sat with her on his lap.

"What a beautiful girl," he murmured.

He lifted her arms up and down while nuzzling her cheek and saying "Papa! Papa!" over and over again in a singsong voice.

Maria rested comfortably in her father's arms. Then Canelo rose from his chair and walked her around the room on her unsteady legs, holding both of her arms above her head from behind.

He looked like a man playing at home with his daughter, not a warrior readying for war.

Jaime Munguia vs. Brandon Cook—the third fight on the pay-per-view telecast—began. It was over in three rounds. Canelo put his daughter down and began stretching with Eddy Reynoso, his first boxing-related exercise of the evening.

Miguel Cotto, who Álvarez defeated in 2015 to win his first middleweight belt, came in, hugged Canelo, shook hands with Eddy, and chatted for several minutes with Chepo.

There was more stretching.

At seven o'clock, Eddy began wrapping Canelo's hands with a representative of Golovkin's camp looking on. Right hand first, then the left.

At 7:15, inspectors Alex Ybarra, Francisco Soto, and Charvez Foger cleared the room of camera crews, family members, and friends. In forty-five minutes, Canelo would leave his sanctuary for the ring.

Tami Cotel returned with the request that Canelo sit for a brief interview for HBO social media.

"I'm sorry," Robert Diaz told her. "This isn't a television show now. He has to get ready for a fight."

Canelo put on a protective cup and black trunks with gold trim. Eddy applied Vaseline to his face. There was more stretching followed by a brief interlude of shadow-boxing.

Eddy gloved Canelo up.

There was some padwork.

Cotel returned. "You walk in twelve minutes," she instructed.

Chepo draped a black serape emblazoned with a Mexican-flag emblem over Canelo's shoulders.

The dressing room had been remarkably quiet from start to finish. Now only the soft Latin music could be heard.

Canelo began signing in tune with the music. A love song.

★★★

A. J. Liebling once wrote of rematches, "The spectator who goes twice to a play he likes is pretty sure of getting what he pays for on his second visit, especially if the cast is unchanged. This is not true of the sweet science."

With Canelo–Golovkin II, fight fans got what they paid for.

The crowd was divided with vociferous partisans on each side. Chants of "GGG! GGG!" were met with "Ca-nel-o! Ca-nel-o!"

Golovkin looked flat in the early going. Or was it old? He was thirty-six, eight years older than Canelo. Either way, he didn't fight the way the world was used to seeing him fight.

A lot of that was due to Canelo. Looking back on their first encounter, Álvarez had realized that Golovkin was wary of his power. Very wary. In his dressing room after that bout, Canelo had told his team, "The judges think he punches like a monster. My punches were just as hard as his, harder."

So this time, Canelo decided to test Golovkin early with more aggression and see how he responded. By moving forward and holding his ground, he deprived Golovkin of the ability to set up at his leisure and gave Gennady less room to mount an attack. This time, Canelo was the man stalking. This time, Canelo moved forward constantly and gave ground more grudgingly while fighting a measured, disciplined fight.

And this time, Golovkin was the more cautious fighter. He jabbed effectively. But Gennady has built his reputation and dominated opponents with the power punching that follows his jab. And that power was absent here because, like all boxers, Gennady throws with less authority when his forward momentum is stalled.

Canelo went to the body consistently and effectively, fighting like the more confident man and forcing the pace of the fight. When Golovkin hit him solidly, he fired back.

Gennady's face started to show bruising as early as round two. Canelo was cut on the left eyelid in round four.

After five rounds, Golovkin was breathing heavily in his corner. After nine rounds, he looked to be fading. Canelo's power was influencing him more than his power was influencing Canelo. It was clear that Gennady needed another gear to win. And digging deep, he found it.

Midway through round ten, Golovkin shook Canelo with a straight right hand and followed with a barrage of punches. Most of them missed, and Canelo regrouped to fire back.

In round eleven, Gennady shook Canelo again. Round twelve saw toe-to-toe action as both men sensed that the outcome of the fight was in doubt. At the final bell, they embraced. Two men who understood that, in the ring, they were the equal of each other.

"I scored the fight even," Abel Sanchez said afterward. "I thought that the twelfth round was the pivotal round. We've got to give Canelo credit. He was able to do the things that he needed to do tonight."

The judges also thought the fight was close but favored Canelo by a 115–113, 115–113, 114–114 margin.

LeBron James, who was sitting at ringside, later tweeted, "One of the best fights I've ever seen! Ultimate competitors in @Canelo and @GGGBoxing! Salute to both of you. Could watch y'all fight any day."

Most athletes believe they won't get hurt in competition. Boxers know they will.

Sergiy Derevyanchenko
and the Harsh Reality of Boxing
Gennady Golovkin vs. Sergiy Derevyanchenko—
October 5, 2019

When Oscar De La Hoya was nearing the end of his career as an active fighter, he offered a stark assessment of the risks inherent in the trade he had chosen.

"I hate getting hit," De La Hoya said. "Getting hit hurts. It damages you. When a fighter trains his body and mind to fight, there's no room for fear. But I'm realistic enough to understand that there's no way to know what the effect of getting hit will be ten or fifteen years from now."

Boxers are not like ordinary people. They court danger and have a tolerance for pain that most of us think we can imagine but can't. That harsh reality was on display when thirty-seven-year-old Gennady Golovkin and thirty-three-year-old Sergiy Derevyanchenko met in the ring at Madison Square Garden on October 5, 2019, in a fight that will be long remembered as a showcase for the brutal artistry of boxing.

Derevyanchenko was born in Ukraine and had roughly four hundred amateur fights in the Ukrainian amateur system. That gave him a wealth of experience but also put considerable wear and tear on his body. He moved to Brooklyn, turned pro in 2014 and, prior to facing Golovkin, had a record of 13 wins against 1 loss with 10 knockouts. The loss came in his one outing against a world-class opponent—a 115–112, 115–112, 113–114 split-decision defeat at the hands of Danny Jacobs.

Derevyanchenko is soft-spoken with a brush haircut, often impassive face, and eyes that can be hard. He understands some English but prefers to have questions translated into Russian and answer in his native language.

"I don't like to talk about myself," Derevyanchenko said during the days leading up to his fighting Golovkin. "I'm a private person. The attention that comes with boxing is a double-edged sword. For the money it helps me make, the attention is good. But the loss of privacy sometimes, especially when I am out with my family, it is not so good."

Golovkin is well known to boxing fans. Born in Kazakhstan, living in Los Angeles, he brutalized a succession of pretty good fighters like Matthew Macklin and David Lemieux en route to becoming the best middleweight in the world. But in 2017, Gennady struggled to win a narrow decision on points over Danny Jacobs at Madison Square Garden. Thereafter, he'd had four fights—gimme knockouts of Vanes Martirosyan and Steve Rolls and two outings against Canelo Álvarez. The first Golovkin–Canelo fight (which most observers thought Gennady won) was declared a draw. The second ended with a credible 115–113, 115–113, 114–114 decision in Canelo's favor, the first loss of Golovkin's ring career.

Golovkin–Derevyanchenko crystalized how bizarre the business of boxing has become in recent years.

One year earlier, the IBF had stripped Golovkin of its 160-pound belt for not fighting a mandatory defense against Derevyanchenko. Then Jacobs beat Derevyanchenko for the vacant IBF title but lost to Canelo Álvarez in his next outing. Thereafter, the IBF stripped Canelo for not fighting a mandatory defense against Derevyanchenko despite the fact that Sergiy's only win after losing to Jacobs was a decision over lightly regarded Jack Culcay. Thus, Golovkin was fighting Derevyanchenko for the same belt he was stripped of for not fighting Sergiy the previous year.

If that sounds strange, the money being thrown around was stranger.

Traditionally, a fighter had to win one or more big fights before getting a seven-figure purse. But DAZN, ESPN, FOX, and Showtime were locked in a bidding war that had led to the payment of huge license fees that often bore no correlation to the revenue generated for a network by its fighters.

DAZN (which had a multi-fight deal with Golovkin) wanted Golovkin–Derevyanchenko as the launching pad for the final quarter of its 2019 season. The network was already locked into a deal that would pay Gennady a reported purse of $7.5 million in cash plus $7.5 million in stock in DAZN's parent company to fight on October 5. DAZN then leaned on promoter Eddie Hearn to contribute significantly to Derevyanchenko's purse to bring Sergiy into the fold.

Thus it was that Derevyanchenko (a largely unknown fighter with thirteen pro victories on his résumé and who had never beaten a world-class fighter) was rewarded with a purse totaling $5.2 million to fight Golovkin. Training expenses, manager Keith Connally's share, taxes, and whatever Premier Boxing Champions took (Derevyanchenko is a PBC fighter) came out of that total. Still, very few fighters in history have had a payday approaching that number. A marketable belt was at stake, but the fight wasn't even for "the" middleweight championship of the world (a title that resided with Canelo Álvarez).

"I like the sport," Sergiy said when asked about boxing three days before fighting Golovkin. "I like the business. The business is crazy now."

There was no trash-talking by either side during the buildup to the fight. The only sour note came at a sit-down with reporters just prior to the final pre-fight press conference when Golovkin was asked one question too many about a possible third fight against Álvarez.

"All these questions about Canelo," Gennady answered. "It's your problem, not mine."

Golovkin was a 4-to-1 betting favorite over Derevyanchenko. He and Sergiy had each fought on even terms against Jacobs. But styles make fights. And the feeling was that, while Gennady and Sergiy had similar styles, Golovkin did everything a little bit better. He hit harder, took a better punch, was a shade faster, and so on down the line. ESPN asked eleven of its boxing reporters to predict the outcome of the fight. Ten thought that Golovkin would win by knockout. The eleventh chose Gennady by decision.

But while few insiders predicted that Derevyanchenko would win, no one was counting him out either.

The question most often asked when the outcome of the fight was discussed was whether Golovkin had slipped with age. And if so, how far? Also, Derevyanchenko was in the best condition of his life, having spent six weeks in California preparing for the bout at Victor Conte's SNAC conditioning facility.

This was Sergiy's chance to prove that he belonged at the table with boxing's top-echelon middleweights.

"Gennady has been a great champion but his time is coming to an end," Derevyanchenko prophesied. "I want to be the one who makes it come to an end."

★★★

Wearing a black Nike track suit with white trim, Derevyanchenko arrived in dressing room #3 at Madison Square Garden on fight night at 8:20 p.m.

The room was roughly thirty feet long and twenty feet wide with a linoleum floor styled to look like hardwood planks. Ten cushioned metal-frame folding chairs were set against the walls. A two-seat, green imitation-leather sofa fronted a large flat-screen television mounted on the wall opposite the door. A college football game was underway.

Some fighters like lots of action in their dressing room. Derevyanchenko preferred calm with no distractions. For the next two hours, he was quiet and self-contained. Except for manager Keith Connolly, no one even looked at a cell phone. From the moment Sergiy entered the room until he walked to the ring, everything was businesslike and low key.

After leaving the room briefly for a pre-fight physical, Derevyanchenko returned, sat on a folding metal chair with his hands clasped behind his head, and stretched out his legs. Then he moved to the sofa and adopted a similar position.

A handful of people came and went—Iryna Derevyanchenko (Sergiy's wife), Pat Connolly (Keith's father), PBC representative Sam Watson.

Co-trainers Andre Rozier and Gary Stark, Sergiy Konchynsky (a friend of Derevyanchenko's since childhood), and cutman Mike Bazzel were a constant presence. Unlike Jacobs–Derevyanchenko, when Rozier (who trained both men) worked Danny's corner, Sergiy's team was now unified.

At nine o'clock, Sergiy rose from the sofa, walked over to a shrink-wrapped package that contained twenty-four bottles of Aquafina, opened a bottle, and took a sip. Then he began changing into his boxing gear, folding his street clothes neatly before putting them aside.

At 9:05, referee Harvey Dock came in and gave Sergiy his pre-fight instructions: "There is no three-knockdown rule. . . . If your mouthpiece comes out. . . . If you score a knockdown. . . ."

When Dock was done, Keith Connolly raised the issue of Golovkin hitting opponents on the back of the head and asked the referee to affirm that he would take strict action in the event of a foul. Dock promised to enforce the rules. Connolly repeated his point and got the same answer the second time around.

At 9:15, Stitch Duran (Golovkin's cutman) came in to watch Stark wrap Sergiy's hands.

Rozier fiddled with the TV remote until the DAZN undercard appeared on the screen.

At 9:34, the wrapping was done.

Sergiy began stretching on his own.

Connolly handed him a smartphone. Al Haymon was calling to wish Sergiy well. The conversation was short, ten seconds of best wishes for the fight.

Sergiy put a white towel on the floor and continued stretching. When that was done, he stood up and Stark led him through more stretching exercises.

Konchynsky approached Maggie Lange (the lead New York State Athletic Commission inspector in the room) and showed her a silver canister labeled "Boost Oxygen."

"Is it all right if we use this?"

"What is it?" Lange countered.

"Oxygen."

"I don't know," Lange said. "Let's go for a ruling."

Konchynsky and the inspector left the room to consult with the commission's medical staff.

Derevyanchenko began shadow-boxing.

"It's your night, bro," Rozier told him.

Konchynsky and Lange returned. The powers that be had said "no" to Boost Oxygen.

Stark gloved Derevyanchenko up.

Sergiy pounded his gloves together and hit the pads with the trainer.

Mike Bazzel greased him down.

Rozier led the group in a brief prayer.

Golovkin's image appeared on the TV monitor. If he and Sergiy weren't about to fight each other, one could imagine them sitting side by side in someone's living room watching the fight together on television. By virtue of their trade, they had more in common than most people in the arena.

Sergiy shadow-boxed a bit more, then paced back and forth, deep in thought. He had followed these rituals many times before. But the stakes had never been this high. Glory and a possible eight-figure payday for his next fight if he won. And the very real possibility that he would be physically damaged before the night was done. This wasn't a movie about life. It was the real thing. More than anyone else, fighters know what's at stake every time they enter the ring.

Golovkin was the crowd favorite. Both men began the fight cautiously. Then, two minutes into round one, Derevyanchenko ducked low as Gennady threw a right hand. The punch landed just behind the top of Sergiy's head and put him down.

"He hit me in the back of the head," Derevyanchenko said later. "I didn't see the punch, but it didn't really affect me that much. I got up and I wasn't really hurt, so it was nothing too bad."

But the round had been up for grabs until that point. Now it was a two-point round for Golovkin. And the next stanza brought something very bad for Sergiy. A left hook landed cleanly and opened an ugly gash on his right eyelid.

Referee Harvey Dock mistakenly ruled that the cut had been caused by an accidental head butt. And because the New York State Athletic Commission doesn't allow for instant video review, that ruling stood. Be that as it may, Derevyanchenko was now at a distinct disadvantage.

Cutman Mike Bazzel swabbed adrenaline into the cut and applied pressure after every round. But he was never able to completely stop the flow of blood. The dripping was a distraction. And as the bout progressed, Sergiy had increasing difficulty seeing Golovkin's punches coming.

"The cut really changed the fight," Sergiy said afterward. "I couldn't see at times. And he was targeting the eye."

Now Derevyanchenko was in a hole. But a fighter can't let his mind wander to what happened the round before or several punches ago. He has to stay in the moment.

Sergiy's response to adversity was to fight more aggressively. "When I started [the fight] moving," he explained later, "I felt like I was giving him room and I was getting hit with those shots that he threw. That's why I started taking the fight to him and getting closer and not giving him room to maneuver."

The strategy worked. Golovkin appeared to have the heavier hands. But Derevyanchenko began winning the war in the trenches. Several body shots hurt Gennady. He seemed to be tiring and losing his edge. One had the feeling that, if Sergiy's eye held up and he was able to take the fight into the late rounds, an upset was possible. Golovkin had a look about him that said, "Either I'm getting old or you're good."

Brutal warfare followed. Choose your metaphor. Two men walking through fire. A dogfight between pit bulls.

The crowd roared through it all.

Neither man shied away from confrontations. In round eleven, Sergiy's left eyelid (the one that hadn't been cut) noticeably puffed up. In round twelve, it looked like a balloon. Both men dug as deep as it was possible to dig. And then some.

Most ringside observers thought Derevyanchenko won the fight by a narrow margin. But before the decision was announced, DAZN blow-by-blow commentator Brian Kenny observed, "[The judges] come into the fight with a certain mindset. Golovkin is the favorite. You expect him to do better."

That mindset was reflected in the judges' verdict: Frank Lombardi 115–112, Eric Marlinski 115–112, Kevin Morgan 114–113—all for Golovkin. The crowd booed when the decision was announced. They weren't booing Gennady, who had fought as heroically as Sergiy. They were booing the decision. A draw would have been equitable. One point in favor of Golovkin was within the realm of reason. 115–112 (7 rounds to 5 for Gennady) was bad judging.

Golovkin himself seemed to acknowledge the iffy nature of the decision when he said in the ring after the fight, "I want to say thank you so much to my opponent. He's a very tough guy. This is huge experience for me. This was a tough fight. I need to still get stronger in my camp. I need a little bit more focus. Right now, it's bad day for me. It's a huge day for Sergiy. Sergiy was ready. He showed me such a big heart."

That thought was echoed by Johnathon Banks (Golovkin's trainer), who later acknowledged, "I don't remember the exact scores, but I thought the fight was a lot closer than that."

After the fight, the skin around Derevyanchenko's eyes was swollen to the point where each eye was almost shut. His right eyelid was purple, bulging, and sliced open. There was a huge pocket of blood beneath his left eyelid.

Neither fighter attended the post-fight press conference. Sergey Konchynsky came into Derevyanchenko's dressing room, packed Sergiy's civilian clothes in a gym bag, and left. Then he and Keith Connolly went with Derevyanchenko to Bellevue Hospital where they were joined by Golovkin, who was brought in as a precautionary measure.

"It took forever at the hospital," Connolly later recalled. "Sergiy and Gennady might have been the only patients there who weren't handcuffed to a gurney."

Derevyanchenko was stitched up and released from the hospital around 5:00 a.m. Then he, Iryna, Konchynsky, and Connolly went to the Tick-Tock Diner on Thirty-Fourth Street, where Sergiy ate blueberry pancakes before going back to his hotel to sleep.

Boxing fans should celebrate the courage and fortitude that Sergiy Derevyanchenko and Gennady Golovkin showed in the ring while battling against each other. And they should remember—fighters are damaged every time they step into the ring. Fights like this take a heavy toll on both fighters. And sometimes the winner is damaged more than the loser.

Prior to fighting Sergey Kovalev, Canelo Álvarez observed, "It's a challenge. But I won't know how big a challenge until I get in the ring with him."

History in the Making
Canelo Álvarez vs. Sergey Kovalev— November 2, 2019

On November 2, 2019, Canelo Álvarez and Sergey Kovalev met in the ring at the MGM Grand Garden Arena in Las Vegas to do battle for the World Boxing Organization 175-pound title.

Canelo's credentials are a matter of record. At age twenty-nine, he was boxing's biggest star and the #1 pound-for-pound fighter in the world. Early in his career, his red hair had been a much-publicized marketing tool. And because of that, some people were slow to give him his due as a fighter. It was also fashionable in some circles to demean Canelo because his power is sometimes overshadowed by his finesse. This, critics said, was a betrayal of his Mexican roots ("He's not a Mexican-style fighter"). Bart Barry rebutted that notion, writing, "Mexican prizefighters do not wish to get struck in the face any more than any other type of prizefighter does."

Canelo spoke to the same point, saying, "In boxing, you have to take care of yourself. I haven't had as many wars as others have had. But there is no need for you to let yourself take a beating and to be bloody to be a great fighter. I am not going to stop what I'm doing to get all bloody and get knocked down all over the place if I have no need to."

Elite fighters have self-belief. Canelo believes in himself and radiates quiet confidence without the loud bravado often associated with boxing. He has the mindset of a fighter and is fundamentally sound with speed, power, and a solid chin. When speaking in public, he chooses his words carefully, keeping his guard up during interviews as he does in the ring.

Prior to fighting Kovalev, Canelo had compiled a 52–1–2 ring ledger. One of the draws came when he was fifteen years old. The other was against Gennady Golovkin. The loss was to Floyd Mayweather when Mayweather was at his peak and Canelo had yet to mature as a fighter.

He has worked hard to get better and has tested himself at every level. He embraces challenges.

Initially, it was expected that Canelo would fight Golovkin for the third time in Las Vegas on September 14 in conjunction with Mexican Independence Day weekend. But bad blood between the two camps led Canelo to seek another opponent. That left DAZN in a quandary. DAZN needed a marketable opponent for Canelo, who was its flagship attraction. The nod went to Kovalev.

Kovalev came into the promotion with a 34–3–1 (29 KOs) record. Once, he'd been the best of boxing's 175-pound champions, having torn undefeated through the light-heavyweight division. He dominated an aging Bernard Hopkins en route to a unanimous shutout decision in Atlantic City and knocked out Jean Pascal twice before losing a controversial verdict (114–113 on each judge's scorecard) to Andre Ward in 2016. Meanwhile, two months prior to Kovalev–Ward, Canelo had fought Liam Smith at 154 pounds. The idea that Canelo and Kovalev might meet in the ring someday would have been derided as fanciful three years earlier. But after Kovalev–Ward, Sergey faltered. He was knocked out in a rematch against Ward. Then, subsequent to reclaiming the WBO belt by stoppage over Vyacheslav Shabransky, he was KO'd by Elieder Álvarez. Kovalev later decisioned Elieder to win the WBO belt a third time. But in August 2019, he struggled to defeat Anthony Yarde.

Canelo, who had grown comfortable at 160 pounds during the preceding two years, would be moving up two weight classes to challenge Kovalev. To his credit, he did not demand a catchweight.

The promotion was about Canelo. The storyline wasn't whether the thirty-six-year-old Kovalev could withstand the challenge from his twenty-nine-year-old opponent. Nor was it a defining fight for boxing's light-heavyweight division. But it would be a defining fight for Canelo.

Canelo was a 7-to-2 betting favorite. The case for an upset rested in large measure on the size differential between the two men. Canelo had turned pro at 139 pounds. Kovalev had fought at light-heavyweight for his entire ring career.

Canelo is five feet, eight inches tall. Sergey is four inches taller. Canelo would have to get inside Kovalev's jab to nullify Sergey's advantage in reach and work the body. It's a good jab. Kovalev hit harder than anyone

Canelo had fought before with the possible exception of Golovkin. And how effective would Canelo's punches be against a man who was bigger than anyone he'd previously fought?

"It's going to be a hard fight," Kovalev acknowledged. "Canelo is very dangerous. He is strong. He smashes you with body punches, hooks, uppercuts. He has good technique. He is great champion. But this is my division, not his. I am bigger. I am taller. I make the fight my way."

That said, Kovalev had been known to wilt when his body was effectively attacked. Canelo had "man strength" now, coupled with a ferocious body attack. And the 175-pound contract weight was a double-edged sword, as revealed by the satellite tour interviews that the fighters engaged in two days before the bout.

Canelo looked hale and hearty. He hadn't put on weight to fight at 175 pounds. He had simply lost less weight while adding muscle in the process.

"Do you like fighting at a heavier weight?" he was asked.

"Sí," Canelo answered. "More eat, more happy."

Kovalev, by contrast, looked tired and drawn. When asked about Canelo coming up in weight, he answered, "He is more dangerous now than ever because he does not have to lose energy to make weight. When you are losing weight, you are losing energy. He is saving energy. For me, it is more difficult now to make weight, but next division is very high for me. One-eighty-five would be best, but there is no title at 185. I will be very happy for the weigh-in."

When the weigh-in came, Canelo registered 174½ pounds; Kovalev, 176.

Sergey removed the crucifix from around his neck . . . 175½.

He took off his shorts . . . 175¼.

He excused himself, went to the restroom, vomited, and returned to the scale . . . 175.

★★★

Canelo Álvarez arrived in his dressing room on fight night at 6:35 p.m. Eighteen camp members wearing matching navy-blue tracksuits with white-and-lime trim were with him.

The room had industrial carpet and cinderblock walls painted ivory white. Two black sofas and fourteen cushioned folding chairs were spread about. A large flat-screen television mounted on the far wall faced a six-by-twelve-foot Mexican flag.

Ryan Garcia, who would fight Romero Duno for a minor WBC title in the next-to-last bout of the evening, was already there. Garcia was sharing the dressing room with Canelo because Eddy Reynoso trained both men. The two fighters greeted each other warmly.

A rectangular table had been set perpendicular against the wall near one end of the room to create a small alcove in front of the television. Canelo settled in the alcove on a folding chair opposite the TV. Chepo Reynoso (Eddy's father and Canelo's longtime manager) sat beside him.

Garcia turned off his music in deference to the champion. It was Canelo's room now.

At seven o'clock, Shane Mosley came in to wish Canelo well. Mosley had turned pro in 1993 and blazed through the lightweight division before moving up in weight to conquer Oscar De La Hoya at 147 pounds. Then came the fall. In Shane's last 21 fights, he suffered 10 losses—an all-too-common endgame for a once-great fighter. One of Mosley's losses was a lopsided decision defeat to Canelo.

Garcia started warming up.

Canelo watched as a bloody bout between Seniesa Estrada and Marlen Esparza unfolded on the television in front of him.

At 7:35 p.m., Nevada State Athletic Commission executive director Bob Bennett entered with referee Russell Mora and assorted dignitaries who listened as Mora gave Canelo pre-fight instructions.

The thud of Ryan Garcia hitting the pads with Eddy Reynoso resonated throughout the room. Then Eddy began wrapping Canelo's hands.

The bloody mask that was Marlen Esparza's face grew bloodier. After nine rounds, the fight was stopped.

A cape was draped over Ryan Garcia's shoulders.

"Looking good," Canelo exhorted.

Then Canelo's two-year-old daughter (Maria Fernanda) and infant son (Adiel) were brought into the room. This was Maria's fourth pre-fight dressing room experience with her father. Her first appearance had been at Canelo–Golovkin II when she wasn't old enough to walk. Now she was able to navigate her way around the room on her own.

"Papa!" Maria Fernanda cried out as she rushed toward him.

Father and daughter embraced.

Then Maria Fernanda examined her father's hands and announced that she wanted her hands to look like papa's.

Canelo put a strip of tape on the back of her hand.

Maria Fernanda informed him that this was unsatisfactory. She wanted the real thing. So on a night when his place in boxing history hung in the balance, Canelo Álvarez took gauze and tape and elaborately wrapped his daughter's hands.

"This is not a distraction," he explained. "It is motivation. Having my children here reminds me of what I am fighting for."

Almost unnoticed, Ryan Garcia left the room with Eddy Reynoso at his side for what was expected to be the biggest challenge of his ring career.

Maria Fernanda, her hands now properly wrapped, began an impromptu dance recital for her father.

At 8:25 p.m., Canelo lay down on the floor for a series of stretching exercises. Maria Fernanda climbed on top of his chest and kissed him. Then, while physical conditioner Munir Somoya stretched Canelo's legs one at a time, Maria Fernanda simultaneously tugged on the other.

A loud "OOOH!" resounded through the room. Ryan Garcia had scored a devastating first-round knockout.

Canelo stopped stretching and looked at the television to watch a video replay of the knockout. . . . Jab, straight right, left hook. KO at 1:38 of round one.

Three minutes later, Eddy was back in the dressing room. Garcia was still being interviewed in the ring.

Eddy gloved Canelo up.

Garcia returned and Canelo embraced him. Minutes later, Duane Ford (president of the WBC North American Boxing Federation) came in and told Garcia that the belt he'd just won had to be returned to Duno.

"The WBC will mail you a new one next week," Ford explained. "This one belongs to him. If you want to present it to him personally, come with me."

Garcia left the room with Ford and returned alone minutes later.

"That was hard to see," Ryan said. "In the ring, you do what you do. But just now, Duno was crying. I felt bad for him."

Canelo paced back and forth, stopping occasionally to rotate his torso. Then absurdity set in.

It was 9:05 p.m. Team Canelo had been told to be ready to walk by 9:15. But earlier in the week, DAZN had made the decision to delay the start of Canelo–Kovalev until after the conclusion of a UFC pay-per-view card that was being contested in New York. Thus, there would be an unconscionably long delay between the end of Garcia–Duno and the start of Canelo–Kovalev, which wouldn't begin until 10:18 p.m. (1:18 a.m. Eastern Time).

That was insulting to fans who had traveled to Las Vegas and bought tickets for Canelo–Kovalev. It was off-putting to DAZN's East Coast subscribers (Canelo–Kovalev didn't end until after 2:00 a.m. Eastern). And it was both disrespectful and grossly unfair to Canelo and Kovalev.

As one disgruntled media scribe noted afterward, "You can't spell 'fuck' without a U, an F, and a C."

The delay was more compatible with the rhythms of Canelo's dressing room than it would have been for most fighters. There's very little physical exertion on his part in the hours before a fight and his psychological make-up minimizes tension. If anything, during the next hour, he got a bit bored; that's all. He chatted with Chepo and Eddy, watched DAZN's filler content on the television, and rose occasionally to shadow-box.

Finally, at 9:52 p.m., a DAZN production coordinator came into the room and announced, "You walk in eleven minutes."

Canelo hit the pads with Eddy . . . ferociously . . . with power . . .

Inside the arena, three national anthems—Russian, Mexican, and United States—were sung.

Eddy massaged Canelo's shoulders while the Mexican anthem sounded.

Chepo draped a serape over Canelo's shoulders.

At 10:08, Canelo left the sanctuary of his dressing room for war. In a matter of minutes, he would climb into a small enclosure that was both a stage and a cage. Fifteen thousand people in the arena would be focused on his every move. Millions more would be watching on electronic platforms around the world. Most would be rooting for him to succeed. Some would hope for him to be beaten into unconsciousness. Only a handful would see or feel the humanity in him. He'd be a symbol, a commodity, a video-game character come to life. That's all.

If Canelo were to be knocked flat on his back, he'd find himself staring up at the cupola of the video board suspended above the ring. The inside of the cupola is black, as dark as the nighttime sky when the moon and stars are in hiding. The referee would flash fingers in his face. Optimally, he'd recognize the numbers from the start of the count. If the first number he heard was "seven," he'd be in trouble. As he rose, the black above would give way to a swirling image of the crowd. The roar would be deafening.

He wouldn't think about whether or not he was fit to continue. It wasn't his job to assess that. Maybe he'd be hurt. Hurt as in physical pain. Or worse, hurt as in being unable to fully control the movement of his body. If the referee asked, "Are you all right? Do you want to continue?" he'd answer "Yes" even though some part of his mind and body—his instinct for self-preservation—might be shouting "No!"

If the fight continued, the same man who'd knocked him down would try to destroy him. The roar of the crowd wouldn't stop. Canelo would be in the fire. And when it was over, the people who'd been watching would go on with their lives. They might talk about the fight, but they wouldn't have bumps and bruises and swelling and pain. If their thoughts were fuzzy, it would be from too many beers, not punches they'd taken.

Canelo had never been knocked down in his ring career. But he knew what he'd done to other fighters. Could it happen to him? Of course it could.

The live gate for Canelo–Kovalev had been hurt by the fact that Canelo's fans were used to traveling to Las Vegas to see him fight on Cinco de Mayo and Mexican Independence Day weekends, not in early November. The casino ticket buy had been smaller than usual.

The announced crowd of 14,490 was heavily pro-Canelo.

The notes I took as the fight progressed read as follows:

Round 1—Kovalev throwing a probing jab with his right hand cocked. Canelo biding his time, processing Kovalev's timing and rhythm.

Round 2—Kovalev busier, keeping Canelo at bay with his jab. Canelo has to find a way to pressure more effectively. He can't let Kovalev control the fight from the outside with his jab.

Round 3—Canelo advancing. Kovalev still dictating the
   terms of the fight with his jab. Sergey has won the first
   three rounds.
Round 4—Kovalev sticking to his fight plan. Canelo fighting a patient fight, starting to land to the body.
Round 5—Canelo the aggressor, looks like the more powerful fighter. Kovalev circling away, jabbing.
Round 6—Good body work by Canelo. The body shots are
   starting to break Kovalev down. Kovalev not throwing
   his right hand much because it will open him up to
   hooks to the body. Fight even after six.
Round 7—Kovalev looks to be tiring, throwing a stay-away-
   from-me jab. Holding when Canelo gets inside or pushing him off with his shoulder.
Round 8—Canelo backing away, going to the ropes, trying
   to lure Kovalev in. Poor strategic decision. Giving away
   the round.
Round 9—Kovalev seems rejuvenated by the last round.
Round 10—Canelo more aggressive now. Kovalev still holding when Canelo gets inside or trying to push him off
   with his shoulder (and maybe break Canelo's nose). The
   fight is even after ten.
Round 11—Canelo in control again.
BOOM! ! !

With 53 seconds left in round eleven, Canelo landed a chopping right
hand that shook Kovalev, then followed with a left hook to the side of
the head that put Sergey on spaghetti legs. Kovalev started to fall and a
crushing right rendered him senseless with his upper body draped over
the lower ring strand. There was no need to count, and referee Russell
Mora didn't.

Canelo hadn't needed a knockout to win. But he needed a knockout
to make his point. And he got it.

Great fighters have very little ambivalence about fighting. They love
it. Canelo loves the challenge of competing in the ring at the highest
level. When asked just prior to the final pre-fight press conference for
Canelo–Kovalev where he thought he stood on the list of great Mexican

fighters, Canelo answered, "The day that I retire is the day that we can judge my place in history." When asked, as he often is, to compare himself with Julio César Chávez (Mexico's most storied ring icon), Canelo has said again and again, "I want to make my own history."

He's doing just that. Canelo might not be as beloved as Chávez in his native Mexico. But he's starting to look like the better fighter. He's also continuing to build his legacy the way a fighter's legacy should be built. Not by self-aggrandizing talk but by deeds in the ring, one fight at a time.

Epilogue

I began this book with the thought that being in a fighter's dressing room before and after a fight is a privilege that I never take for granted. It also gives rise to a range of emotions.

Over the years, it has become increasingly difficult for me to watch fighters I care about in the ring. Maybe that's because I've seen two men beaten to death in front of me. Maybe it's because, as I've grown older, I've been imbued with a greater sense of mortality coupled with a fuller understanding of loss. There are times when I sit at ringside and feel my heart pounding. During the early rounds of the first fight between Jermain Taylor and Bernard Hopkins, my hand was shaking so much that my notes were an almost illegible scrawl.

On December 1, 2019, I received a telephone call from Ed Brophy (executive director of the International Boxing Hall of Fame in Canastota, New York) telling me that I'd been chosen by the electors for induction into the Hall of Fame. It's the most meaningful honor that I've received as a writer and I'm deeply grateful for it. But as the preceding pages make clear, if I'm in the Hall of Fame, it's simply as a guide who helps visitors find their way through a Pantheon of Gods.

Thomas Hauser
New York